WHO IS IT?

WHO IS IT?

KATHRYN CERVERA

Copyright 2019, Kathryn Cervera

All rights reserved. Printed in the U.S.A.

No part of this publication may be reproduced or transmitted in any form or by any means, electronic or mechanical, including photocopy, recording or any information storage and retrieval system now known or to be invented, without permission in writing from the publisher, except by a reviewer who wishes to quote brief passages in connection with a review written for inclusion in a magazine, newspaper or broadcast.

Published in the United States
by eBooks2go, Inc.
1827 Walden Office Square, Suite 260, Schaumburg, IL 60173

ISBN-10: 1-5457-4771-7
ISBN-13: 978-1-5457-4771-1

Library of Congress Cataloging in Publication

*For my father,
Joe Cervera*

CONTENTS

Chapter 1 1
Chapter 2 14
Chapter 3 23
Chapter 4 31
Chapter 5 45
Chapter 6 57
Chapter 7 71
Chapter 8 90
Chapter 9 101
Chapter 10 112
Chapter 11 126
Chapter 12 138
Chapter 13 154
Chapter 14 164
Chapter 15 173
Chapter 16 189
Chapter 17 205
Chapter 18 224
Chapter 19 235
Chapter 20 246
Chapter 21 262

CHAPTER 1

The first bell rang throughout the halls of Rorertown High School, giving students a five-minute warning. Teenagers wandered the crowded hallways; darted off to different classrooms; talked with their friends; and hurried to their lockers, making every minute of procrastination count. Their loud and high-pitched voices echoed through the long building.

Fourteen-year-old John Dolton was one of six guys standing in a row, taking up the hallway. Tall and lean, he had curly, shoulder-length black hair, matching dark eyes, and a light complexion. The group split up, darting down different halls toward their classes. His pace quickened, with Tom and Chad racing to keep up with him.

A girl stepped in front of him, blocking his path. He came to an abrupt halt, almost bumping into her. "I like your hair."

"Uh, thanks," John said.

"It's so long," another girl said, appearing by his side.

The next thing he knew, girls surrounded him in a tight circle. They talked all at once, tangling their hands in his hair. He shifted back and forth uncomfortably on his feet. Class would begin any minute, yet he couldn't move. He glanced over at his buddies for help and glared at them for laughing.

"Dude," Tom called out. Taller than most seniors, he had short, spiky black hair offset by a light complexion with matching acne. "Come on."

"We're going to be late," Chad slurred. Short, husky, and hairy, he had dark circles under his eyes, matted dirty-blond hair, and a speech impediment.

"I have to go." Seeing an opening, he darted through the girls and caught up with his friends amid the giggles and shouts trailing after him.

"You little whore," Tom said, "you can have any girl you want. All you have to do is stand there and let them come to you."

"Whatever."

John turned a corner and came to a complete stop. He saw a girl coming toward them. Not just any girl—the girl. She was tall and slender, with wavy dark-brown hair flowing past her shoulders. Her dramatic eyes complemented her light-brown complexion. He had first noticed her six weeks ago in one of his classes, so he knew she was also in the ninth grade. But he never had the guts to approach her. Basketball practice kept him busy every day after school. The only time he saw her, aside from class, was between classes. If other girls weren't surrounding her, she was always heading off to her classes or out the front door.

But this time his eyes remained on her. She walked by the group and smiled at John, their eyes meeting briefly.

Wait a minute, he thought, *she's in my next class. Here's my opportunity to talk to her*. It was time to make a move before someone else stole her away.

"I'll catch up with you guys," he said to Tom and Chad. He turned around and followed her.

"Man, he always gets the pretty ones," he heard Tom say to Chad.

He shot Tom a look over his shoulder, who smirked in reply. Chad hit him on the shoulder playfully, and they resumed walking toward the classroom. Shaking his head, he scanned the students and saw the girl had stopped at a locker. He paused, took a deep breath, and then slowly walked up next to her.

"Hi, I'm John." Some pickup line.

She looked over and smiled, making eye contact. "I'm Lisa." "You're in my English class, aren't you?"

Lisa studied his face.

"With Mrs. Braughan." He held his breath. "Yes, that's right." Her eyes lit up.

"Can I walk you over there?"

"Sure." She shut her locker, and they walked back the way he came. "Are you new here?"

She looked over at him, raising an eyebrow.

"Oh. I mean I don't recognize you from my junior high school."

"I went to Swedson."

"That explains it," he said. "I went to Westchester." "I've lived in Rorertown my entire life," Lisa added.

"Same here."

Her eyes swept around and he followed her gaze. Several heads turned their way. He looked all around him but saw that the oncoming looks were curious. Ignoring the stares, he turned back to her.

"What kind of music do you like?" "Rock, pop, and R and B."

"Good answer."

They entered the room, where more heads turned in their direction, eyes lingering on them for a while before returning to their own business.

What's going on? he thought. He couldn't tell who the stares were directed toward. *I know she's pretty, but I approached her first.*

John spotted Tom and Chad, already seated in the back. He nodded to them, then followed Lisa down a middle aisle and sat behind her. A boy abruptly stopped in front of the desk, staring at him.

He had taken the boy's seat.

Before John could say anything, the boy turned on his heels. Muttering under his breath, he walked to the back of the room, where the only empty seat remained. John smiled, dumped his book bag on the floor, and leaned forward to be closer to Lisa. Close enough to smell her shampoo. Honey and vanilla?

Quick—think of something to say. She's looking back at you, he thought.

But John couldn't. He didn't know much about her. His eyes widened. *Basketball—why didn't I think of it before?* He could ask her to the game tonight.

Lisa turned sideways. "Is your hair naturally curly?"

His eyebrows shot up. "Uh, yeah." He hadn't expected that.

She laughed. "You don't like it?"

"It can be a real pain sometimes." He moved his hair out of his eyes. "I like it."

"Thanks." He smiled.

He heard snickering behind him. He glanced over his shoulder and saw Chad giving him the thumbs up, while Tom hollered away. Shaking his head, he faced forward. Lisa leaned back in her seat, looking past John and at his buddies. Right when she looked back at him, Tom whistled loud and long.

They're killing me, he thought, meeting Lisa's questioning gaze. He threw his hand up, rolling his eyes in disgust. *And they wonder why they have no girl.*

"Your friends?" she asked, raising an eyebrow.

"I've never seen them before," he said with a straight face, and she laughed. "So, do you like basketball?"

"Yes." Lisa nodded.

"Our first game is tonight, if you want to come," John said.

"Sure. What time?"

"Six o'clock."

"I'll be there," she promised.

During the rest of the school day, John walked Lisa to her classes and then made a mad dash to his classrooms.

But he didn't care. Her eyes lit up each time she spotted him by the door, waiting. Her subtle perfume lingered after they parted ways. Her giggles echoed in his ears.

He could see her beautiful smile while he counted the minutes until the next period. Just to be around her was intoxicating.

After school let out, John said bye to Lisa, then walked to the gymnasium. He entered the locker room, where he found his buddies already changing. Only then did he realize how the day had flown. He had been too distracted.

"There you are," Tom said. He smacked him on the leg with a towel. John dodged it too late. "Been looking for you."

"Sorry," John muttered, opening his locker. He dumped his book bag and grabbed his uniform to change.

"It's all good," Chad slurred.

"Who's that chick you've been with?" Ben asked. He also had black hair, thick and long that framed his head. He stood medium height, with broad shoulders and black eyes.

"Lisa."

"The one that you ditched us for?" Adrian piped up. He had a bony frame, tanned skin with dark-brown hair, jetting brown fuzz on his upper lip.

Ben punched his shoulder, and Adrian grabbed the towel out of Tom's hands, smacking him. Ben flinched. "Dude, that was my ear."

"But it's true," Adrian whined.

"She's hot," Jason added. "I'd dump your ugly face for her any day." He had a dark complexion with matching dark hair, complete with hazel eyes.

"Thank you," John spoke up. "I knew you'd see it my way."

Laughter erupted in the room. John quickly changed his clothes while his friends continued to joke around and punch each other. Fishing a hair band out of his book bag, he pulled his hair away from his face into a ponytail. Dressed and ready, John shut his locker when Jason approached him.

"Hey, man," Jason said, "you going to hook up with her?"

"Working on it," John said. He scanned the crowded locker room, noticing that it suddenly turned quiet. He turned back to Jason. "Why? What's up?"

"We overheard some guy telling his friends earlier that he also liked her," Adrian told him. "Just so you know, he got pissed when he saw you hanging around her."

John frowned. He thought back but didn't remember anything unusual. But then again, his attention had been solely on Lisa. They did get a lot of stares, though. "Who?"

"His name's Danny." Ben shut his locker. "He's in one of my classes. We can point him out to you."

"Think he'll come tonight?" Chad slurred. "She's coming," John added.

"Then he'll come," Tom confirmed. "And we'll kick his butt. Don't worry."

John smiled, shaking his head. More hollering erupted in the room. He looked around, seeing that the entire team stood ready to go. "All right, you guys," he yelled, "let's go kick some butt."

"Yeah!"

The team piled out of the locker room and into the gymnasium to begin their workout.

Students filled both sets of bleachers, which faced each other on the sidelines of the court. The cheers, shouts, and stomps flooded John's ears. Not surprising for the first game of the season. They were playing Doverly High School—their rival—the Dogs. Since Rorertown was a small city like Doverly, they each had one high school, though the distance between them was five minutes driving. It was the Dogs versus the Rangers.

There were two games tonight: the junior varsity and the varsity. John was captain of the junior varsity team, which consisted of freshmen and sophomores. Besides himself, his friends made up the freshman half, and the rest of the team members were sophomores. The varsity players were juniors and seniors. They stood off to the side, waiting for their game and watching the junior varsity warm up.

But John wasn't fazed. He stood hyped and ready to win. He surveyed his team piled in two lines, practicing lay ups. He drilled the team a long time until he felt certain they had loosened up. Now they were focusing on their skill. As he waited his turn, he watched the guys dribble down the court and make their layups. No one had missed a shot yet. He nodded, feeling certain that they were ready.

Five more minutes, he thought. *Then the game should start.* John caught himself seeking out Lisa but couldn't find her anywhere. She promised to come. Now concentrate. He shook his head to clear his mind.

Adrian threw him the ball and then jogged to the back of the other line. John made a perfect layup, passed the ball to Chad, and then trotted to the next line.

"John," shouted a voice behind him.

He turned around and there was Lisa on the third row of the bleachers with two other girls and guys. His eyes widened briefly upon seeing the guys. But then he noticed they sat on the other side of the girls who were sitting to the right of Lisa. He shook off the feelings, figuring they were the other girls' dates.

Lisa waved at him, and he smiled, nodding to her.

Man, she looks pretty. He reluctantly turned away, but soon he felt self-conscious of his every movement. He knew exactly where she sat. But was she watching him? He snuck a glance at her out of the corner of his eye. Yes, she was watching him. Chills crept down his back. *Damn, she is distracting*, he thought. Suddenly he felt someone else staring at him.

John looked to the left and saw a guy standing by the steps of the bleachers, watching him intensely. He stood about medium height, with a bony frame, straggly brown hair covering his eyes, and a light complexion. John recognized the guy—he had been suspended the other day for fighting some kids in the parking lot.

They locked eyes for a second, before the guy glanced at Lisa, then back to John. He bolted up the bleachers and sat directly behind Lisa, one row up. He leaned his elbows on his knees until hovering over her.

What the hell? John thought.

The guy shifted to one side, then to the other, but Lisa never turned around. Her eyes remained on John. The guy turned red, glaring at him.

"That's Danny," Adrian spoke up.

So that was Danny. It explained his behavior, but there wasn't anything John could do. "We'll keep an eye on him," Chad added.

"No," he said. "Focus on the game." He stole one last peek at Lisa. Right on cue, the referee blew the whistle to start the game.

At the tip-off, the Rangers grabbed possession of the ball, taking it straight to the basket and scoring. The Dogs did the same, slipping through their defense and scoring.

The game continued on this way for some time. Each team dashed up and down the court. Players dodged, fought, dribbled back and forth, and raced the ball to the basket. Every time the Rangers scored, the Dogs stole the ball, only to run down to the other side of the court and make a basket.

By halftime, they were tied 60–60.

During the third quarter, they continued to sprint, to fight, to try something new to outdo each other, but nothing worked. The score climbed slowly, neck and neck—62–62, 66–66, 70–70. Good, but not good enough.

It was now the fourth quarter, with two minutes left in the game. The Dogs had the ball. As a Dog rushed down the court, John ran alongside of him, keeping up, and moved in on him, closing off his space until forcing him out of bounds.

The referee blew the whistle. It was their ball.

John started to switch places with the Dog to throw the ball in when he looked up at the Ranger's bleachers, noticing that Danny now sat on the left of Lisa. But she paid him no mind, not noticing him at all. This thought made John smile. They locked eyes again. It was time for this guy to back off already. But Danny remained where he was. John turned around, his back to the bleachers. He needed to concentrate on the game.

Sweat matted his hair to the sides of his face and rolled down his back as he took a breath, his hands on his knees. They had to do something if they were to win this game. And quick. Several students stood in the bleachers, their cheers bouncing off the walls and stomps vibrating beneath his feet. He straightened when the referee handed him the ball.

"Go, John," he heard Lisa yell behind him.

His smile diminished when his peripheral vision showed Danny leaning toward Lisa. *He will not stop*, he thought. And he couldn't do anything right now. But what about when the game ended? *Focus*!

John slapped the ball in frustration. "Break!"

Both teams spread out around the court. Seeing Jason open, John passed him the ball, but a Dog charged ahead and knocked it out of bounds. It soared through the air, and John realized the ball might smack Lisa. He dove, nearly missing it, but he managed to knock the ball to the left. As John flew, students past him before the bleachers rushed up to meet him. He crashed, landing hard on the steps. That's going to leave a mark. The whistle blew.

Laughter erupted. John sat up slowly and saw that the students were turned away from him, laughing at something else. But he couldn't see what. He picked himself up gingerly, with the help of some students, and moved back on to the court. His buddies surrounded him, asking if he was OK, then slapped his back and shoulders, before repositioning themselves.

A dull ache throbbed on his right side. He would feel it in the morning. But at least the ball didn't hit Lisa. He glanced at Danny and then did a double take. A circular red imprint burned on his cheek. He watched as Danny's face turned a deeper shade of red. Danny abruptly stood up, stormed out of the aisle, down the steps and out the gymnasium.

Good! Now he could concentrate. John sneaked a glance at Lisa, who smiled. He shrugged.

They had less than thirty seconds, and the Dogs had possession. A Dog threw the ball in, and Tom jumped, slamming it down and away from the player. Adrian charged through and snatched up the ball. He pivoted and passed it to John.

He raced down the court, heading toward their basket. A Dog appeared by his side, but Chad jumped in the way, blocking him. John turned and went around, noticing Jason underneath the basket and passed the ball to him. Two Dogs surrounded Jason, who passed it to Adrian. John came up the center, and Adrian passed it to him. He shot right at the free-throw line and made it. 72–70.

They were down to fifteen seconds, and the Dogs had the ball. John grabbed his buddies, keeping them on the Ranger's side of the court. A Dog threw the ball in, and Tom jumped, tipping it toward Adrian. A Dog ran up and jumped in front of him, stealing the ball. Chad stepped in front of the Dog, freezing him in his movements. Chad's hand came up and knocked it out of the Dog's hands. Jason ran on the inside of them, grabbed the ball, turned around, and passed it to John. He shot from the three-point line just as the horn went off.

Swoosh! Nothing but net. They won the game. 75–70. "Yeah!"

John started jumping up and down, hollering. The Rangers ran over and surrounded him on the court. Before John knew what was happening, his buddies picked him up and placed him on their shoulders, carrying him around the court and cheering. Everyone in the gymnasium stood, shouting and clapping. John looked at the blur of faces hollering, applauding, and stomping all around him. The Rangers jogged two laps, carrying him the entire time, and when they passed Lisa, John saw that she stood cheering as well.

"All right, all right, all right!" John yelled, laughing. "Put me down!"

They stopped by the Ranger's bench, where John touched solid ground again. Coach Winston—Coach W—caught up with the team, congratulating them and giving a quick pep talk while the varsity team waited for the bench. John only heard half of the talk, but his buddies kept slapping his arms and shoulders in approval.

As soon as Coach W excused them, John turned and pushed his way through the crowd amid the pats and handshakes. Voices called out to him, and he glanced over his shoulder, seeing his buddies waiting for him.

"I'll catch up with you guys," he called out. They nodded and headed to the locker room.

He walked through the gymnasium, straight to Lisa. "Good game," she said.

"Thanks." He stood a few feet from her since his body was drenched in sweat. "I'm going to shower real quick."

She smiled. "OK. I'll be right here—no rush." "I'll be right back."

He sprinted to the locker room, where his buddies were changing and others already showering. Cheers broke out when he entered, making him stop briefly. He smiled. He grabbed a towel off the rack and headed to his locker, quickly patting down his sweat-drenched body.

"Good game, you guys." John draped the soaked towel over his shoulders. Cheers erupted again.

"We kicked butt," Tom yelled. "There was no time for jelly. They had to bend over and hold their ankles."

Laughter echoed.

"Did you see that jump shot, man?" Jason flicked his wrists at an imaginary basket. "Right when the horn went off."

"What about Chad's block?" Adrian slapped Chad on the back. "Knocked the ball right out of the guy's hands. He don't mess around."

Chad flexed his muscles, causing laughs and hollers to spill around the room.

"Or when Tom threw it down," Jason continued.

But John paid them no heed. He rushed around, quickly showering, and donned his clothes, thankful for something clean and dry. He fished in his locker, spotted his deodorant and cologne, and sprayed himself down. Much better. Now he smelled musky instead of like dirty socks. Steam already filled the locker room from the showers, mixing with the sweaty clothes and boys' body odor—a smell he didn't want to have lingering. He needed to jet before it became too stuffy.

"You going to stay for the other game?" Ben asked. "No, I'm going to hang with Lisa," John replied. "Right." Ben turned abruptly, heading to the showers. "Next time."

"Yeah, yeah."

"Don't be a dick," Adrian yelled after Ben. "He approached her first." John looked at Adrian, who sat on the bench, taking off his shoes. "Don't worry about him." Adrian said.

"He probably has a thing for her too," Jason added.

John looked back and forth between them, and then threw up his hands in frustration. "What the hell?" he asked. "I start talking to Lisa and now everyone likes her?"

"She *is* hot," Tom interjected.

Rolling his eyes, John grabbed his book bag and shut the locker. "Coach W also yanked him out of the game," Chad slurred.

John's eyebrows furrowed, thinking. Coach W had pulled Ben out during halftime, but not because he did something wrong. He certainly wasn't yanked. There were twelve guys on the team. They had to let everyone play somehow. Coach W alternated players to give the team a breather. "He didn't yank him."

"You played the entire game." Tom slammed his locker shut. Hard. Too hard. It echoed through the room, silencing everyone.

All eyes turned to the two of them. Was that anger in Tom's voice? Their gazes met briefly. John started to say something but stopped, realizing Tom was right. He had played the entire game. But it was the first game. Didn't mean it would be this way for every game. So Ben was angry because he played only half?

"That's not my decision to make."

The guys knew it too. Coach W decided who played. Tom turned his back on him and entered the showers. John looked at Jason, Chad, and Adrian. They shrugged. First Ben, now Tom. He ran a hand through his hair. There wasn't anything he could do about it. Besides, Lisa was waiting. He swung his bag over his shoulder.

"All right, you guys," he made his way toward the door. "I'll see you next practice." "You better get some for me!" Adrian yelled out, and the guys started hollering.

John shook his head, throwing the towel in the dirty bin. "Maybe if you take after him, you would get some," Jason said.

The shouts drifted through the open doorway, where he emerged from the locker room.

CHAPTER 2

John scanned the gymnasium until he spotted Lisa waiting for him. She stood near the side of the bleachers with the same group of guys and girls who she sat with. He walked over to her, and they surrounded him. He had been anxious to get back to Lisa, not wanting to keep her waiting long. But the varsity game had already started.

"John, this is Sarah, Tony, Meg, and Martin," Lisa said.

"Hey, what's up?" He shook hands with Tony and Martin. Now that John saw the group up close, he recognized them from school.

"That was a good game, man," Tony said, putting his arm around Sarah. He was tall with short, spiky dirty-blond hair, blue eyes, and beige undertones.

"Thanks."

"Yeah, congratulations," Meg added. She had brown undertones like Lisa, but short, dark curly hair and wore glasses.

"That was funny how you smacked that guy," Martin said. He had short, wavy brown hair with a light brownish complexion and was muscular in his upper body.

The group laughed.

"I didn't want it to hit Lisa." He met her gaze briefly, and she smiled.

"You guys going to state this year?" Sarah asked. She had sandy-brown hair pulled back in a bun, highlighting the freckles on her face and matching her light complexion.

"Hopefully," he replied.

"When is the next game?" Meg asked. "Next Friday."

The girls stepped aside and formed their own little group, allowing the three guys to continue talking. Stealing a glance over at Lisa, he saw her whispering to the other girls and laughing, while periodically looking over at him. *She's talking about me to her friends.*

Definitely a good sign.

"Dude," Martin stepped closer, lowering his voice, "is that your chick?"

"Not yet." John shook his head. *I wish she was.* "This is our first time going out." "Go for her," Tony said.

"Yeah, I'm trying to."

"Oh yeah, man, that's cool." Martin slapped his hand.

"We'll leave you two alone." Tony started walking over to the girls, raising his voice again. "We'll see you at the next game."

"Yeah, we'll definitely be there."

Martin joined Meg's side, and Tony stood by Sarah. John also walked over to the group, but Lisa was the furthest one away. She stood between the two couples, so he wasn't able to stand next to her.

"Nice meeting you, ladies." He waved to Sarah and Meg. "Bye, guys. I'll see you at school."

"Bye," the four of them replied in unison. "Bye, Lisa."

He moved closer to Lisa once the others left. She seemed quiet all of a sudden, looking down at the ground. He lifted up her chin to where he could see her eyes. "Your friends?"

"Sarah and Meg are my two closest friends." Lisa nodded.

"That's cool."

"Tony is Sarah's boyfriend, and Martin is Meg's boyfriend."

John nodded, figuring as much. "So, where's your boyfriend?" He looked around the gymnasium.

"Hey."

He smiled and wrapped his arms around her. Jason, Adrian, and Chad appeared. They each slapped his hand and patted his back again, before sitting on the bleachers to watch the next game.

"Quite the popular one, are we?" Lisa asked.

"What?" he said. "Not really. They're from the team." "Sure, whatever."

"Come on, let's go." He shook his head. "I'll walk you home."

John steered her from the bleachers and along the side of the gymnasium amid the crowds, where a few people called out to him, cheering. Lisa clung to his side as they pushed their way through the crowds. Smiling, he offered his elbow, and she grabbed it. The stares came again from several students who were seated in the bleachers or standing in corners talking, but he ignored it and kept going.

They exited the gymnasium, walking among the quiet school grounds and over the parking lot. Hoisting the book bag to his other shoulder, John lowered his elbow and grabbed Lisa's hand. She glanced at him and smiled. He stopped and looked around the vast parking lot, where they had almost reached the edge. All the cars were parked near the school, away from them. She glanced up at the dark, clear sky. Nighttime had already approached. He watched her until she noticed his locked gaze. Meeting his eyes, she smiled and looked down, blushing. It was the perfect moment to be alone with her—and he chickened out, hesitating too long until the moment became lost.

Don't want to rush it and scare her away, he thought. "Where do you live?" "Oh, this way." She nodded her head to the right.

They turned in that direction and continued walking on the sidewalk, outlining the streets and along the school grounds.

"I live this way too." He glanced at her. "Which subdivision?" "Deer Creek."

"I know where that is," John said. "It's across my subdivision."

"Thanks for inviting me to your game."

"No problem." He squeezed her hand.

"I liked how you passed the ball under that guy's legs," she said, laughing.

"That was the only way I could pass it." He laughed as well. A silence washed over them. "Tell me—what do you like to do? Hang out with your friends?"

"Well, of course," she answered. "Although I'm not as popular as you."

"I'm not popular." Surprised, John looked over at her, studying her face, but she seemed nonchalant.

"You ever thought about becoming a professional basketball player?" she asked. "Hmm, I don't know." He shrugged. "Haven't really thought about it."

That was only half the truth. He had thought about it several times but didn't want to get his hopes up too much. He figured he would play his best throughout high school and see what happens. If anything, he hoped to get an athletic scholarship for college.

"You should," Lisa confirmed. "You're really good at it."

"Thanks. I also know a lot about computers. If it doesn't work, I can become an engineer or something." He looked at her. "What about you?"

Lisa thought for a minute. He steered her across a street. "I honestly don't know. I mean, there are several things I would like to do."

"Such as?"

"Maybe become a fashion designer or go into public relations."

"Public relations." He rolled the words over his tongue. "Like communications?"

"Yes." She glanced at him, surprised. "You can go into either field or a number of fields, but I would be a more behind the scenes person in communications. Work for a company to promote them or their product."

"What about mass communications?"

He smiled when her eyes widened. "That's more television or radio, like broadcast journalism or news media. It's interesting, but I prefer to create rather than report. Anyone can report what's happening. Boring."

They both laughed at her bluntness. He dropped her hand and moved to the other side of her when they reached another intersection, so he would remain on the outside by the street.

"Such the gentleman," Lisa interjected, and he grabbed her hand again.

"And the fashion shows?" John was on a roll. The questions flew out before he even thought about them.

"It'll be an either or." Lisa shrugged. "Right now, I need to concentrate on finishing school, but then I want to see the world."

"You could do both."

"Yeah?" Lisa questioned, raising an eyebrow with her head turned at an angle.

Man, she's hot. "Why not?"

"I guess it could work," she mumbled.

"That would be cool," he insisted, stepping in front of her and forcing her to stop. "Think about it. We could travel together while I play basketball games, and you could have a fashion show in each city."

"Yeah, I like that," she agreed. "And we would always be together."

He caught her gaze while smiling. He was really glad that he had worked up the nerve to talk to her. So far things were going great between them. They resumed walking down the street toward her neighborhood. The moon and stars lit the dark sky, but the temperature had only dropped a few degrees, giving them a little relief, though no breeze. The long, hot days could seem like torture sometimes, but he liked it here. There were a few streetlamps on so they could still see their surroundings.

It can't be that late, he thought, looking around.

"Let's take a shortcut to my house," Lisa suggested, glancing at her watch.

"OK."

She led him toward some trees and bushes that outlined the subdivision from the rear.

They walked, still holding each other's hands tightly. Together they climbed over fallen tree branches, stepped over rocks, through patches of tall weeds, up dirt hills, and down grassy trails. He could see backyards of houses visible on the far left side behind fences.

"Careful," John said, grabbing her waist to guide her down a steep path. She was thin, so it was easy to carry her. But the moment was too short. She was on steady ground again, and he had no choice but to let her go. His hands had already lingered too long, itching to wrap around her completely. To pull her close to him and hold her in his arms.

When she looked at him, he reluctantly dropped his hands and looked around, seeking a way out. *I know where we are*, he thought.

He recognized the area, though not entirely familiar with it. He knew where they were, but he didn't know which house Lisa lived in. By taking this path, they should reach the rear of her house or come up along the side of it. The streetlamps on their left provided enough light to maneuver without any difficulty.

This looks like a good place to play a trick. An idea popped into his mind. "You sure you know the way?" he asked. "I think you got us lost."

"Yes, I know the way."

"OK." He headed off in a different direction. "Hey, where are you going? John."

He jumped behind some bushes, crouching down low and clutching his bag to him to minimize the noise. Holding his breath, he heard her footsteps crunching over the leaves.

"John, this isn't funny," Lisa called out.

When the footsteps stopped, he peeked over the top of the bush and saw that she had her back to him. He slowly stood up, shifting his bag on his back and coming out from behind the bush. He tiptoed around the trees slowly, trying not to make a sound. He crept up behind her.

"*Aauugghh!*" he said, grabbing her waist.

She screamed flinging her arms around, and he burst out laughing. Lisa turned around. "You dork." She started to playfully hit him, and he blocked the hits by grabbing hold of her hands.

It was now or never. He leaned over and kissed her on the cheek. Her eyebrows shot up, and then she burst into a smile. He held on to one of her hands, and their eyes locked. "Come on." He led her through the bushes. "Which way now?"

"This way. No, wait. I don't want to go home." Lisa stopped walking and grabbed his arm, making him stop in his tracks. "No, I eventually have to."

They started walking again toward where the backyards stood. He looked over at her, wondering what she meant. Maybe she enjoyed his company and didn't want the date to end. Here was his chance to ask her out again. After all, they were still holding hands.

"Want to go on a real date?"

"Oh, uh," Lisa stammered. "Yes. That would be great." "Want to go to the movies tomorrow?"

"Oh, I thought you meant tonight," Lisa said softly.

"Well," he fumbled, trying to think of a reply. "I would, but it's late." "Tomorrow's fine."

"Sorry." He felt like an idiot, not knowing what else to say. But it was late. They couldn't do anything now.

"That's OK," Lisa said reassuring him. "I can't stay out much later tonight anyway." "You have a curfew?"

"Something like that," she mumbled. "It's just ... nothing." "What? What is it? You can tell me."

"Do you have any siblings?" she asked instead. "Nah, just me and my parents," he replied. "Oh."

"Why?"

"Oh, never mind." She stared at the ground while they walked. An uneasy silence fell over them.

"You have siblings?" he asked. "How many?" When she didn't reply, he continued. "Let me guess. They get to stay out later than you."

"No ... I mean, yes." Her voice tapered for a split second.

"Oh," John stammered, wondering what she wanted to tell him, but decided to drop it. Better to change the subject. "Are we still up for tomorrow?"

They walked along the side of a house, and she pulled on his hand, stopping him by the fence, before reaching the front lawn. He looked around the fence at the house, noticing that they remained out of view from anyone, and he turned back to her.

"Is this your house?" He nodded his head toward it.

"Yeah." A smile appeared on her face again. "So, what time tomorrow?"

"Noon. I'll meet you at the mall by the food court entrance."

There was only one mall in Rorertown. If only he was old enough to drive, then everything would be better.

"Sounds good." Lisa dropped his hand and retreated a few steps back. "I have to go now, but I'll see you tomorrow."

"Bye," he called out.

She turned and disappeared behind the fence. John peered around it, watching her dash over the lawn and on to the front porch. Fishing a key out of her pocket, she hurried inside, looking flustered and anxious. She closed the door quickly, and John remained by himself on the side of the lawn. He glanced at the surrounding subdivision so he could remember where she lived. He located the crossing streets, jotting the names to memory, and then took off toward his house.

He smiled briefly, but his eyebrows furrowed by her actions just now. She appeared apprehensive about getting home promptly and unnoticed. John shook his head and shrugged away his thoughts. He had another date with her tomorrow, so no need to worry.

She probably had a curfew, he thought, pulling out his watch from his book bag.

Glancing at it, he quickened his own pace. More time had passed than he initially thought.

CHAPTER 3

The sun shone brightly the next day, and John decided to walk to the mall. He liked Rorertown, since it was small and easy to get around. The several blocks passed by unnoticed. He glanced at his watch and quickened his pace, realizing he would be late. He had intended to arrive early but kept getting interrupted. His mom wouldn't let him leave until his room was clean; then Tom dropped by to see if he wanted to shoot some hoops, not knowing that John already had plans.

He stopped and stretched, raising his arms over his head, working out the cramped muscles. The throbbing on his right side wasn't as bad today. He just needed to keep it loose. It was singing by the time he came home last night. He entered the house with a slight limp, and his mom made him soak in the hot tub. But it did wonders. The limp was gone, and he was better. He would stretch again later. Maybe run tonight.

John arrived at the food court entrance on the second level and immediately spotted Lisa waiting for him. She looked prettier than ever. "Hey," he said approaching her. "Sorry I'm late."

"Oh, that's fine," she replied, but he still felt bad.

"Have you been waiting long?"

"Nah."

"Don't lie."

Lisa laughed at his comment, which made him feel even worse. He knew she had probably been waiting for a while.

"Come on," he said and grabbed her hand. He led her toward the entrance doors. "I'll make it up to you."

She smiled, and he opened the door for her. John also smiled, walking in behind her and quickly falling into step alongside of her. Her soft silky hand entwined with his hand, and her other hand rested softly on his arm. He felt good with her by his side, mostly because they acted like a couple so quickly after he had approached her yesterday. It already seemed like she was his girl, even though he hadn't officially asked her yet.

He looked over at her. They strolled passed the stores, oblivious to other people. He only had eyes for her. Their gazes met and locked on one another before bursting into laughter, shy yet blushing smiles and soft laughter.

Now if only he could work up the nerve to ask her.

John glanced over to his right side briefly and stopped in his tracks, realizing they had passed the movie theater.

"What's wrong?" Lisa asked, also stopping.

"We passed it," he said, making her laugh. "Come on."

"Oops," Lisa said. "You were too busy gawking."

"I can't help it you're beautiful." They turned around to retrace their steps. "Yeah, yeah."

He led her to the box office gate, where they looked over the movies playing. John saw that they had some time to kill. "How about we eat first?" he suggested, gazing at her. She looks so pretty.

"That sounds good," she agreed.

They resumed their strolling, heading toward the food court this time. "Do you have to practice today?" she asked.

"Oh no," he said. "We practice after school for two hours."

"Every day?"

"Yeah," he confirmed. "But our weekends are free. I get to spend today with you."

She smiled at this comment.

They approached the food court, scanning the various choices while lost amid the crowds gathered to enjoy the day. They were surrounded by numerous people: families spending time together; young and old couples, like the two of them, on outings; children of all ages, crying, laughing, and talking as their parents kept them occupied; and kids their own age, hanging out in small and big groups. John recognized a few faces here and there from school. Mostly big crowds from the high school—some his age and some older kids who he knew but didn't associate with.

As they walked around the food court, a few kids nodded to him, whom he recognized from their attendance at the game. He nodded back and smiled, acknowledging them before turning back to Lisa.

"What do you want to eat?" he asked her. "Pizza."

John led her to the pizza restaurant, where he bought each of them a slice of pizza and a drink. As he carried the plates and she held the drinks, they found an empty table and sat down across from one another. He caught himself watching her eat, finding it harder to tear his eyes off her. She looked up from her plate and made eye contact, freezing her movements after seeing that he hadn't even touched his plate.

"What?"

"Nothing." He nodded, hesitating. "It's just …" His voice trailed off, making her gaze stay locked on his face, her eyes searching and waiting patiently for him to finish speaking. *Should I ask her now?* He thought, biting his lip. *Or is it too soon?* But he didn't want to lose her, not after discovering that two other guys liked her. "I have a question for you."

"OK …"

"I was wondering if you would be my girl?" John held his breath. Lisa's eyes lit up.

"Really?"

"Really."

"Oh wow." Her eyebrows rose briefly, silencing John again. "I mean yes." He extinguished a sigh of relief, making them both laugh. She said yes!

"I'm sorry," Lisa said, smiling. Her hand covered her mouth, displaying long fingernails.

He saw her cheeks turning slightly pink. She was so cute. "You had me there for a moment. I wasn't expecting that."

His smile slowly disappeared. "Why not?"

Now she hesitated. Her eyes lowered to her plate, her shoulders shrugging. "No one has ever asked me before," she whispered.

"You're kidding." She shook her head no.

"Hmm," he uttered for lack of a better word.

Her eyebrow rose. "You find this hard to believe?"

"Yeah," he responded. "I know of two other guys that like you. But I don't know how I became the lucky one."

"Because you asked first," she answered, smiling. He rolled his eyes. "Although I'm not as popular as some people."

Taking a sip of his drink, he shook his head. "I'm not popular. I play for the school team. I don't even know most of the people that cheer for us."

"It's easier for guys, I think."

He caught a hint of something in her voice. "What's easier?"

"To make friends and be liked," she said. "Girls have it harder."

His brows furrowed, caught off guard by the topic of conversation. He hadn't expected this comment, nor did he know exactly how to respond. "What? How?"

"You guys do," Lisa said. "Your friends don't judge you by how you look, what you wear, how you act, or who you hang around."

He saw her point. "True. We say how it is. Or fight if it gets bad."

"Last year, my friends and I had a falling out with the popular group," she continued. "The girls ended up spreading false rumors about us. I lost several acquaintances. But I barely saw them because we were spread out among Swedson and Westchester. Now I only have a couple of classes with my best friends and have all my classes with at least one of the popular girls. Every day is practically another battle where I face off with them."

He rolled her words in his mind. "Who are the popular girls? Our grade, right?"

"Yeah." Lisa nodded. "There are seven of them now. It used to be ten with the three of us." She paused. "You know that one corner between the hallway and the cafeteria, where the benches are?"

John nodded.

"They always hang out there."

"Ah, OK." John realized who she meant. He remembered seeing the group of girls several times but never spoke to them. They were usually surrounded by guys in the upper grades. He didn't know what was the big deal. He considered the group snobby and stayed away from them, since the girls seemed too much into their looks. He had also heard some nasty things about their reputation. "You hung out with these girls?"

"We all went to school together, so I've known them for years," Lisa explained. "But last year we had a big fight. I don't remember what it was about, probably something stupid. But my friends and I became more serious about our studies and grades. Now I remember." She set her cup on the table. "They were always into boys, sneaking out and partying. They became really snobby and were always mouthing off to everyone: students, parents, and teachers. It didn't matter who it was; they simply didn't care."

"What do you mean by battle?"

"Oh." She rolled her eyes. "They're always making snide remarks to my face about everything: my looks, my social life, my clothes, my belongings, and so forth. They always compete with one another for the most expensive stuff, to be the prettiest, the skinniest, to party the most, to experiment the most, and to always have a boyfriend." He saw her face fluster.

"Well," John said, looking around them. He lowered his voice and leaned toward her. "Want to know a secret?"

Lisa met his gaze. "OK."

"I didn't know them last year," he informed her, spreading his hands out in front of him. "Or you. But they're considered a joke now."

"Seriously?"

He nodded. "They're popular, but that doesn't mean they're liked." Her head tilted to the side. "What do you mean?"

"They're an easy lay."

Lisa paused. "Oh wow." Her brows furrowed. "I didn't know that, though it shouldn't surprise me."

"You were smart to get away from them," he said. "They've said things to me and my friends too. But no one likes them."

"What kinds of things?" She took a sip of her drink.

John rolled his eyes and shook his head, trying to remember the comments. The girls had said so many things it was not what, but where to begin. Might as well start with himself. "They said to cut my hair."

She threw her hands in the air. "Your hair is cool."

He waved his hand, dismissing the comment. "I don't care what they think."

She shook her head. "They've turned really nasty this year." Her face turned pink again.

He could tell she was angry. Irritated. *Why was it bothering her so much?* John thought, taking a bite of pizza. Then he remembered. Lisa had lost a lot of her friends, though he was glad she no longer hung around them. But it had to be more than that. It finally hit him. The girls made fun of her for only one reason—they were jealous. She was prettier than them, but she didn't realize it. He preferred it that way too. It kept her from becoming conceited like the other girls.

John chuckled, and her movements froze. If only she knew how many guys liked her. How he fought with his friends in the locker room because of her. His friends. Who knows what will happen when he encounters Danny. Maybe all Lisa needed was a reminder.

"You realize the girls are jealous, right?"

"Why would they be jealous?" "Because you're perfect," he said. Lisa gave him a sidelong glance. "You are," he said, making her smile.

After they finished the meal, they cleaned off the table and threw their trash away. Cradling her hand in the crook of his arm, they headed back to the theater. Once he bought the tickets, they sat down as the movie began. John put his arm around Lisa, and she scooted closer to him. He still couldn't believe how lucky he was. He had thought guys would be hitting on her all the time, and he would never stand a chance. He wasn't even surprised that other guys liked her. She was beautiful. But it didn't matter now. She was his girl.

The movie turned out to be hilarious, a real hit. They couldn't stop laughing. Afterward they walked around the mall hand in hand, looking at the stores while commenting once in a while about the movie.

"Where do you want to go next?" he asked.

"I don't know." She glanced at her watch. "Do you need to go?"

"Huh? Oh no. Not for a while," she replied, seeming a little distracted. "You sure?"

"Yeah."

John glanced over at her, not quite sure if something was wrong. She always looked at her watch. Now he wondered why. He thought everything had gone smoothly between them. After all, she was his girl now. He waited to see if she would tell him what he did wrong or if she wasn't enjoying herself, but she only smiled. "Is something wrong? You can tell me. Did you—"

"Nothing's wrong." She stepped closer to him, so he dropped the subject. "OK. Do you want to go to my house and hang out?"

Lisa smiled. "Sure."

"Come on." They headed out of the mall, and he led the way to his house.

CHAPTER 4

On Monday morning John waited by Lisa's locker. A few kids glanced at him here and there as he stood there obviously waiting but he didn't care. He smirked, remembering their date Saturday night. They had left the mall and gone to his place, where she met his parents. They played a little basketball in the driveway, where he showed her some moves; using every excuse he could to touch her. Her waist, her arm, her shoulder.

Then they went inside and ate dinner with his parents. He could tell they instantly liked Lisa. She was beautiful, charming, and easy to talk to. She seemed more relaxed and laughed easily. Once his dad started telling joke after joke, John knew she had won them over.

John and Lisa moved to the living room to watch a movie. His parents join them for a bit, much to John's annoyance, forcing them to sit on the couch awkwardly, separated from each other. But the moment his parents left them alone, he scooted closer to her and wrapped his arm around her. Lisa instantly snugged against him, leaning her head on his shoulder. He could smell her perfume, feeling her hair tickle his face. She sat that close to him. God, she was intoxicating.

He no longer paid attention to the movie. Instead, he kept sneaking glances at her, waiting for the right moment, trying to restrain himself. It took every ounce of will power not to do anything more. He couldn't. Not with his parents in the next room. When she lifted her head and looked up at him, he leaned in and stole a kiss.

John smiled, remembering the taste of her. But then his eyebrows burrowed over briefly, remembering how Lisa glanced at the clock and saw the time. She jumped off the couch in a panic, saying it was late and she had to go. He offered to walk her home, but it was her face that made him take a double look. Her face turned from panicked to scared, and she bolted out the front door.

Lisa called him when she got home to let him know she made it OK. But she could only talk a few minutes. Even then she whispered, talking fast. Like she couldn't be on the phone. *Or couldn't be up maybe?* he thought. *It wasn't that late to still be awake.*

He shook his head. It didn't matter. He straightened up, seeing Lisa in the hallway. She lit up upon seeing him and walked right up to him.

"Hey." John pulled her to him and kissed her on the lips, which she eagerly returned. They hugged each other tightly. He could feel her moaning against him. *Oh, shit*, he thought, stepping back from her. He glanced down, hoping nothing showed or that she felt anything.

John looked up and saw Tom, who smirked, nodded to him, and kept walking. He looked back at Lisa, noticing Sarah and Meg standing a few feet behind them near their lockers. They were also smiling and silently cheering on Lisa. John smiled, grabbing Lisa's hand.

"Come on," he said.

They were officially a couple now, and the whole school noticed as they walked down the halls hand in hand. Everyone stopped and stared as they passed by. Some students smiled, calling out, congratulating them. Some threw them dirty looks and started whispering among other students. But John didn't care. He had Lisa. He grabbed her hand and stuck it in the crook of his arm.

The whole day they were the talk of the school. John kept getting stares from everyone when he wasn't with Lisa. The ones from the girls were worse. The guys just nodded in approval or shook his hand. They only had one class together, which sucked. They didn't even have the same lunch period. He made it a point to see her in between classes as much as he could.

Before he knew it, the day was over and he was saying bye to Lisa, then sprinting off to his basketball practice. Practice lasted easily two hours every day after school. Just depends on the coach and how they were doing. Sometimes it lasted three hours if they kept messing up. He had wanted her to stay and watch so he could spend more time with her afterward. But he didn't know her schedule or routine yet. They were still new as a couple. He hadn't had time to ask either. Instead, John promised Lisa to call her when he got home.

John burst into the locker room, seeing that the whole team waited on him. They were all dressed and ready to practice. Even the sophomore guys were waiting, though they talked among themselves. He suddenly felt bad, remembering his responsibilities as captain. He couldn't be distracted or have a bad day, because then it affected his team members, who counted on him, and they wouldn't perform as well.

We need to get out on the court before Coach W starts looking for us, he thought.

It was his responsibility to get the team warmed up and ready for practice by leading them through the workouts and the drills before they concentrated on skill. They usually ended practice with a scrimmage. He quickly changed.

"You guys ready?" he asked everyone.

"Yeah!" Their voices carried throughout the room.

"All right," he raised his voice to be heard, "we played a good first game. Let's keep our focus up and our spirits on the prize to make state this year."

"Yeah!"

"Let's go," he shouted.

The Rangers piled out of the room and entered the gym to begin their workout.

Try as he might, John couldn't stop thinking about Lisa. All throughout practice, his mind kept wandering. When could he see her again?

I could walk by her house on the way home, see if I can visit her, he thought, running down the court. Just for a little bit.

Now focus on the game!

John turned around, and the ball flew past him, bouncing out-of-bounds. Coach W blew the whistle, calling a time-out. He looked back at the court to find all eyes on him. He realized Ben had passed him the ball, since he stood open and right next to the basket for an easy shot.

"John, get your head out of the clouds," Coach W yelled.

"Sorry, sir," he said. "It won't happen again."

Ben, appearing angry and holding his hands up, approached him, yelling, "What the hell?"

He ran his hands through his hair, letting out a deep sigh. "Sorry, man."

"Sorry," Ben bellowed, stepping up to John's face. "You're sorry. You're the captain, and you can't catch a pass."

He backed up a few paces, but Ben stepped closer until he remained screaming in John's face, spit flying everywhere, his face hard and angry. Before John realized what was going on, all his buddies stepped forward, surrounding the two of them.

Adrian reached them first, stepping between them. He pushed Ben back. "Step off, man."

John saw his buddies break off into two sides. Adrian, Jason, and Chad stood next to him, while Ben and Tom stood facing him.

"You step off," Tom yelled, pushing Adrian, then turned to John. "And you be the captain you're supposed to be."

"Watch who you're talking to," Jason bellowed, pushing Tom back.

"What happened to bros before hoes?" Ben shouted to Jason, stepping closer. "Shut up, you little dick," Adrian said to Ben. "You like her too, and you know it." All at once, Ben and Tom started fighting with Jason and Adrian.

"Guys, stop it," John yelled, running forward.

He stepped between Adrian and Ben. Chad stepped between Tom and Jason, pulling them apart. John continually ducked to stay away from the swinging fists that kept popping out all around him. He grabbed the nearest guy from behind and pulled Adrian back. He pushed Ben back until they stood at arms' length from each other.

"Stop!" John yelled at Ben. "That's enough!" He looked over at Chad, who had Tom in a headlock while Jason stood back, panting with his fists clenched. Tom swung his fists around, trying to free himself, and finally relented when it was hopeless for him. "Let him go."

Chad instantly released Tom, who straightened, his face bright red. John looked around at his buddies, who still stood facing each other but no longer swinging. Ben's eye was swollen. Jason had a little blood seeping out of his nose. No one said anything. He turned back to Ben, who remained glaring at him.

"It was an accident," he said firmly. "Now chill out. We'll do the play over and get it right."

The whistle blew loud and long, silencing them. The Rangers looked over at Coach W, who appeared angrier than any of them. John noticed that the sophomores were gathered near the basket and away from the scene, watching the entire time. *Those little punks*, he thought. *They just stood there*. He turned back to Coach W, who had walked out to half-court, facing the team that stood on one side.

"All right, you knuckleheads," Coach W bellowed. His eyes shifted to each member. "This isn't the time or the place to be screwing around. You want to fight, take it outside. Five laps—all of you. Now!"

The Rangers grumbled. They formed a single line on the outlining of the basketball court and started running around it. John sprinted. He led the guys around the court, finding himself pulling too far ahead, blowing off steam.

"Pick it up," Coach W shouted. "Stay together. You wanted a captain; now keep up with his pace."

John heard curses muttered behind him. He continued running, pumping his arms and legs. Sweat trickled down his temples and back. He puffed and puffed, pacing himself. He blew air out of his mouth, feeling bad about what happened. First for losing control of the team and then for letting his friends fight it out in front of everyone. But he mostly felt bad about his distractions earlier that started everything.

What really set it off for Ben and Tom? There was no reason for them to blow up over missing a pass. Was Ben still hung up on Lisa or angry from the first game? And what was Tom's deal?

The Rangers never finished the game. Instead, they spent the rest of the practice between running and doing drills. Every time someone screwed up, the whole team had to run two laps around the court.

By the end of the practice, Coach W yelled at them some more. "Everyone screws up now and then."

They stood around the coach in a semicircle, exhausted and out of breath. Every member panted, every face looked beet red, every guy drenched in sweat. The whole gym reeked of bad odor and dirty socks. John used the front of his shirt to wipe the perspiration off his face. No matter how many times he tried, the sweat continued to flow.

But Coach W wasn't finished. "That doesn't mean you lose your head over it," he continued. "From now on, you screw around on my watch, you'll run like you did today. We don't have time to be wasting. Our next game is this Friday. If you lose, you'll have no one to blame but yourselves, because you were too busy screwing around instead of practicing." He paused, glancing at John, who briefly closed his eyes. His head bowed, feeling ashamed of himself. "Now hit the showers."

John turned on his heels and bolted to the locker room. The rest of the Rangers trudged along. His muscles ached and burned from the extra hard workout. Sweat drenched his entire body. He desperately needed a hot shower. He entered the room and headed straight to his locker, grabbing a towel on his way. He fished out his school clothes from his bag and quickly showered and changed, oblivious to his buddies. Only when he emerged from the showers did he find his buddies squaring off against one another. They stood on opposite sides of the aisle between the lockers.

Damn it! They're not going to stop. Throwing his dirty towel on the bench in disgust, he stepped between his buddies before more fists started flying. He turned, facing Ben and Tom.

"What is your deal?" John stepped up to them. "You have something to say, say it."

Ben and Tom finally backed down, retreating to their lockers instead.

"All right, then," John said, looking around him. "Let's chill and forget about it. We'll do better next practice." Shaking his head, he grabbed his book bag and headed toward the door. His buddies called out to him, but he merely waved his hand, letting the door slam, shutting out their voices.

John walked home by himself, still fuming and aching all over. He took his time walking, allowing his muscles to stretch. The sun beating down on his shoulders felt good. He crossed the street and continued walking past his subdivision, heading over to the next subdivision, where Lisa lived. The surrounding neighborhood stood alive with cars passing, kids laughing and talking as they strolled by, and families jogging with their young ones or pets.

He kept an eye out for Lisa, wondering if she was out and about right now. Seeing no sign of her, he crossed the intersection and turned left on to her street. He pressed on, searching. The trees and bushes they had taken last time were on his right. He crossed to the other side of the street, staying on the sidewalk, looking at all the signs.

It should be around here somewhere, he thought, and then recognized the crossing street.

He remembered that the house stood at the corner of two streets. He looked to his right and spotted the fence where they said goodbye. That meant the house loomed right in front of him.

John sprinted over to the fence, hiding his body for cover, and peeked around it. The two-story house looked nice, but it appeared to be quiet. Not a sound emerged nor a light shone. The curtains were drawn shut, the door closed. No car stood in the driveway. He looked at each window carefully, looking for any sign of her. Or someone. But he didn't know which room was hers. Shifting his bag on his shoulders, he strolled over to the sidewalk and up the front steps. He rang the doorbell and waited, glancing at his watch. It wasn't too late, remembering she had a curfew.

A few moments later, Lisa opened the door and her eyes grew wide. Really wide. She closed the door halfway, only showing her face. "John, what are you doing here?" she whispered firmly, anxiously looking back over her shoulder.

He instantly regretted being there. "I just wanted to see you. Thought we could hang out." He shrugged, the words coming out fast and weak.

"I can't," she said. "Not on school nights. I'll see you tomorrow."

And with that, the door closed in his face. John's head slumped as he turned around and walked toward his home.

Now he felt worse. This day was not ending well for him. He probably got her in trouble. It was his fault. He should have checked with her first before showing up unannounced. Well now he knows.

* * *

The next day John stood by Lisa's locker, waiting. He kept rehearsing his apology over and over. She saw him and lit up, breaking into a gorgeous smile. He exhaled, his shoulders relaxed, and smiled, knowing everything was all right. She ran into his open arms and hugged him fiercely. John held her to him, digging his face into her hair. He pulled his head back, still holding her is his arms, and placed his hand under her chin, lifting her face up until her eyes met his.

"I'm sorry."

"It's OK," she replied. "You didn't know."

"Yeah."

"I can't hang out on school nights," Lisa said.

"Ok, fair enough," John said. "What about Friday nights?"

"That's fine."

"Then this Friday, we're going out."

She smiled. "Ok. Though you'll probably have to meet my parents."

"Deal." he instantly replied.

"Wait," she said. "Don't you have a game?"

"Ah, shit."

Lisa laughed and he pulled her to him again, hugging her one last time as the final morning bell rang.

The week flew by fast for John. It was Friday, and he was supposed to meet Lisa's parents that night. Kids were heading out the front door, with the final bell still echoing throughout the halls. He said bye to Lisa and headed to the locker room for the game.

She couldn't stay, which made no sense. *She stayed for last week's game*, he thought. *Or maybe she went home first and then came back*. He shook his head.

Several heads turned his way. He ignored the stares. Some girls stepped in front of him, blocking his path, reaching out to touch him, to touch his hair. He merely dodged their hands and walked around them.

Geez, he thought. They don't stop. Even knowing he had a girlfriend, they still tried. If anything, it was worse.

Tony and Martin passed him, nodding to him. He nodded back, wondered if they were coming tonight with Sarah and Meg. A few of his buddies yelled for him to wait, running to catch up, and John slowed down until Adrian and Jason caught up with him.

"Oh, damn, that's nice," Adrian said, spotting a girl walking toward them. "I like that."

"Ask for a quickie," Jason said.

John laughed and they took off so Adrian could work his game. He spotted Chad talking to a girl too. Jason called out to Chad, hollering. He continued pressing his way through the crowds, entered the locker room and quickly changed.

He stood with the team, but his thoughts were miles away. His buddies remained by his side. Or rather Jason, Adrian, and Chad stood by him. Ben and Tom stood apart facing them, glaring at them. They were still acting like little dicks, so John just left them alone, no longer caring.

The Rangers lost the game that night.

He had been distracted. His mind was constantly thinking about Lisa, slowly learning the rules of the household. He knew she had a curfew. He knew she could not go out on school nights. He knew she could not stay up late. Not even on the phone. He could not stay up too late either but if his parents knew where he was, they were ok. It was not this bad for him. He did not understand why her parents were so strict.

John realized he was distracted when Lisa was at the game, but even more so when she wasn't.

Lisa's house loomed in front of him. The sun was setting on the horizon. He was tired, hungry, and his muscles ached.

Yet John had never been more nervous than he was now. He rang the doorbell and waited.

A man opened the door, tall and big, with broad shoulders, looming over the doorway.

"Hi, I'm John," he said, extending his hand.

"Carlos." Lisa's father shook his hand, squeezing it hard.

It took every ounce of John not to wince out in pain. The father was big and strong and could snap him into two pieces. Yes, he got the hint. Don't break his daughter's heart.

Carlos stepped back and let him inside. John spotted Lisa coming toward him with her mother by her side, giving him the once-over.

"John," Lisa exclaimed, breaking into a smile, "this is my mother, Sylvia."

"Nice to meet you," he said shaking her hand, smiling at what he saw. He could see where Lisa got her looks. The mother was an attractive older version.

"You must be hungry," Sylvia said.

"Very." They all broke out laughing.

Dinner was quiet and awkward, as the four of them sat at the table. He had to be on his best behavior and keep his hands to himself. But it was not just the dinner table that was quiet. The house itself was quiet. And big. Too big for just the three of them. John glanced at Lisa out of the corner of his eye. He could also see she was nervous and uncomfortable, as she focused on eating her food. Yet he found it odd. She seemed more relaxed at his house with his family then with her own.

He kept trying to think of something to talk about but couldn't. Of course, it didn't help that her parents kept looking at him. And they weren't hiding it.

"So," Sylvia said, finally breaking the silence, "Lisa tells me you play basketball."

"Yes, I'm the captain of the junior varsity team," John said, hoping to impress her.

"I'm surprised they let you have your hair that long," Sylvia shot back.

Ooh, John winced at that dig, having been silenced. Apparently, she was not impressed. Carlos simply grunted.

"Mom!" He could hear the embarrassment in Lisa's voice. Embarrassed by her mother's behavior. John glanced over at her, seeing her cheeks burn pink. He gave her a small smile, but she avoided eye contact. Too upset to do anything except stare at her plate. He dropped his hand and placed it on her leg, squeezing it to comfort her.

Carlos grunted louder, having seen what he did. John quickly took his hand off Lisa's leg. Apparently, he didn't like that either.

Oh, this is going to be a long night, John thought, stealing a glance at the kitchen clock.

"I'm just saying," Sylvia continued.

With dinner finally over, John helped clear the dishes from the table over to the kitchen sink but was quickly shooed away by Sylvia. They moved to the living room to watch television, seating themselves on the couch, only for Carlos to sit between them. Now they were on opposite sides, with Carlos in the middle, taking up most of the couch.

He grunted, feeling squashed. *Man, he's a big dude*, John thought. *Subtle much?* He looked around, thinking it was time to make his escape and leave. He did his part. He met the parents. Surely, they would kick him out soon.

Some framed photos on the wall caught his eye. Family photos it looked like, except there were five of them. Beside Lisa and her parents, there were two other guys in the picture—teenagers who looked more like Carlos. They were slightly older than Lisa too. Her brothers? Lisa had never mentioned brothers to him. Only alluded when he pressed her that one time. So where were they now?

John glanced over at Lisa, seeing that both her and Carlos watched him. He was about to ask but stopped. Something told him not to. Lisa's face looked frightened. Carlos looked angry, daring him to ask. His mouth opened and closed a few times, before realizing Sylvia stood next to him. He looked up at Sylvia and sighed in relief.

Right on cue, Sylvia said, "It's getting late. It's time for you to leave, John."

He smiled and instantly stood up, eager to be gone.

Lisa also jumped up. "I'll walk you out."

"Nice meeting you both," John said. He shook their hands once again as Carlos also stood up, joining Sylvia's side.

He joined Lisa's side as they walked to the front door, aware of the parents right on their heels. "I'll call you tomorrow."

"Ok, bye."

Lisa opened the door and John stepped over the threshold, calling out and waving to them, "Bye."

The door closed behind him as he made his way down the front lawn. His eyebrows burrowed over. That didn't quite go so well. And he didn't know why. Or what he did wrong in their eyes. Other than they were overprotective of Lisa. He had wanted to give her a proper farewell but knew that wasn't happening. He also knew calling her tonight was out of the question. But it was the photos that had cut the evening short. Lisa's face had looked so frightened of him asking. Almost like she was shaking her head no.

He shook himself, dismissing it. Nothing he could do now. *Next time*, he thought, *we're hanging at my house.*

* * *

Lisa seemed better the next day when John called her. They didn't mention anything about the night before at her house. Instead he asked her to come over to his house to hang out. And much to his surprise, she said yes.

She was all smiles when he opened the door, causing his shoulders to relax as he broke out in a smile. *Man, she is hot*, John thought. He let her inside and his parents came out to greet her, hugging her this time. They spent the afternoon hanging out and watching television in the living room. His parents had left them alone, much to his relief.

There was no reason not to, John thought, holding Lisa in his arms. *They like her.*

When the pizza arrived, they settled in to watch movies. John glanced at his watch. The afternoon had flown by. He knew she would have to leave soon. He wasn't quite sure what time she had to be home by. But he didn't want the night to end.

Maybe we can hang out tomorrow at the arcade, he thought.

He paused the movie. Lisa looked up at him questioningly. "What time do you have to be home?"

She glanced at the clock on the wall. "In an hour."

"OK, let's get going," he said. "I'll walk you home."

"Already?"

"I don't want you to get in trouble," he replied.

"True."

"And then you'll get grounded and not be able to go out at all," John pointed out.

"Also true," Lisa said, groaning. "That almost happened the other day."

"Come on." He stood up and helped her off the couch, smiling as she protested, not wanting to leave. "We can hang out tomorrow."

Lisa brightened up by that remark. "OK."

They said bye to his parents and started walking to her place.

"Let's take that shortcut," John suggested.

There was still time. He held her hand following as she led the way, getting a nice view of her. He waited until they were in the middle of the forest before pulling her to him. John wrapped his arms around her and kissed her on the lips. She eagerly returned the kiss, pressing herself against him. Without another word, John lowered her to the ground, kissing her.

CHAPTER 5

Two months had flown by.

John went through the motions of practice halfheartedly. Their practices were getting worse and worse over the days. All they did was run. Their next game was quickly approaching, yet they weren't ready.

The weather also changed from hot to cool and windy. The Rangers continued to run during every practice and lose every game they played. The team members actually looked fit from all the workouts. His buddies had either packed on pounds of muscle or trimmed down to a defined cut. John was the latter.

Between trying to balance his schoolwork, his girlfriend, basketball and his friends, he had lost control. By the time John realized why they were losing the season, it was too late. The damage had already been done. There was no chance for state this year.

His friends split up into two groups. Ben and Tom went off on their own, having joined up with some other guys. John recognized the guys when seeing them but couldn't put any names to the faces. Nor did he care. Adrian, Jason, and Chad remained by his side. Once leaving practice or a game, the group split up and parted ways.

During practice, the guys went through the drills and rehearsed the plays. But John soon discovered it was all an act. Once it was game time, all hell broke out. No matter how many times the team tried, Coach tried, or John tried; Ben and Tom messed it up. They hogged the ball, passing it between them only. They dribbled down the court and go for the layup, only for it to be intercepted and the other team to score.

Tom grabbed the rebound and dribbled down court.

"Tom," John shouted. "I'm open."

But Tom ignored him and kept dribbling, trying to go around the Snake.

"Tom!!!!" John yelled again. He was standing right under the basket, waving his arms. Come on, man. They were already losing. He was wide open and had an easy shot.

More Snakes surrounded Tom and he looked around for Ben, but Coach didn't play him this quarter, having caught on. John could see the frustration on his friends' faces. Chad bulldozed his way in and knocked the ball out of Tom's hands. Anger flashed on Tom's face and he pushed Chad.

Here we go, John thought, sighing, his shoulders drooping.

Chad pushed Tom back harder, sending him sprawling across the court on his butt. Ben jumped up from the bench, causing Jason to jump up and trip him as Adrian ran to Chad's side.

The whistle blew long and hard as Coach W and John ran up, trying to separate the fights.

John shook his head, clearing his thoughts from last night's game. Luckily, Lisa hadn't been there.

He had spent the afternoon with Lisa at the arcade. They walked quickly; heads bent from the wind. He wrapped his windbreaker around her tightly and they burst into his house. He closed the door, glad to be out of the fierce wind that made his teeth chatter.

"Mom, Dad," he called out, "we're home."

No one answered.

Lisa looked over at him questioningly. "They go out?"

"Huh, I guess so." He thought back, trying to remember what his parents told him about today. Surely he had told them they were coming over later, right? He shook his head.

Then he realized they were alone. This was the first time they had been alone together at their houses. Completely alone.

Lisa had taken off his jacket and hung it on the coat rack. She must have thought the same thing, as her posture suddenly changed. She stood awkwardly, almost shyly, glancing at him.

He smiled and pulled her to him, kissing her on the lips. Her stomach growled, loud and long. They broke out laughing.

"Come on," he said, pulling her to the kitchen. "Let's find something to eat."

They scrummaged around in the cabinets, but with no such luck. It was Saturday. Tomorrow was grocery day. *Damn it*, he thought. He was about to close the door when something caught his eye. In the back of the cabinet was a bottle of liquor. Hmm, this will warm us up.

He grabbed the bottle and held it up to Lisa. She smiled and nodded. Why not? He fished out two shot glasses and they took a swig. The liquid burned going down. Lisa made a face.

"Too strong?" He asked.

"No, it's fine."

They took another shot and it went down smoother, warming his stomach. John went to the living room and turned on some music. He pulled Lisa to him, holding her close in his arms, and they swayed back and forth. He could feel her loosening up. He spun her around, making her laugh.

The afternoon turned into a blur, as the shots went down, and they danced and danced. But then John realized they still hadn't eaten. His head became instantly clear. He stopped the music and grabbed the phone.

"What's up?" Lisa asked, her face beet red.

"I'm going to order a pizza," he said. "We need to eat something." He found the number and placed the order.

Shit, they don't deliver. It was too far and too cold to walk. He walked to the garage and opened the door, spotting his dad's 1981 Pontiac Bonneville inside. His parents took his mom's car somewhere and still weren't back.

He would have to drive.

"Come on." He grabbed the car keys from the bowl.

"What are you doing?" Lisa asked.

"I'll drive us," he replied. "It'll be faster this way. By the time we get there, it'll be ready."

"What? Are you crazy?"

"It's fine. I've driven before." Which was true. His dad had taken him out driving several times to get use to it. He even let him drive home once or twice when his parents were too buzzed or too tired.

"Are you sure?" Lisa continued.

"Yes, it's close by," John said.

"They won't get mad?"

"Nah."

They got in the car and he started the engine, opening the garage door. After they buckled up, he adjusted the mirrors and reversed slowly from the driveway. Then he shifted to drive and turned the car to the left, accelerating down the street.

"Oh, the garage door," Lisa said.

"Oh, shit."

John reached up for the garage opener and it fell out of the holder, landing somewhere on the floor. "Where did it go?"

"I got it," she said, bending over and fishing around on the floor.

"No, wait. I see it," he said. "It's over there."

"John!"

He looked up as a car came right at them, blaring the horn. John served to the right, and then saw the parked car too late, and slammed on the brakes.

They screamed. The impact of the car jarred him forward. His head crashed into the steering wheel, the seatbelt cutting into his chest and waist. He saw black dots, blurring his vision. His head and jaw throbbed in pain. He couldn't breathe.

John tried to lift his arm but couldn't; it felt heavy. A loud horn blared, echoing in his head, making his ears wince. It wouldn't stop. He turned and his arm fell off the steering wheel. The horn stopped. Now he heard sirens. He looked down at his lap. His arms were throbbing, sitting idly on his legs. He wanted to reach over and unbuckle his seatbelt but couldn't. He realized he couldn't move. The pressure on his chest was killing him, making it hard to breathe.

He heard a soft moan next to him. Lisa! He looked over and saw her stir. There were cuts and bruises on her face. She had been leaning forward when they hit the car. Her face must have hit the deck.

"Lisa," he said. "Are you OK?"

"Yeah, I think so." She moaned, turning her head slowly.

The cuts on her face made him wince. Feeling came back to his arms. He tried to lean toward her only for his head to start pounding, the black dots appearing. His surroundings turned blurry, fading in and out. He shook his head, trying to clear his vision but it only intensified the throbbing.

The sirens echoed in the distance coming closer. John covered his ears as the sound grew louder. It sounded like the police, or maybe an ambulance. Someone must have called.

"It's OK," he shouted over the noise, hoping she could hear him. "We're going to be OK."

He couldn't hear. He couldn't see. He could barely move. The chill hit him first, wind gushing in, the sound roaring in his ears. Hands reached in, talking to him, feeling his face, arms, and chest. Strong hands. A light shined into his eyes, making him turn away.

He was lifted, floating on air. The black dots swarmed his eyes.

"Lisa!" John yelled.

But he couldn't see her. He couldn't move again. Something restrained him. He was laying down now. A warm fluid flooded his body. He felt so good. And tired. So tired.

Wait, he thought, struggling. *What was he trying to remember?*

"Don't fight it," a voice said. "Let the medicine work."

Lisa, he thought. *Where's Lisa?*

"She's OK," the voice said. "We're taking you both to the hospital."

She's OK. They're going to be OK. *Oh God,* he thought, falling deeper into a black hole, *what have I done?*

"John," a voice said, from far, far away. It sounded sad, worried. Anxious. He recognized that voice from somewhere. "John." His mom.

No, wait a minute, he thought. She's right here. He slowly opened his eyes to find his mom sitting in a chair, staring at him.

Relief flooded her face instantly. "Oh, good. You're awake." She leaned forward. "How do you feel?"

He glanced around his surroundings to discover he was lying on a bed, hooked up to some machines. He was in the hospital. Everything came back to him. The car. The accident. Lisa.

"How's Lisa?" he asked. "Is she OK?"

"She's fine," his mom replied. "Just some cuts and bruises."

The dark room and quietness of the hallways told him it was nighttime. Probably the wee hours of the morning. How long had he been out?

John watched his mom fidget by biting her nails. She only did this when she was angry or nervous. He saw the resemblance between them. His mom had black curly hair, flowing past her shoulders. She never looked her age, which was forty-three, and probably wouldn't for a while. She was considered tall for a woman and carried a slender figure. She stayed a young, creamy beige color, always burning but never tanning.

"How are you feeling?"

He shook his head. "My head hurts a little but I'm fine." That was only half true. His upper body felt sore. Even his face hurt. But he wasn't about to worry her. "Can I go?"

"Not yet. The doctors want to keep you for observation."

"Why?"

His mom hesitated.

"What?" John asked. "Mom, what are you not telling me?"

"What happened, John?" she asked instead. "Do you remember?"

"Mom, tell me. What did the doctors say?"

She sighed, looking down at the ground. John sat up, pulling the covers off him. He paused briefly, having sat up too fast. He tore off the tape from his arm and took out the needle, wincing. The machine went off, beeping.

"John, stop. You need to rest."

He was naked, the only thing covering him was a gown barely big enough to wrap around his entire body. It opened in the back and he held onto it tightly, standing up on the cold tile floor impatiently. It worked. His mom averted her eyes as he fished for his clothes, quickly changing.

Nurses came in.

"Where's Lisa?" he yelled.

"John!" He heard her voice.

He walked around the nurse, ignoring her protests, and futile attempts to stop him. Like she could stop him. One sweep of his arm and she was out of his way. He went to the next room, spotting Lisa on the bed, also hooked up to machines. Her face looked like she had been in a fight, covered in black-and-blue bruises. He ran to her side, ignoring the pain in his chest, and the throbbing in his face. He sat on the bed and grabbed her hand.

"Lisa," he said. "I'm so, so sorry."

She smiled or tried to beneath a swollen lip. "You're fine, John. It was an accident."

"Oh good, you're both awake," a deep voice said entering the room, making them turn to the door. The doctor introduced himself, moving to the other side of the bed, looking at Lisa and her vitals. "You're the father I presume?"

John's eyebrows burrowed over, confused. Seriously, dude? "I'm not her father. I'm her boyfriend." He turned to Lisa. "Is she OK?"

"She's fine," the doctor continued. "A few cuts and bruises. We just want to keep her here overnight for observation and monitor the baby. Make sure everything is OK."

Baby? "Wait, what?" John exclaimed.

"Baby?" Lisa asked.

"You're pregnant," the doctor replied.

His mouth dropped open, then shut. His eyes widened. The news hit him like a rock, straight to the stomach.

Lisa was pregnant.

He looked over at her, seeing that she was also shocked. She met his gaze. He could see she was scared. *Damn*, he thought. John squeezed her hand tight, giving her a small smile. He placed his hand carefully onto her stomach, the doctor's voice rambling on in the background.

He was going to be a father.

Oh, shit, he thought, trying to think back to the night it happened. *Which night was it? Does it matter?* He shook his head, clearing his thoughts. He was fourteen and going to be a father.

The doctor finally left them alone.

"Did you know?" he asked her.

"No." Lisa sighed. He could see she was fighting back tears.

"Hey, hey, it's OK." John laid on the bed next to her, holding her in his arms. "We'll figure it out." He stroked her hair, feeling her body tremble, crying silently against his chest. "Shh." He held her close to him, rocking her back and forth until she fell asleep.

* * *

His dad woke him up this time.

John opened his eyes to find his father standing in the doorway, appearing very angry. He stepped forward, making John shrink back into the bed. John had never seen his dad this angry before, which made him scared. He didn't know why either. He had no reason to be afraid of him. It wasn't like his dad ever beat him, but then again, John never saw him this upset.

His dad was a few inches taller than him. He was also on the slender side, but built, especially in his upper body. His jet-black hair and mustache were thick but kept short, making it easier to manage. He also had a light complexion, but with yellow undertones. His dad entered the room and John felt Lisa stir beside him. He turned toward her when movement from his peripheral vision caught his eye. John looked up to find Lisa's parents sitting in the corner, watching them silently.

Uh-oh, John thought. *How long have they been there?* He wasn't sure when they had entered the room, but he could tell they were upset. Furious. Carlos looked like he wanted to beat him up. Sylvia seemed outraged, livid.

They knew. Both of their parents knew. They haven't even met each other. *Geez, this is a great first meeting for them*, John thought.

"Mom, Dad," Lisa said, awake and now sitting up.

"John, let's give them the room," his dad said.

He met Lisa's gaze. She looked frighten, like she didn't want to be left alone with her patents. He didn't want to leave her side. Not like this. But he knew he had to. They had to face the music and answer to their parents. He certainly couldn't meddle in her family. Not yet anyway. Not until they figured it out and came up with a plan. Reluctantly, he squeezed her hand and stood up from the bed. John threw Lisa a smile, trying to tell her it would be OK, before following his dad out of the room.

As soon as they entered his room, his dad turned on him. "What's the matter with you, boy?" he demanded, closing the curtain behind him. "What did you think you were doing?"

"Dad ..." John walked backward, toward the bed. His hair fell over his face, blocking his vision. He was at a loss for words. "I... don't...know..."

"Of course, you don't," his dad yelled. "You were thinking with your little head and not your big one."

His shoulders slumped. The curtain moved and his mom entered the room. John averted his eyes, glancing at the floor, feeling ashamed of himself.

"I cannot believe you would do something like this," his dad continued. His hair stuck up in all areas. His black eyes bulged out. "We raised you better than this. I ... I ..." He stopped midsentence, pacing around in front of John, his hand on his forehead.

"Well," his mom said, crossing her arms over her chest. "What do you have to say for yourself?"

John collapsed on the bed. "We'll figure it out."

"Oh?" his mom asked "Yes, we'll make it work."

"You better," his dad shot back, turned on his heels, and stormed out the room.

* * *

A few days had passed. John had finally been released from the hospital and was at home, resting. The doctors said he was fine, just to take it easy so his body could heal. He had been excused from school. His parents didn't want him to overdo it at basketball. And John didn't want any questions. Besides his bruised face, he had bruises on his chest and waist from the seatbelt. He found out he had been going faster than he realized.

His friends had called, asking where he was. And to get his lazy ass to class. He joked around with them, evading their questions. Oh yeah, he was fine. Probably a bug. Would be back soon enough. They better not be slacking at practice.

John tried to see Lisa before leaving, but her parents weren't having it, refusing him entry into the room. He didn't know if she was still at the hospital or if she had been released. He didn't know how she was doing. He called her house a few times, but no one answered. They knew his number by now. Either no one was home, or her parents weren't letting her answer the phone.

He was sitting on the couch, when his mom came in, looking upset. Now what?

"I received a call from Lisa's parents," she said. "They are taking you to court for reckless endangerment."

"Reckless endangerment?" John shouted. He could feel his cheeks burning, the anger rising throughout his body. First the crash, then the hospital, and now this. Haven't they gone through enough? "Seriously?"

"Yes," his mom replied.

"I was in the car too."

"Reckless endangerment of a minor and infant."

His mouth dropped open. The baby. Is something wrong with the baby? "Is the baby OK? Did something happen?"

"I don't know."

"The doctor said the baby was fine," he said. "I should know if something happened."

"They didn't say," she replied.

"Well if they would let me speak to her," he roared back. He reached over for the phone, but his mom stopped him.

"John, listen to me. You can't talk to her."

"What?" he asked. "Are you kidding me? She's my girlfriend."

"The parents don't want you talking to her right now," his mom said.

"Why not?"

"Well can you blame them?" she shot back. "You took the car without permission and got into a car accident. And then come to find out, their daughter is pregnant."

John winced at her words. She had a point. He hesitated, not knowing what to say. "How long are they going to act like this?"

"What?" his mom asked.

"How long are her parents going to keep us apart?" he asked. "She's pregnant and I'm the father. At some point, we must talk and see each other. We must raise the baby. They can't keep us away forever."

Now his mom was at a loss for words. She averted his eyes, looking down instead.

"What exactly did they tell you?"

"Let's just take it one thing at a time and go from there," she replied. "Starting with the court date."

CHAPTER 6

John waited by Lisa's locker. He was finally back at school, even if it was Friday. The final bell rang, and she still hadn't showed up. He ran to his class, making it just in time. All through the day, he kept looking for Lisa but never found her.

Maybe she's still home and healing, he thought. She had a few bruises on her face. Probably wanted them to heal before stepping out in public again. It would raise too many questions. I'll stop by her house after school. The parents can't expect me to stay away forever.

The day passed by in a blur. His friends surrounded him now that he was back. The stares continued from the girls, but they were bolder now that Lisa was nowhere in sight. They kept trying to reach out and touch him or talk to him as he passed by. But he paid them no mind. He just wanted the day to be over already so he could go check up on Lisa.

He turned the corner and saw Meg and Sarah in the hallway. They turned around and spotted him, calling out to him. "John."

Oh, crap, he thought, walking up to them. Did they know? Their faces looked worried. No, they didn't know.

"Hey," he said.

"Have you seen Lisa?" Sarah asked.

"She's been absent all week," Meg said.

"She's been sick," he lied. "I'm going to check up on her today." He held his breath, hoping they would buy it. He didn't see them that much as it was so they may not have noticed he was gone too.

"Oh, OK," Meg said.

"Well, that's good to know," Sarah added. "We were getting worried."

"It's not like her to miss school," Meg continued. "When I call, no one answers."

"I'll let you know," he fibbed.

"John, come on, "Adrian said thumping him on the back. "We got a game."

The game! He forgot all about the game tonight. He groaned then said bye to the girls and took off with Adrian to the gym. At least he had been saved from the questions. But he hadn't worked out or practiced all week. He was out of shape. He entered the locker room and quickly changed into his uniform. His friends hollered when they saw him, surrounding him but his mind was miles away.

He didn't want to be here.

He wanted to go check up on Lisa, which meant it would be late by the time the game ended. *Just get through the game, and then you can see her*, he thought. *Now focus*!

But John was rusty. His legs felt heavy when he ran, his reaction time slower. He was out of breath from simply running down the court after the ball tipped in their favor. Jason passed it to him, and he missed it, the ball flying by him. His teammates yelled at him. Coach W shouted at him. He sighed.

This was going to be a long game.

He heaved and heaved from all the running, his face feeling hot. His chest hurt and his muscles strained. By the end of the first quarter, his teammates caught on that his game was off. He could see it on their faces. He was letting his team down. There was too much going on right now. He was too distracted.

John took a deep breath. Even the cheering in the gymnasium had died down. The whistle blew and Coach W pulled him, replacing him with a sophomore. He sighed in relief, glad to be sitting on the bench to catch his breath. He could hear the comments from the guys on the bleachers, but simply ignored them. Ben and Tom smirked.

"Now you know what it feels like," Ben muttered.

"Oh, shut up," John shot back.

They lost the game.

He saw the disappointment on his friend's faces. It was his performance this time. Not Ben and Tom hogging the ball. They barely played anymore.

I'll work out this weekend, John thought. *I'll make it up to them*. He looked up at Lisa's house in front of him. The front-porch light was on, and he could see the living-room light was on from the window. And one of the bedroom's lights on the second floor was on. *Good, they are home.*

He rang the doorbell, his heart pounding in his chest. He didn't know why he was so nervous. He should be excited to see Lisa. But he was both. It would be the first time seeing her since the hospital. They had parted with tension in the air. Not the way he wanted to at all. He didn't want to leave her side but knew he had to. He didn't know how her talk went with her parents. Not easy, he was sure.

It was also the first time he'd see her parents as well. That's why he was nervous, he realized, his cheeks burning. What do I say to them? They wanted to kill me.

The curtain pulled back and Carlos's head appeared, looking out. He saw John and the scowl retuned instantly. Carlos wagged his finger back and forth at him. No. The curtain dropped, and the footsteps retreated.

John's mouth fell open, aghast. He shut it, at a loss for words. They wouldn't even open the door. Instead Carlos told him to go away. He couldn't see Lisa. His shoulders slumped over, and he turned heading home.

* * *

John was in a courtroom, sitting next to his family's lawyer, feeling speechless and dumbfounded. His parents were in the row behind him. He still couldn't believe this was happening. That he was being charged with reckless endangerment. Worst of all, Lisa's parents were the one accusing him—his own girlfriend's parents. He knew this was all their doing. Lisa wasn't even here.

The prosecuting attorney sat at the table on the other side of the room from where John sat. He glanced at the row behind him, where Lisa's parents sat. They stared straight ahead, avoiding eye contact. Yes, it was their doing. He could see it on their faces. They wanted justice.

John looked over his shoulder. His mom shot him a sideways glance before returning her attention to the front. He tried getting his dad's attention for some help, but he only sat there. Outrage, disgust, worry, and disappointment clouded his face.

He tried paying attention to the prosecuting attorney and his lawyer, ranting back and forth. It was hard to keep up at times. All he kept hearing was reckless driving, child endangerment. His head throbbed from lack of sleep. He spent the entire night worrying about today and what would happen.

Suddenly the judge banged his gavel on his bench, silencing the attorneys. All eyes turned to the front.

"All right, I have made my decision," the judge said. "Will the defendant please stand."

He stood up next to his lawyer, holding his breath. The prosecuting attorney sat down.

Here it comes.

"The facts of this case are the following: You drove the car without permission and crashed it. Now since you are underage, and the plaintiff, Lisa Ramirez, was pregnant at the time, you are hereby charged with reckless endangerment of a minor and infant. Do you understand the charges brought against you?"

His eyes shifted downward, and his shoulders slumped. Slowly nodding, John said, "Yes, Your Honor."

"Since you are a minor and this is your first offense, I will take that into consideration," the judge continued. "You made a mistake. Now you have a choice on how to carry out your sentence. You can serve it in a juvenile detention center for four years or military school for four years until your eighteenth birthday. Consider this your second chance at life. Which will it be?"

John's eyebrows shot up. Neither choice sounded good, but he immediately knew the answer. "Military school."

"Very well. Military school it is. Case closed." The judge banged the gavel on his bench.

Four years in military school! He collapsed in his seat, burying his head in his hands. Now what was he going to do? What was Lisa going to do? What was going to happen now?

He glanced back at his parents, and his mom burst into tears. His dad pulled her close to him, trying to comfort her, but to no avail. They were no longer furious. They were in shock. And the worst part was Lisa wasn't here. He couldn't talk to her. He couldn't even say good-bye to her. He would be shipped off to military school for the next four years. He didn't even know where the school was.

But he knew one thing for sure. Her parents had charged him. They wouldn't let them talk. They wouldn't let her answer the phone when he called. Just like they wouldn't even open the door. How could they do this? How could they just send him away? What about Lisa and the baby? How could he support them?

Carlos and Sylvia stood up, shoulders back, and walked out of the courtroom without a single glance in his direction.

*** * * ***

"Mom, I'm home," Marisa Perez yelled, shutting the door. "No one home as usual."

She collapsed on the couch and sighed. All her life Marisa lived here, and her mom was never home early. Since her mom worked close to ten hours a day, Marisa took care of the house. She kind of felt sorry for her mom, who was really young, only twenty-seven going on twenty-eight. And single. Her boyfriend dumped her for someone else when she was five months pregnant. Therefore, Marisa didn't really care much about her dad. She figured he was a jerk to get her mom pregnant and then run off.

She stood up and went to the kitchen, checking the messages. None. She looked in the kitchen cabinets and started making supper.

Marisa liked living with only her mom. They were really close and looked so much alike. They were both tall, had brown eyes, creamy skin, and wavy brown hair, but hers was slightly curlier and more of a hassle than her mom's. Sometimes Marisa thought of her as an older sister.

"Hello," said a voice.

"Hey, Mom," Marisa called out. She checked the oven after a quick glance at the clock. Almost seven. Her mom was home early, earlier than last week. "Dinner's almost ready."

The kitchen door swung open, and her mom entered, looking exhausted yet grateful to see a meal being prepared.

"Honestly, Marisa," her mom said. "I don't know what I would do without you."

The one thing she really liked was how her mom appreciated everything Marisa did. Most importantly, she respected her. She would do everything possible to compensate for her support.

As an executive assistant for a public relations company, the duties consisted mostly of data processing, filing paperwork, meeting clients, following up with clients, and running errands. Her mom also completed anything that the CEO needed, and she consistently worked long hours to meet the job demands and support Marisa. She never had a set schedule for work either. It usually consisted of getting there after Marisa headed off for school and coming back whenever she finished her workload for that day.

Working so many hours as a single parent was not easy. There were times when Marisa longed for company or missed being around her. Even spending time with her now was becoming less frequent. Usually she didn't see her mom until late at night after work, who by then was too tired to do anything. Her mom would simply collapse on the couch, never making it any further into the house.

Nonetheless, Marisa loved her mom.

After the last few details of the dinner were attended to, they sat down to eat. "You know that guy Jeff I told you about?" Marisa said. "Jenni said he likes me."

"All right, that's great," her mom said, smiling.

"How was work?"

"Same as usual," her mom replied. "Tomorrow we have a meeting because we're getting a new boss."

"You don't think they'll fire you, right?" she asked.

"Oh no," her mom said. "They want to go over a few things and change some of the system. Our other boss retired, and a new guy bought the company. I'll simply be assisting the new boss."

"Fingers crossed."

* * *

John Dolton pulled into the driveway of his old home. He stepped out, stretched from the long drive, and looked around the neighborhood. Even though it remained the same all these years, his eyes saw everything for the first time. He focused on the children smiling and playing in their front yards. His thoughts were miles away. John watched them, wanting to enjoy the moment but he couldn't. Instead, he watched the sun setting on the horizon.

He was back in his old town. It had been a little over a year since he'd been back.

I should have visited more often, he thought, frowning slightly. *I owed them that much. I have no excuse for the past year.*

But thirteen years had already vanished. He served his sentence at the military school until his eighteenth birthday. The school had been a strict place that emphasized discipline, respect, and following orders. John quickly discovered there were two types of kids there. Either they were like him, teens who had clean records and made a mistake, or they had long juvenile records, and this was the last effort to straighten them out before prison. John was one of the few good kids without many offenses. He only had one charge against him, the lawyer informed him. After he served his sentence, his record would be expunged.

"Do the time, then you'll be free," his dad said during one visit. "You can move on and put this experience behind you. No one will ever know."

"Take advantage of what this school can offer you," his mom said. "It's a great school. You can finish your education and still get a job."

"Have you heard from Lisa?" John asked instead, not hearing them at all. His parents grew quiet and shook their head no for the umpteenth time. His shoulders slumped, and he sighed. It was always the same answer. No word. John wrote letters to Lisa whenever he could, telling her what happened, where he was, that he missed her, and that he hoped to see her. How he wouldn't forget her. Asked if she was OK, if their kid was OK, and he never got a response, though he wasn't sure what he was expecting.

"Maybe it's best you let her go," his mom suggested gently.

"What?" John exclaimed. "Are you serious right now?"

"John," his dad chimed in.

"I have a kid that I know nothing about," he said.

"If she had the kid," his dad added.

John's eyebrows shot up. He hadn't thought of that.

"We don't know anything," his mom continued. "We don't know if she had the kid, or if she kept the kid. You've reached out to her numerous times. She knows where you're at. It's in her court now. If she wants to see you, she will. Maybe it's best to focus on you for now."

The words rang through John's ears. *Focus on you.*

John shook his head. His poor parents. They visited him every Saturday. John wasn't sure who suffered more: him spending time in a military school, or his parents traveling many miles to see their only child. He knew they must have been questioned. Why their only kid wasn't around anymore. With his sentence almost up, he looked forward to getting on with his life.

As soon as he graduated, John had a choice to make. He took his parents advice and joined the air force. He focused on his computer skills and IT, learning everything he could. He served eight years in the air force, and his assignments took him to new locations. He welcomed the change of scenery, only too happy to get away from his past. With a new start, surrounded by new faces and challenging jobs, he sharpened his skills. He welcomed the people who knew nothing about his past.

After eight years, he was honorably discharged, and reentered civilian life. He stayed in the same location. Close enough to drive to his parents' house for a visit. But not for a day visit. *You did visit them*, he told himself. That part was true. He came when he was on leave after each of his assignments. But the last year he could have been by more often. He had the vacation time. And now here he was, on leave for two weeks.

He clearly remembered the day his world ended—the day the lawyer called him up. His parents were killed in a car accident. The news stunned him, but he barely had time to grieve, since there were necessary matters to handle immediately. He planned and saw to his parents' burial.

Now he was back to handle the paperwork involving their finances, assets, and bills; and to turn everything over to his name since he was now the family's only living heir.

John now shook himself from his thoughts by the sound of children laughing, realizing he still stood on his driveway. *Quit wasting time*, he thought. Yes, he was stalling, and he knew it. Just like he was still grieving.

He took a deep breath and fished out the key to his parent's house, as he made his way to the front door. Best to get to it.

When John entered the quiet, empty house, he immediately noticed how it looked the same after all these years. They never changed anything. He roamed through the house silently, walking from room to room. Seeing everything for the first time. The house had a total of three bedrooms, with the intention of them being put to good use. But John's mom had two miscarriages before becoming pregnant with him. After giving birth to John, his parents decided to make the third bedroom into a guest room.

The furniture, appliances, even the family photos on the walls were the same. The biggest photo of his family hung in the living room above the mantelpiece. He was only a teenager in that photo, but his parents didn't care. His mom managed to get a photo here and there when he came by to visit. The one of him in his uniform was up. The most recent one was already on the wall, but it hadn't been blown up.

The house seemed big and vacant on the inside, dark. He turned on every light, looking at all the stuff. The clothes in the closet, the kitchen appliances, the boxes in the garage surrounding his mom's car. He opened the door to his old room, seeing it was exactly the same as he left it. His mom got a bigger bed for when he came to visit. Maybe hoping he'd stay and move back in, he was sure.

There were only two topics his mom had discussed these days. When was he was coming home, and who was he dating?

"Are you seeing anyone right now?" his mom asked.

The questions began when John had finally stopped asking about Lisa. That didn't happen until this past year.

He smiled softly. "No, mom."

Her smiled faded looking disappointed. He knew she wanted grandkids. Just like she wanted him home. She may already be a grandma. But he couldn't stop wondering about Lisa and his kid. Every time he started talking to someone, Lisa came back into his mind. And he could never pursue anything. Always worrying. Every time he saw a mother and daughter together, his heart leaped in his chest. Only to be saddened.

They could be out there, John thought. *Anywhere*. And now here he was, back where it all started.

He closed the door and entered his parent's room.

This might take a while, he thought, frowning slightly. He found the filing cabinet and opened it. There were rows and rows of papers. John sighed. He closed the cabinet and returned to his car, getting his suitcase out of the trunk.

* * *

He was barely back a week when he ran into his old buddy Jason at the grocery store. "John," a familiar voice said on his right side.

He turned to find Jason standing there, looking as stunned as he felt. "Jason," John said, shaking his hand. He briefly glanced Jason over, seeing that he still looked the same, though more muscular in his upper body. His skin was darker, and his face jetted a goatee.

"Man, I haven't seen you in years," Jason said, smiling. "How've you been?" "I've been good," he replied. "Real good. You?"

"Working nonstop," Jason said. "Can't seem to get a day off."

John noticed Jason wore a company shirt and recognized the name. "You work for the telephone company?"

"Yeah," Jason confirmed. "Installation and repair service calls. Six years now. You?" "Well I'm back in town for now," John answered.

"Oh?"

"My parents were killed in a car accident," he replied.

"Oh, dude." Jason's jaw dropped. "Damn. I'm sorry."

This was the first time he said it out loud to anyone else. The news was still fresh, sadness still raw. He cleared his throat.

"When did this happen?" Jason asked.

"A few weeks ago," he said. "I'm here taking care of all their assets."

"Oh, ok."

"But I might stay," John added. Which was true. He had been debating whether to stay all week. The house was in good condition and paid for. He had his mom's car, which was paid off. He turned everything over to his name. The only thing he had brought with him was his car. His apartment was a rental. It was easy to cancel the lease. "I just need to look for a job."

"Oh, nice. What are you looking for?"

"Computers."

"Hey, that's where the money's at," Jason said. "Where you staying?" "Same house."

"I bought my first house over here on Spice Oak." Jason beamed. "You'll have to come over for a barbeque. Shoot some hoops."

John nodded. "Sounds good." "You still play?"

"Not like I use to," he admitted. "More fooling around." "Maybe I'll kick your butt this time," Jason said, grinning.

"Quit dreaming," John said, smiling. "You still talk to any of the guys?"

"Nah." Jason shook his head. "I haven't seen any of them in years. After you disappeared, everything fell apart. Tom and Ben started hanging with some dicks and ended up quitting the team."

"Why?"

"Tom tried out for the captain position after you left and lost it to a sophomore," Jason explained. "And Ben kept getting pulled out of games. We left them alone. After that it was only Chad, Adrian, and me. We all went to different colleges, so I lost contact with them. Last I heard, they moved out of state."

"What about Ben and Tom?" John asked. "They still live around here?"

"They were kicked out of our high school shortly after the second semester started," Jason said, shrugging. "Never saw them again."

John shook his head. The news didn't really surprise him. His last few memories of high school were blurry, but he briefly remembered Ben and Tom acting weird.

"Where did you go, anyway?" Jason asked.

He hesitated, knowing the question would come up eventually. Yet he still didn't know how to answer. But it was his buddy Jason. Still, he couldn't tell him everything right here. Only half the truth. The whole truth was better said over a bottle of beer. "I joined military school," he said. "Then I enlisted in the air force."

"No way," Jason said, punching him in the shoulder. "You flying airplanes now?"

"Oh, no." John laughed. "I was in IT. Got out last year."

"Ah, man. I wanted to go up in a plane."

"I got stories to tell," he said. "Next time."

"For sure," Jason said. "Hey, the next Saturday I get off, you should come over for some hoops."

"Definitely," he said. "I'll go easy on you."

Jason smiled, shaking his head. "Still have the same number?" "Yep."

Shaking his hand, Jason said, "All right, man, I'll see you soon. We'll get our game on." "All right, bye."

* * *

John looked around the master bedroom. *Not bad,* he thought. It was no longer his parent's bedroom. It was now his room. He had also fixed the other rooms, turning his old room into a guest room and the other room into a workout room. Not that he needed a guest room. He didn't know what else to do with it.

Some of the clutter had been cleared from the closets and the garage. But he found there wasn't a need to change a lot of the house or get rid of stuff. It was the papers he still had to go through.

Now he just needed to get the rest of his stuff from his old apartment. It wasn't much besides his clothes. He could knock it out in a weekend.

But first thing's first.

Going straight to the closet, he pulled out his best business suit. It was time to get a job.

CHAPTER 7

The halls of Westchester Junior High School were crowded and noisy in the early morning. Students prepared for the school day by getting their books at the last minute, talking to their friends in groups, and racing off to classes in every direction. School had been in session for over a month.

"Where did you get that picture, Marisa?" Patty asked.

Thirteen-year-old Marisa, currently in the seventh grade, was at her locker, waiting for the first bell to ring. Her best friend, Patty, stood next to her, staring at the picture on the inside of her locker. Patty had a medium complexion, a little darker than Marisa, but with black hair and black eyes. She was fit and toned from playing sports.

"Magazine," Marisa replied. She adjusted the book bag on her shoulder. "I'll buy it from you."

"No way," she said, smiling and shutting her locker.

She walked with Patty to their first class of the day, math. She usually liked math, but the teacher made it sound so boring that she hated it. As usual, she spent the period talking with Patty to pass the time. When class ended, they met up with their other best friend, Jenni. The three of them have known each other since they were little. Jenni was tall with blond hair that fell above her waist. She had a light complexion, striking blue eyes, and was very skinny. Marisa swore the girl could be a model.

They walked over to the computer classroom, and right when they entered Marisa noticed a man sitting at the teacher's desk instead of their regular teacher. Talk about gorgeous—the guy was hot! She found herself staring at him. He looked up, and his big dark-brown eyes met hers. She quickly turned away and headed toward her seat in the back row. She sat down on the other side of Patty, who sat next to Jenni by the end of the aisle. Her eyes returned to the man.

"Dang. Who's that?" Patty asked them.

Marisa shrugged, her eyes never leaving him.

"Where's Mrs. Hager?" a kid asked the man.

"She's sick, so I'm taking her place," he replied in a deep, dreamy voice. She looked up at the board and saw the name "Mr. Dolton" written on it. "He's cute," Jenni whispered. She nodded in reply.

"He looks young too," Patty said.

He did look young. He looked about late twenties, early thirties. He had long, black curly hair that fell around his face, shaping it; a strong, angular jawline; and dramatic brown eyes with a light skin complexion. He was so incredibly fine!

The class whispered about the substitute teacher. Marisa soon noticed every girl switch from staring at him longingly to glancing at their friends in between giggles. The whole class became silent, and all eyes followed him. He stood up when the bell rang, turning out to be tall and slim.

"If you open your books to page seventy-six, we will continue from where you left off last class," Mr. Dolton announced.

"Boring," Marisa said jokingly. Jenni and Patty covered their faces, laughing in their hands.

Suddenly Mr. Dolton stood right by their row, looking at her. The entire class became silent. Heads turned in her direction. "Excuse me, what did you say?" Mr. Dolton asked.

"Uh …" She faltered for a few seconds. "I said boring."

"I'll see you after class," he said. He returned to the front of the room and started teaching.

Really? she thought, frowning. *All I said was boring.*

As if reading her thoughts, Patty asked, "What was that all about?"

"I don't know, but he has some major attitude problem," Marisa replied, rolling her eyes.

She looked at Mr. Dolton, wondering what was his problem. She didn't think she said it that loud. No one else heard it. Her eyes shifted around the room, noticing a few students glancing her way before whispering to one another or following Mr. Dolton's movements around the room.

He may be cute, but he didn't have to be so rude. Marisa shook her head, trying to focus on the lecture. But soon found it hard to concentrate. All throughout class, Mr. Dolton kept eyeing her.

"He sure keeps looking at you," Jenni whispered, leaning forward in her seat to look past Patty.

She nodded. When class ended, Marisa said bye to her friends and approached Mr. Dolton at the front of the room. He stood by the board, waiting until everyone left.

"Now do you want to tell me why you said that?" Mr. Dolton asked. He walked over to the desk until standing directly in front of her, folding his arms across his chest.

Marisa met his gaze, having to step a few feet back. He turned out to be a good deal taller than her. "All I said was boring." She shrugged. "I don't see what the big deal is."

"I hadn't even started teaching," Mr. Dolton said. "That was very rude." "Sorry," she said. "I didn't mean to embarrass you."

"What's with this attitude?"

"Can you please hurry up?" she asked. "I'm late for class."

Study hall was next. But she wanted to leave already. Without saying a word, he walked around his desk and sat down. He took out a detention slip and started filling it out.

"Why am I getting a detention slip?" Marisa asked. Her cheeks burned. "Because of your attitude," Mr. Dolton replied. "What's your name?" "None of your business."

He glanced up, giving her an all-time famous teacher look. Their eyes met. Marisa noticed every time he looked at her, they held each other's gaze for a while. He had such beautiful eyes.

Quit checking him out, she thought, scowling.

"Marisa Perez." Her gaze shifted, searching for the clock. The bell rang, announcing the next period. Great. Now she needed a pass or would be counted late.

"I'm going to call your parents tonight to make sure they see it," he informed her.

"How can you?" she asked. "You don't have access to my number. You're just a substitute."

He handed her the detention slip. "I'll see you tomorrow after school."

She took it and abruptly turned, leaving the classroom. *I cannot believe this*, she thought, *He can't do this to me.*

The empty hallways greeted her. Closed classroom doors whizzed by. Marisa felt her cheeks burn. Mr. Dolton didn't give her a pass, and in her eagerness to get away from him, she forgot to ask. If anyone roamed the halls, she could get into more trouble. Her pace quickened. She entered study hall and joined her friends at a table.

"What did he tell you?" Jenni asked.

"He gave me a detention slip," she exclaimed. "For what?" Patty asked.

"That's what I want to know," she commented. Jenni leaned forward. "When is it?" "Tomorrow after school."

"Dang, and to think I thought he was cute," Patty said.

"I know right." Marisa shook her head. She never heard of cute teachers who were mean, let alone cute.

"Can substitutes do that?" Jenny asked.

"Good question," Patty replied.

It was a good question, one none of them could answer.

At lunchtime, Marisa entered the noisy cafeteria, where she bought a meal. She walked over to an empty table and set her tray on it, sitting down. Soon her friends joined her. Jeff, Mark, and Sean also came up to the table, making her blush. They each pulled a chair over and sat between them. Marisa exchanged glances with her friends, who were also blushing.

She noticed where the guys sat. Jeff sat between Marisa and Jenni, Mark on the other side of Jenni, and Sean next to Patty and on the other side of Marisa. These guys were popular and hot, having computer class and study hall with them.

Marisa liked Jeff the most, first noticing him during class when school began. Slowly but surely, the guys talked and hung out more with the girls. Jeff had a dark complexion, slightly darker than Patty, with black hair and black eyes. Tall, slim, and built, not too much, but enough not to start a fight. Mark had brown hair, brown eyes, and a light complexion, the tallest of the three. His face carried a tough yet sleepy look, like he just rolled out of bed. Sean also had brown hair and brown eyes, but his skin was tan like Marisa's. His hair came past his ears, long in the front, which he wore hanging over part of his face.

"What do you guys think of the substitute?" Jeff asked.

"I think he's mean," Marisa interjected.

Jeff smiled, catching her gaze.

"He looks young," Mark said yawning.

"I know right," Sean said, staring at Patty.

She looked over at Patty, whose cheeks were pink, more so than the three of them. Marisa smiled. Sean liked Patty—and she knew it too.

They do like us, she thought. They're sitting by the girl they like. Her smile became brighter. She glanced at Jeff, whose eyes remained on her.

Patty tore her eyes away from Sean long enough to glance in Marisa's direction. "He made a big deal out of nothing."

The rest of the group nodded.

When school ended, Marisa shut her locker and turned toward Jenni and Patty, who were waiting with their book bags.

"He's definitely going to ask you," Jenni said to Patty.

Marisa fell in stride with them, heading toward the front door. Kids pushed pass them in all directions. She glanced around the crowded hallways. "Guys, lower your voice," Marisa said quietly. She scooted closer, steering them to one side of the hallway to avoid being trampled over. "They might hear you."

"Oh, he'll ask you," Jenni added, glancing at Marisa. She smiled. "And you. I saw the way he looked at you."

They almost reached the front door when a voice behind her said, "Marisa, wait up."

A glance over her shoulder showed Jeff coming toward her. *Yes*, she thought, and stopped, waiting.

"Can I walk you home?" he asked, approaching her.

Her eyes widened briefly. She couldn't believe it. He wanted to walk her home. This was definitely a good sign. "Sure." She turned to her friends, who also stopped walking, and waved goodbye. "I'll see you guys later." She fell into stride with Jeff.

Jenni waved back, and Patty made kissing sounds. She rolled her eyes, making them laugh.

"Call me," Patty called back.

Marisa nodded and turned back to Jeff, hoping he didn't see that exchange. He walked slowly, staying in step with her. They exited the front doors, walking side by side down the few steps, crossing the parking lot before reaching the sidewalk. Jeff stopped in his tracks, looking at their surroundings.

"Which way?" he asked her.

"This way." She nodded her head to the right. "It's the second street on the right side."

"Oh wow," Jeff said. They turned in that direction. "You live really close. I'm the subdivision behind this one."

"That's not much further."

"Nah, it's not bad at all," Jeff said.

They started walking the few blocks toward her house. Students poured out of the school building and headed off in different directions. Some were staying in big groups, and others were venturing on in pairs or by themselves. Chatter could be heard all around the school premises.

The sun was shining, hot and humid with the smell of rain lingering in the air. Marisa walked everywhere so the weather never took a toll on her, no matter how hot or cold it became. She loved the fall season, which signified change and offered some relief.

"How come I haven't seen you around before this year?" Jeff asked, glancing at her.

She shrugged and glanced shyly at him, turning her face to the side to see him better. He was so cute. Their gazes met, making her heart pound in her chest. She was surprised but glad he asked to walk her home. This was their first time alone together.

"I don't know," she answered. "Did you go to Appleville Intermediate?"

"Yeah," he replied. They crossed the street. "I guess we didn't have any classes together last year."

"You do look vaguely familiar," Marisa admitted. "Maybe I saw you in the halls. Your friends do too."

"Probably," Jeff said. "Can't seem to get rid of those dorks." She laughed. They turned right onto her street.

"Man, you live close," he said, gazing at the surrounding street.

"My house is up ahead," Marisa said, nodding to the one-story house already in view.

"Thanks for walking me home." She turned up her driveway and stopped on the front lawn.

"No problem," Jeff said, shifting his bag on his shoulders.

Their eyes locked. She glanced at the ground before meeting his gaze again. A silence fell between them. She didn't know what else to say, but she didn't want to say goodbye either. Marisa knew she couldn't very well invite him in the house alone, though. She saw his feet shift around. He didn't want to leave either. The walk had been too short. An idea came to mind.

"Do you need to be anywhere right now?" she asked him. He shook his head. "Not really."

Marisa plopped on to the grass, where Jeff smiled and instantly sat down next to her. She spread her long legs over the freshly cut grass, stretching her arms over her head from being cooped up inside all day. The sun beamed down on them from above, warming her skin.

"That's a nice house," Jeff said. "Thanks."

"What time do your parents get home?" he asked, looking around. "My mother gets home late," Marisa informed him.

"Oh, OK," Jeff said, catching her gaze. "I'll just have to walk you home from now on." "Quite the smooth one, I see," she said, laughing.

"Any siblings?" Jeff asked. His eyebrows scrunched over.

"Nope." Her voice grew quiet, her gaze diverted to the ground, anticipating the next question.

"What about your dad? When does he get home?"

"It's only my mother and I," she said softly, meeting his eyes. He nodded. "You have any siblings?"

"I have an older sister and brother at the high school," he answered. "My brother is eighteen, and my sister is seventeen." He paused. "I think I was the oops baby."

Marisa's mouth dropped open, and Jeff burst out laughing, making her shut it. He was kidding. She could feel her cheeks burning. "You're terrible."

Jeff shook his head. "That face you made was priceless." She smacked him on the arm.

"Tell me about your mother."

"She's single, so she works long hours," Marisa began.

The two of them continued talking until the sun started to set on the horizon. Jeff glanced at his watch and stood up, picking his book bag off the ground.

"It's getting late," he pointed out.

He held out his hand for Marisa. She also grabbed her book bag off the grass and grasped his outstretched hand with her other hand. He pulled her up from the lawn until her feet met solid ground.

"Yeah, I know."

She didn't want the moment to end, but she knew it must be close to dinnertime. Her stomach would start growling soon. She had a few assignments to finish, about an hour's worth. She couldn't very well stay out here all night, though. There was no telling when her mom would arrive.

"So I'll see you tomorrow," Jeff said. "Yeah," she said, smiling. "This was fun." "It was."

She waited for Jeff to leave, but he made no move.

"I'll wait until you're inside," he said. "Make sure you're safe." "Oh, OK." She turned toward her house. "Bye."

"Bye," Jeff called out. He stood on the lawn, watching until she entered the house.

Marisa closed the door and locked it, before collapsing momentarily. She leaned against the frame. *He is hot indeed*, she thought. *And he waited to make sure I was safe before leaving.* Smiling, she picked herself up and walked through the living room.

The one-story brick house was a basic three-bedroom and two-bath home. She considered the outside of the house deceiving since it was bigger on the inside, extending quite long in the rear. But the wooden fence surrounding the small backyard hid the majority of it. It looked small, but cozy, and the perfect amount of room for the two of them. She entered her room and dumped the book bag on the bed. She returned to the kitchen, where a note sat on the table.

It said: "Honey, I won't be home until dark. There are leftovers in the refrigerator. Don't wait up for me."

Great, Marisa thought. *I'll have to wait until tomorrow to give my mom the detention slip.*

She ate a quick supper, finished all her homework, and watched a movie before her mom finally arrived at the house. It was after nine when her mom entered through the front door, looking so exhausted and stressed out. Her steps were slow; her arms weighed down by the numerous bags she carried.

"I thought I told you not to wait up for me," her mom said, fumbling with the door.

Marisa jumped off the couch and ran over to her mother. She grabbed the bags about to fall out of her mom's hand and set them down on the armchair, then quickly closed and locked the front door.

"Thanks, sweetie," her mom said, dropping the remaining bags on the chair. She rubbed her tired eyes. "Now what are you doing up?"

"It's only nine o'clock," Marisa replied, running to the coffee table. She picked up the detention slip and returned to the front hallway, handing it over. "I need you to sign something."

"Who's Mr. Dolton?"

"A substitute," she replied. "He's taking Mrs. Hager's place."

Her mom's eyes grew big for a little bit, reading it. She glanced up and stared off in the distance, seeming a little worried, but soon shook her head, muttering, "Nah." She returned her attention to Marisa. "Why did you get this?"

"I don't know." She shook her head. "I said boring in his class. You know how teachers are."

"Substitutes can give out detention slips?"

Good question. She shrugged. The substitute's reaction seemed harsh, but there wasn't anything she could do about it. For the first time in her school career, she had after school detention. Would he be there tomorrow? If Mrs. Hager returned, maybe she didn't have to go.

Her mom fished a pen out of her purse, signed the note, and gave it back to her. Marisa's eyes widen briefly by the response, or lack of it. This was the first time any teacher reprimanded her.

"Don't get anymore. OK?"

"OK," Marisa said. "You hungry?"

"No thanks. I'm too exhausted to eat."

"I'll go to bed now." She kissed her mom on the cheek. "Night." "Night, hon."

Marisa walked to her room but paused in the doorway. She glanced over at her mom, who collapsed face-first on the couch and fell into a deep sleep. Marisa set the slip on her desk and retreated back to her mom, covering her with a blanket left by the couch.

Poor Mom, she thought. *All she does is work. She never has any free time. She comes home so exhausted that she doesn't have any energy to do anything else.*

* * *

"You forgot to call me," Patty declared.

"Sorry." Marisa shut her locker. "I ended up talking to Jeff all afternoon, then waited for my mom to get home."

"How did it go with him?" Jenni asked. "Yes, details please."

"We only talked," Marisa admitted, smiling. She could feel her cheeks turning hot. "Sean gave me his phone number this morning," Patty said.

"Cool."

They stopped momentarily in the hallway before splitting up to go to their classes. Mark suddenly appeared by their sides.

"Ladies," he said, nodding to them, and turned to Jenni. "Hey."

"I'll see you guys in class," Jenni said. She headed off in the opposite direction with Mark by her side.

"Bye."

"They make a cute couple," Patty declared.

"One more class, and we get to see our honeys," Marisa added, making her laugh. "Or soon-to-be honeys." She glanced around the packed halls. "I don't know where their lockers are or where they hang out between classes."

"All in good time we shall," Patty pointed out.

"That would be nice."

Marisa walked among the crowded halls, heading over to their first class. They entered the room and sat in their usual seats. They passed notes back and forth to each other. The last ten minutes they were allowed to talk. When class was over, they walked to their computer class.

Actually, Patty walked and Marisa trailed behind, once remembering her stupid slip.

If the substitute is even here, she thought. *Maybe Mrs. Hager is back today.*

She entered the classroom after Patty only to be disappointed. Detention was on. Marisa glanced to the left and saw Jenni already seated. She approached the desk, avoiding eye contact, and dropped the slip on it without saying a word. She turned and headed over to her seat, catching Jeff's gaze. He smiled as she passed his row where he sat with Mark and Sean. Smiling back, she entered the row behind them and sat down.

Mr. Dolton stood up from the desk and started teaching. Eyes followed his every move, particularly from the female students. The substitute walked through the aisle in the center of the classroom, passing by each row. When he stopped at their row, his eyes rested on Marisa.

"Was it me or did he just *look* at you?" Patty asked once he had moved on. "He looked at her," Jenni answered.

"Why is he doing that?" she asked. "I don't know," Patty replied. "Marisa," Jeff whispered.

She looked between the computers. He leaned back in his seat and passed her a note. "Oohh," Patty teased, receiving a swift jab in the ribs. "Ow."

Holding the note above her lap so it remained hidden by the table, she read: "Will you be my girlfriend?"

Oh my, she thought, feeling her pulse race. *He just asked me out.*

Marisa wrote "yes" and passed it back to him, smiling. He read it and responded. By the time Jeff handed over the note, she had forgotten all about class. She quickly opened the paper, spreading it out on top of the table to read.

Jenni and Patty suddenly whispered, "Marisa."

When she glanced over at them, the note was snatched out of her hands. She looked up to find Mr. Dolton standing next to her. Marisa heaved a sigh. He read it to himself while all eyes stared at her, making her face turn hot. Talking ceased. The only noises in the classroom were the shifting of seats, students straining to see in the back row. Amusement flickered from the guys. Irritation and frowns flashed from the girls. As though she had deliberately stolen all the attention. Only her friends appeared disbelieving—outraged—especially Jeff.

"You two have lunch detention with me," Mr. Dolton said, glancing at Jeff and Marisa.

He crumbled up the note, threw it away and continued teaching, like nothing happened.

She sneaked a peek at Jeff, who rolled his eyes. She couldn't believe what had happened.

Again! Mr. Dolton was really annoying her. What was his deal anyway? It was only a note. Why was he always picking on her?

I've never been in trouble before he arrived, she thought.

When class ended, Marisa followed Jenni and Patty out the aisle. Mark, Sean, and Jeff joined them, pairing up with the girls. The group marched over to study hall, found a table and sat down.

"I cannot believe it!" she exclaimed. "He's always picking on me. What is his problem?" "He has been picking on you," Patty agreed.

"And the question is why?" Jenni pointed out.

Jeff scooted his chair closer to Marisa, making her blush. They were now a couple, but her friends didn't know. Not that she had any opportunity to tell them. "I don't see what the big deal is," he said. "It was only a note."

"He sure is a weird teacher," Mark said, stretching his legs.

"All substitute teachers are weird," Sean remarked, moving the hair out of his eyes. "I wish Mrs. Hager was back," Marisa remarked.

Everyone nodded.

At lunchtime Jeff and Marisa sat across from each other at the teachers table. They kept making funny faces and couldn't stop laughing until Mr. Dolton split them up on opposite ends of the cafeteria. Marisa sat by herself in a corner for the entire lunch period.

After school Jeff approached Marisa at her locker, where she gathered her books together. Patty and Jenni waited, chatting away with Mark and Sean.

"Call me tonight." He handed her a piece of paper. "OK," she said, stuffing it in her pocket. "Bye."

"Bye."

Marisa watched him join Mark and Sean. She smiled and glanced at her friends. "You ready?" Jenni asked. Marisa shot her a look.

"Oh, that's right," Patty said. "You have detention."

She nodded, rolling her eyes. Addressing the whole group, she said, "I'll see you guys later."

"Have fun," Jenni called out teasingly. "Yeah, yeah."

"Call me tonight," Patty said. "OK."

She smiled, realizing her group of friends grew from three to six now. The guys had simply joined the girls whenever they could today, popping out of nowhere in between classes to escort them to another class or to lunch or to walk them home. Sean and Mark were walking home Patty and Jenni this afternoon. This was a good sign for all of them.

The door to Mr. Dolton's room stood open. Marisa entered the quiet, empty classroom, feeling like she had seen enough of him already. He looked up from his desk briefly before returning to his work. She paused at the first table, wondering what to do next.

"Did you bring your book?" Mr. Dolton asked. "Yes," she replied.

"Copy the whole chapter."

Rolling her eyes, Marisa headed toward her usual seat in the back row. "No, up front where I can see you," Mr. Dolton called out.

Marisa stopped in her tracks, turned around and sat in the front row, right next to the desk. She took out her book and notebook to start writing. All the tables had computers on them, leaving little space to work. The first few minutes were spent rearranging the monitor, keyboard, and mouse. After writing a few pages, she paused and counted through the chapter to see how many were left.

She froze, feeling eyes on her. When she glanced up, Mr. Dolton quickly looked down. *How long has he been staring at me?* she thought. Since her hand hurt and she was sick of writing, she studied Mr. Dolton. He appeared to be about her mom's age. He also had a cute dimple on his cheek. He glanced up, and she diverted her eyes to the page.

"Get back to work."

Marisa took one last peek and saw no wedding ring on his finger. When she finally finished, it was after five. Her hand throbbed. She was tired and wanted to go home. She walked up to the desk with her work in hand. Mr. Dolton looked up, caught her gaze, and held it again for a long time. His eyes were big and dramatic—beautiful.

What am I saying? she thought. He keeps getting me in trouble.

She broke the gaze, diverting her eyes away from him, and dropped the work on the desk. As she turned back to the table, her peripheral vision showed his eyes following her movements. She quickly packed up her belongings, whereas Mr. Dolton finally stopped gazing at her.

Why the heck did he stare at me like that? "Can I go?"

"I'll be calling your parents tonight," Mr. Dolton said. "Why?" she asked, looking over at him.

"You have had lunch detention and detention with me," he replied. "I need to have a conference with them on your behavior."

"I said boring and passed a note in class," she pointed out. "You need to have a conference with my mom because of that?"

"Yes," Mr. Dolton said, "and also because of your attitude and the fact that you have been back-talking to me the entire time I have been here."

"Entire time?" Her eyes widened. "You've been here two days. You're the substitute."

"Doesn't matter." He stood up. "It doesn't give you the right to behave however you wish in this classroom."

She rolled her eyes. "Can I go?"

The long day took a toll on her. She hoisted the book bag on her shoulder and moved toward the open door. This should give him the hint and let her leave.

"Yes, but you have to promise me you'll pay attention in class." He started gathering his stuff together.

"Yeah, whatever." "Marisa."

"It's not my fault your class is so boring," she said and bolted out the room.

The halls were empty. Quiet. Her footsteps echoed across the tile floor. She made her way out the front door, the sun hitting her skin and warming her face. She crossed the pavement and turned to the right, heading home. The school grounds showed no students in sight. Only a few cars stood here and there in the parking lot, probably belonging to teachers. She strolled along the sidewalk, taking advantage of the time to release some anger and calm herself. She took a right at her street.

If only Jeff could have walked her home today. It was nice to have some company yesterday rather than walking by herself. Arriving at the house, Marisa entered and closed the door behind her, locking it. She headed straight to her room, dropping the book bag on her bed and stretching for a moment after being cooped up in the school building for hours. Her stomach growled loud, echoing throughout the quiet house. Was it that late already?

Marisa walked to the kitchen to make a quick supper. After she ate, she retrieved the paper from her pocket and dialed Jeff's phone number. She had no idea what to say, but he wanted her to call. Why didn't she give him her number?

"Hello," said a voice. "Jeff?"

"Yeah."

"It's Marisa."

"Hey, how was detention?"

"Stupid. I had to write the whole chapter." "Oh joy," Jeff said.

"You know what's really weird?" She walked over to the living room. "He wants to contact my mom."

"Why?"

"I don't know," she replied, collapsing on the couch. "He said since I had detention with him, he needed to have a parent conference on my behavior."

"He sure has been acting weird," Jeff remarked. "Especially toward you." "No kidding."

"I don't like that at all," he said. "I don't like him very much. He—"

Marisa heard a voice speaking in the background. She paused, listening. It sounded like an older woman's voice, probably his mom.

"I have to go," Jeff said suddenly. "OK. Bye."

"Bye."

She hung up the phone, frowning. There had been no opportunity to talk to Jeff alone today or to really talk to him at all. And he was her boyfriend. Now what could she do for the remainder of the night? There was some homework to finish, but her hands still hurt from writing. She entered her room and approached the computer for some music.

The phone rang. Marisa dashed to the living room and snatched up the cordless phone. Please let it be Jeff.

"Hello."

"May I speak to Mr. or Mrs. Perez, please?" said a voice.

The name on the caller ID said "Dolton John." Who?

"Who's speaking?"

"John Dolton."

John Dolton? she thought. *Who is that?* Oh, wait a minute. It was Mr. Dolton, the substitute.

"My mom's not here," she told him. "Then I'll speak to your father."

Her eyebrows shot up by the audacity of this man. Just assuming she had both parents in her life. Marisa hated when people spoke without common courtesy. Without thinking was more like it. What was his deal?

"My mom isn't here!" she shouted and hung up the phone, shaking her head in disgust.

What was with him? He refused to leave her alone.

Marisa spent the evening working on her assignments and listening to music until the front door opened. She jumped up from her desk and dashed into the living room. Her mom burst inside, dropping her purse and bags on the floor, next to the door. The clock in the living room said almost nine p.m. She embraced her mom.

"Mr. Dolton called."

"Who's he?" her mom asked, locking the door.

"Substitute."

"Oh yeah. What did he want?"

"He wanted to have a conference with you," she replied. "He says I'm a bad girl." Her mom rolled her eyes. "It's late. I'll call him tomorrow."

"OK. His number is on the caller ID." Marisa turned toward her room but glanced back at her mom, who sat on the couch, struggling with her shoes. "You hungry? How about I make you a plate?"

"No, sweetie." Her mom dropped a heel on the floor. "Thanks, though."

"Mom, you need to eat." She crossed her arms over her chest, unable to remember the last time her mom ate. Was it only two days ago? It seemed longer since Marisa rarely saw her.

"I ate earlier," her mom replied. "Really, I'm good. I take enough for lunch and dinner." She nodded. "All right. Night."

"Night."

CHAPTER 8

The three girls stood by their lockers, waiting for the school day to begin. Marisa fumbled with her books, shoving them into her bag before closing the locker. The bell should be ringing any minute now.

"Sean asked me out," Patty announced. "All right!" Jenni exclaimed.

"I cannot believe it," Patty gushed. "I'm so happy." "Has Mark asked you out?" Marisa asked Jenni.

"Yes," Jenni said, smiling. "Yesterday when he walked me home." "Oh wow," she said. "Now all of us have boyfriends."

"Yeah," Patty agreed, then glanced at her sharply. "Wait, Jeff asked you out?" "Yesterday."

"You never told us!" Jenni exclaimed.

"Oops," Marisa said, smiling. Patty hit her on the arm. "That's why we were sent to lunch detention."

The warning bell rang, and they said bye to Jenni, parting ways. She walked with Patty to the math classroom, pushing her way through the students rushing in every direction. Mrs. Hager was there instead of Mrs. Saltinee. Marisa glanced at Patty, raising an eyebrow. This wasn't good.

"Mrs. Hager, why are you here instead of in the computer room?" a student asked.

"Mrs. Saltinee retired," Mrs. Hager replied. "I'm taking her place for the remainder of the year."

"That was a sudden move," another student added. "Why did she retire?" a third student asked.

"Personal reasons," Mrs. Hager said. "Mr. Dolton is the permanent teacher for computer."

Several students cheered, and some students groaned, including Marisa. Today would be his third day here and already she was sick of him.

"This ruins my day," Marisa whispered to Patty, who nodded. He better not get me in trouble anymore.

After math class, the two of them caught up with Jenni, informing her about the switch in teachers. As they headed to their next class, Jeff, Mark, and Sean caught up with them right before they entered the room. Marisa smiled when Jeff joined her side. But her mood changed upon spotting Mr. Dolton. She sat down, avoiding any eye contact. Her friends didn't know he called her house last night. So much had occurred within the last few days, it was hard to keep them up to date. Now that he was the teacher, she needed a plan to stay out of trouble. Should be simple enough. Pay attention and do what he says. Just don't look at him.

Marisa tried her best to pay attention when he began teaching, but it was very hard. "I swear, this has to be the most boring class ever," Jenni whispered.

She nodded and yawned, covering it with her hand. Suddenly Patty jumped straight up in her seat, shaking herself roughly to wake up. Jenni tried to stop a laughing fit, burying her head in a book. Marisa watched half amused. Patty jabbed Jenni in the ribs, who kept laughing.

Shaking her head, Marisa put her elbow on the table and leaned her head against her hand to keep from falling asleep. She saw Jeff also tried to stay awake. He kept picking his head up in order not to doze off. He caught her attention and smiled.

The other guys were just as bad. Mark was dozing silently, slouched in his chair with his head leaning on the top of the seat, not making any attempt to hide it. Sean was dozing off, shaking himself awake every few minutes. At least she wasn't the only one. Her eyes skimmed over the other students to keep herself occupied. The guys were nodding off; the girls were following Mr. Dolton's every move.

When class finally ended, the group headed over to their study hall room. They broke off in pairs, walking through the halls before reaching the room. Marisa walked dazed and half asleep behind her friends, following their footsteps without paying attention to her surroundings. Jeff was by her side; that was all she cared about. They almost entered the room when he placed his hand on her elbow, stopping her movements.

"Hey."

He tilted his head to the side, smiling.

"What?" She wiped her mouth. "Am I drooling?"

Jeff laughed softly and moved the hair out of her eyes. "No, but you are beautiful."

She smiled at his response before rolling her eyes. "What's up?"

"Nothing, I only wanted to say you're beautiful."

"OK," she replied. "I'm awake now."

He laughed, holding out his arm for her. Marisa grabbed on, and together they entered study hall. He led her to the table where their friends were already seated and pulled out a chair for her. She collapsed into it, feeling her eyes droop.

"Aahh," Patty and Jenni said. They placed their heads on the table.

"Shush," Marisa replied. Jeff sat next to her. She yawned and added, "Mr. Dolton put me in a sleeping mood."

"I can't wake up," Jenni mumbled, her head resting sideways. "Neither can I," Patty added a few seconds later.

Mark and Sean were already dozing in their chairs. Marisa also rested her head on the table. Jeff simply leaned back in his chair. Soon the entire group had their eyes closed.

After school Jeff met Marisa at the lockers. She finished gathering her books to leave and shut her locker, anxious to leave the premises. The day had been too long. She grabbed on to the arm Jeff held out for her, turning to where Mark, Jenni, Sean, and Patty talked, shutting their lockers and zipping up their book bags.

"Bye, guys," she said, turning toward the front door. "You better call me, woman," Patty called out.

"I will, I promise," Marisa said, looking over her shoulder. "What about me?" Jenni asked.

"I'll call you, babe." Mark put his arm around her shoulders.

"OK," Jenni replied, smiling. "Later," Jeff also called out. "See you." Sean waved.

Marisa shook her head, laughing as they exited the building together. She raised her head toward the sky, welcoming the instant warmth, waking her fully. She squinted; her eyes adjusted to the sudden change in environments. They crossed the pavement and continued walking on the sidewalk toward her house.

"Man, I finally woke up," Marisa said.

"Has Mr. Dolton bugged you anymore?" Jeff asked suddenly. "Not today," she replied, glancing over at him. "Why?"

"I don't like how he keeps bugging my girl," he said, meeting her gaze. "Aw, that's so sweet."

"Besides, that's my job." "What?" she exclaimed.

Laughing, Jeff lowered his arm and grabbed her hand, holding it. They crossed the street, now walking along the side of the neighborhood in silence, enjoying the moment.

"It's your turn," she stated. They made a right on her street. "For what?" Jeff's eyebrow rose.

"To tell me about your family," she answered. "I told you all about mine the other day."

"Fair enough."

They reached her house. He dropped his book bag on the front lawn and sat down, pulling her with him. Marisa laughed, plopping on the grass, letting the bag slide off her shoulders. Her gaze took in their clasped hands.

"My parents have been married for more than twenty years," he began. "My dad is retired military, but he has a civilian job now. He works for emergency management, writing response plans. My mom is a professor at Saint Elois Community College."

Her jaw dropped. "Oh wow. Good for them. What does your mom teach?"

"Life science, which includes biology, geology, ecology, and environmental science," he continued. "Any of the sciences, basically."

She nodded. "What do you want to do?" "Not sure yet," Jeff admitted. "You?"

"Me neither." She shook her head. "I don't have a clue." "We're only teenagers," he said.

"True." Marisa let out a deep sigh.

"What's wrong?" Jeff asked, peering at her face.

She hesitated before meeting his gaze. Should she tell him? He was her boyfriend; she could tell him anything. What should she tell him? Where to begin was more like it. The empty house, the long hours her mom worked, and hardly eating. Yet she was only a teenager—a factor she often forgot.

"There are times when I don't feel like a teenager," Marisa admitted. "I come home to an empty house every day. I feel like an adult waiting up for my mom." Her eyes shifted to the ground. Jeff remained silent, waiting for her to finish. "I mean, I love my mom," she continued. Their gazes met. "But I don't like her working so much. I always worry about her. Don't get me wrong, she's a great mom. I have everything I need. I'm not deprived in any way. She makes good money, but she always has to work long hours."

"When does she get home usually?"

"Depends on the day." She shrugged. "It could be anywhere from six to nine. She makes it to the couch, where I try to make sure she has eaten before she falls asleep. But on her days off, she's awesome. She'll spend the whole day with me."

"She's an assistant for a company?" Jeff asked.

"She's an executive assistant for a public relations company," Marisa clarified. "Basically, she's at the beck and call of the CEO. She has to stay until he lets her go home. I think she's overworked most of the time."

"Hourly or salary?"

Her eyebrows burrowed over. Shaking her head, she said, "I don't know." "Sounds like she works hard to support you," he pointed out.

"I know." She released a sigh. "And she does. I only wished she didn't have to. I feel bad sometimes."

"You shouldn't," he remarked. "She loves you. She works hard so you won't have to." "I know."

"She's done a great job raising you," he continued. "I know she's proud. You're beautiful and intelligent."

"Yeah, yeah," Marisa said, tossing her hand in the air.

"You know it's true." He smiled briefly. She felt him hesitate and caught his gaze. "What happened to your father?"

"He left when she was pregnant with me," she answered. "Ouch."

"Yeah." She could feel her cheeks burning. "You've never met him?" Jeff asked.

"No."

"If he was still around, your mom wouldn't be working so much," he concluded.

"Yeah ..." Her voice trailed off.

"Understandable." He nodded. "But she wouldn't want you to feel bad. It's not your fault."

"I know, but I can't help it sometimes," she whispered.

A silence washed over them. Marisa raised her eyes to the clear sky, where the sun beat down on them. Her stomach growled, loud enough for both of them to hear. They laughed, making eye contact.

Jeff glanced at his watch. "I should get going."

She stood up, brushing off the grass from her clothes and picking up her bag. "You can always call me if you get lonely," he suggested, standing up. "OK," she said, smiling. "I'll see you tomorrow."

"Bye."

Marisa walked up the front porch and waved at Jeff. She unlocked the door and entered the house. She set her bag down, deciding to eat first before tackling her homework. Man, time flies when I'm with him. It was nearly six. A ham and cheese omelet sounded good right now.

The phone rang, making her pause. She went to answer it then froze, recognizing the name and number. Mr. Dolton. Marisa rolled her eyes and let it ring. A few minutes later the message light was blinking.

Hmm, should I listen to the message? Erase it? she thought. He probably wanted a parent-teacher conference with her mom. Not that she knew why. He was the one always picking on her. Her stomach growled and she entered the kitchen to make dinner. She'll deal with him later.

* * *

The final bell rang and Marisa shut her locker, turning to Jeff, only to find her mom rushing toward her. She blinked a few times, wondering if she was imagining things. No, that was her mom all right. But why was she here?

"Mom?"

Her friends stopped talking and surrounded them as her mom came to a stop in front of her. She took a deep breath like she had been hurrying to get here.

"Your computer teacher, Mr. Dolton, wants to speak to me," her mom replied.

"What?" Marisa exclaimed.

"He's the one that gave you the detention slip?"

"Yeah."

"He wants a conference about your behavior."

Marisa sighed. So that was why he called last night.

"He didn't give me much warning," her mom continued. "I had to plead with my new boss to get off from work so I could come here."

"I'm sorry, Mom."

"This better be good," her mom said. "I still have to go back to work. Now come on."

Without making themselves seen, her friends had slowly back away from them so they could talk in private. She didn't get a chance to look back at Jeff or to say good-bye. Instead, she led her mom down the hallway and to Mr. Dolton's room.

She opened the classroom door and entered, followed by her mom. She approached Mr. Dolton's desk, who immediately stood up with such force that his chair banged into the wall behind him. Marisa frowned, noticing Mr. Dolton looked shocked and speechless. She glanced sharply at her mom whose eyes widened in surprise.

What now? she thought, her gaze shifting between them. Her mom and Mr. Dolton seemed to forget about her as the silence lengthened in the classroom, their gazes locked on to each other.

"Lisa," Mr. Dolton said.

"John!" her mom exclaimed, backing up a few steps. Marisa quickly moved out of her path. She shouted, "What are you doing here? No! No, not you. No, it can't be you. You can't be her teacher!"

"I wanted to talk to you about Marisa's behavior," Mr. Dolton said. He slowly took a few steps toward her.

"You guys know each other?" Marisa questioned, raising an eyebrow. *How did they know each other*? she thought. What was going on?

Mr. Dolton looked over at Marisa as if remembering she still stood in the room, and then back at her mom. "Is she our child?"

"Say what?" Marisa shouted. What was he talking about?

Her mom walked backward to the classroom door and opened it, her eyes never leaving him. "Come om, Marisa. Let's go!"

"Lisa, look," he said, walking up to her. "It's been thirteen years since I've seen you. Can't you give me another chance?"

What? Marisa thought. She needed some answers already.

"Marisa, I'm not going to say it again," her mom said through clenched teeth.

"Whoa, whoa, wait a minute," she said, stepping between them. "Does someone want to tell me what's going on around here?"

"I'm your father," Mr. Dolton announced.

She looked over at him and burst out laughing. "Yeah right." Her gaze shifted to her mom, who became silent, her face contorted. Marisa gazed back at Mr. Dolton, who appeared bewildered, pleading. Marisa stopped laughing. Her mouth dropped open. *Is it true? Is he really my father?* Her cheeks burned. *No, this cannot be true. No! Please don't let it be true.*

Mr. Dolton stared at her mom, who focused her attention on the floor. All the while, she held the door open.

"Marisa, let's go!"

She took a deep breath and left, following her mom, without saying another word. "No, wait!" She could hear Mr. Dolton shouting and his footsteps chasing after them. Her mom closed the door in his face.

She was oblivious to their surrounding as they raced down the hall and out the front door. Luckily, most of the students had cleared out by then. The halls were nearly empty. Marisa waited until they were in her mom's car, away from everyone else, so they could talk in private.

"Mom, is he really my dad?" She asked.

"Yes," her mom replied quietly.

"What?" she asked. "Why did he come back? What kind of jerk would come back thirteen years later after he ditched you and expect you to take him back?"

Her mom didn't say anything for a while. She continued to avoid eye contact, seeming lost in her thoughts. Finally, she replied, "I don't know." And with that, she started the car and peeled out of the parking lot, the tires screeching as she sped down the street and away from the school.

When they arrived at the house, her mom pulled into the driveway but didn't turn off the car. "I have to go back to work," she said. "I'll be home later tonight."

"OK," Marisa replied. She got out of the car and entered the house, watching her mom leave again.

She dropped her bookbag on the couch, grabbed the cordless phone off the coffee table, and dialed Jeff's number. It rang.

"Hello," said Jeff answering.

"Jeff, it's Marisa."

"Hey, what's up?"

"Guess what I found out?" she exclaimed, pacing around the living room.

"What?"

"Mr. Dolton is my dad."

"What?" Jeff shouted. "Are you sure?"

"Yes," she said. "He asked my mom to give him another chance. Can you believe him?"

"No," Jeff said. "Man, that's low. We were just talking about your father too."

"It's a good thing I never wanted to meet him in the first place." She took a deep breath.

"Wait a minute," Jeff said, pausing. "I thought you felt bad about your mom working so much."

"Because he left her," she stated. "After what he did to her, I never had any intentions of meeting him."

"You have a point there," Jeff agreed. "Now what's going to happen?"

Marisa paused, realizing it was a good question. What was she going to do now? What could she do? "I don't know," she replied. "My mom ran out of his classroom."

"That's not really surprising," he added. "Don't tell anyone."

"All right."

"Sorry, but I really had to get that off my chest." "No problem," Jeff said. "That's what I'm here for." She smiled briefly. "I have to go."

"All right."

"Bye." She hung up the phone and lay on her bed. She felt angry and frustrated at the nerve Mr. Dolton had by asking her mom for another chance. She couldn't believe he was her father!

What right does he have to come back for my mom? she thought. *How can it be OK to get someone pregnant, leave them for another person, and then expect them to take you back? After all these years too. Now he suddenly shows up out of nowhere.*

The thoughts continued to run through her head.

Now what? Am I supposed to be mad at him forever or forgive him and accept what he did? Did he change or remain like he was when my mom knew him? What he did was unacceptable and not supposed to be easily forgiven.

Since she didn't know what her father looked like, she was surprised at the news. Nor did she really know what to expect. She didn't know how he could be her father. They looked nothing like each other. Her mom had never told her anything about him, except what he did whenever she asked.

Marisa released a sigh and turned over onto her stomach, clutching her pillows. Today turned out to be a very long day, and she wasn't really looking forward to tomorrow.

CHAPTER 9

The next day Marisa walked to school, fighting the humid day that threatened to rain, predicting her mood. Intolerable and unbearable. She entered the building and approached her group of friends. They stood by the lockers, getting their books for class. But when she saw Jeff waiting, a smile came to her face. She knew exactly why he was there, and it made her feel good to see how much he cared.

"Hey," she said, walking up to him.

"Hey." He grabbed her hand. "Do you want to go to the mall after school?" "Sure."

"Cool. I'll see you in computer," Jeff called out, slowly letting go of her. "Bye."

It was really sweet of Jeff to ask her out. She really needed to get her mind off what happened yesterday and get cheered up. She watched him leave with Sean. Mark joined Jenni's side.

"You ready?" he asked her.

"Yes," Jenni said. She closed her locker and looked over at Patty and Marisa. "I'll see you guys later."

"Bye," Patty called out, standing next to Marisa.

Marisa opened her locker and quickly changed her books, since classes were about to start. Shutting the locker, she turned to Patty, who watched her. "I know," she said. "I forgot to call you."

"Mhmm," Patty said teasingly. They fought the crowds toward their classroom.

"Sorry, I've had a lot on my mind lately," Marisa said quietly.

Patty shot a glance at her as they entered the Math classroom. They sat down in their seats right when the final bell rang. "What's wrong?" Patty whispered.

"I'll tell you later." She had wanted to tell her friends what happened yesterday but decided to wait until they were all together, instead of repeating the story numerous times.

Patty nodded and turned her attention to the front of the room.

But Marisa's thoughts continued to wander about the confrontation that occurred yesterday. She didn't see her mom this morning before leaving, not that she usually did. If so, it was only long enough to say goodbye. Her mother never said anything else during the night about Mr. Dolton. She simply collapsed on the couch and fell asleep. Marisa stayed in her room, thinking the hours away. Her mind raced with questions—so many questions that hadn't been answered yet. She had stayed up late worrying too much about what would happen now that she knew her father.

You're in class. Concentrate!

Marisa looked up, and the bell rang, jarring her thoughts. She stood up and quickly packed her book bag. She exited the room and headed to computer class, with Patty by her side. *Great*, she thought. *I have to face him again.* Her eyes widened upon another realization. He was her teacher. She would have to face him every school day. *I learned only last night he's my dad.*

She entered the room behind Patty, ignoring the front desk. Her eyes swept toward the back where her friends sat. She quickly followed Patty down the aisle until they reached their row and sat down. "I'm so glad it's Friday," she exclaimed. "This has been one long week."

"Really," Jenni added.

"You have plans for the weekend?" Patty asked them.

"Mark and I are going to the movies tomorrow," Jenni said, smiling.

"And I don't have to look at dumb butt for two days," she commented, nodding her head in Mr. Dolton's direction.

Jenni and Patty laughed. Marisa's eyes drifted over to Jeff, who heard the comment and caught her gaze, smiling. Mr. Dolton stood up to begin the lecture. During class she passed notes back and forth with Jeff so they would stay awake. For once she actually avoided getting caught. They continued talking about the discovery they made last night. Jeff had as many questions for her as she did, but she still had no answers.

When class finally ended, Mr. Dolton asked her to stay, which ruined her mood. She didn't feel like talking to him. It was too soon. She wanted answers but needed time to blow off some steam. Her friends threw a worried glance at her before heading over to study hall. Jeff was the last to leave the room, lingering longer than anyone else. Their eyes met before he disappeared out the door. Marisa waited quietly by the front of the room.

"Do you have a class next?" Mr. Dolton asked, turning toward her.

The door was left open. Marisa eyed it, wondering if she could simply leave. She wasn't in trouble or ordered to stay, merely asked. "Study hall," she replied.

"I wanted to talk to you about yesterday."

He sat down on the edge of his desk. Marisa hesitated, knowing he would bring this up and waited for him to continue. Instead, he simply stared at the ground. She couldn't stand the awkward silence and wanted to leave.

"Are you really my father?" she asked. "Yes."

"Why did you come back?"

Mr. Dolton quickly looked up at her as if taken back by that question. He appeared hurt and shocked too, but he didn't say anything. Tired lines etched the corners of his eyes. He ran a hand through his hair.

"Why did you come back?" she repeated.

"I came back for the woman I love," he said carefully. "I also came back to see my child."

"That answer sounds rehearsed," she remarked, making him gasp. "You're probably just saying that rather than admitting you ditched my mom."

"*What?*" Mr. Dolton demanded, jumping to his feet. His face turned distorted and angry, aghast. "What are you talking about? I didn't ditch your mom."

"Sure," she said, heading toward the door. "Likely excuse."

"Marisa."

She exited the room before he could finish his sentence. *How can a person forget ditching someone?* she thought, rolling her eyes. *I don't know what my mom ever saw in him.* Marisa raced through the empty hallways, her footsteps echoing off the walls until reaching the classroom. She quickly entered, spotting her friends at a nearby table and approaching them, collapsing onto the nearest chair.

"What did Mr. Dolton tell you?" Jenni asked.

Marisa glanced over at Jeff, who sat next to her, and caught her gaze. She threw him a look, her eyebrows raised, and he shrugged. It was her call.

"Is everything all right?" Patty asked her.

Hesitating, she looked around the room seeing that it wasn't crowded. The other students were busy working on their assignments or talking with their friends. Gazing back at her friends, they scooted their chairs closer and leaned toward her. "Promise not to say anything to anyone?" Marisa asked. The five of them nodded, throwing each other questioning looks. Only Jeff didn't seem confused. He placed a comforting hand on her shoulder. "I found out yesterday that Mr. Dolton is my father," she whispered.

A glance at her friends showed they appeared dumbfounded and shocked. A silence settled at the table. No one moved.

"What?" Mark finally asked. Everyone seemed to breathe again. "You're kidding, right?" Jenni asked.

"No." She shook her head. "I'm not. My mom confirmed it." "But you look nothing like him," Patty said.

"Thank God for that," Sean remarked, and Patty smacked him on the arm. Her friends continued to throw puzzled looks her way.

"How about you start from the beginning?" Jeff suggested.

Marisa told her friends everything that she knew—from her father leaving when her mother was pregnant and ending with them meeting with him yesterday.

"That seems rather peculiar," Patty admitted.

"I agree," Jenni added. "He starts substituting here, then becomes a teacher, and by the end of the week, you find out he's your father."

"Coincidence?" Patty's eyebrow rose.

The timing had appeared too fast, too coincidental, almost too obvious. But for what? She couldn't answer.

"Now what?" Sean asked her.

"I don't know." She shrugged. "I have to wait and see."

"Is that why he asked you to stay after class?" Mark asked.

She nodded, letting out a deep breath. Her cheeks burned. Her father returned after all this time, bringing along unanswered questions. *If he claimed to love my mom, why did he leave her?* she thought. *Why did he wait so long to come back? Why did he come back?*

He said he came back to see his child.

I don't care, she thought, gazing at the table. He was gone for too long. I never wanted to meet him in the first place.

"Marisa."

She looked up to find her friends staring at her, appearing worried. "You all right?" Jeff asked, grabbing her hand.

"Yeah, I'm sorry," she said. "I'm just confused, angry, frustrated."

The bell rang, and she slowly stood up from the chair. Her friends also gathered their belongings together. Marisa said bye to them, grabbing Jeff's arm and headed to her next class. During lunch, her friends gathered around her, probing her with more questions, but she no longer felt like discussing the subject. She felt the topic had already been exhausted enough. Her friends took the hint and talked about other things without becoming offended. They simply sensed she needed time to adjust. She wanted time alone.

Marisa attended the rest of her classes, lost in her thoughts and oblivious to her surroundings. The shock of the news wore on her throughout the day. She went through the motions of sitting in her seat at each class, staring at the teacher but not hearing their words. The bell rang too soon, the noise in the crowded hallways floated through her ears. The students pushed past her in the hallways, and she walked on in a daze like a zombie.

The final bell rang, and Marisa was more than ready to leave the premises. She changed her books out and shut her locker to find Jeff standing by her side, bringing a smile to her face.

"You ready?" he asked, holding out his arm for her.

"Yes." She grabbed on to it. Glancing over at her friends, she said, "I'll see you guys later."

"Bye," they replied.

Stepping forward, she looked over her shoulder at Jenni, Patty, Mark, and Sean, who stood watching her leave. She turned back around and proceeded walking toward the front door.

Marisa gazed over at Jeff, who was also studying her. "What?"

"Nothing," he said. "Admiring your beauty."

She smiled, glancing briefly at the ground. "Did I offend them by brushing them off?"

"No," he said. "They understand, but they're worried about you."

They exited the building. The hot and humid air cloaked their bodies. They crossed the parking lot, turning to the right and proceeding on to the sidewalk near her neighborhood. Marisa finally became aware of her surroundings. The numbness bounced off her skin in waves like the reflection of light. She glanced around, enjoying the scenery. Students spread out in different directions all around them, their voices drifting off. Soon no one was around but the two of them. Jeff grabbed her hand, making her smile at him.

"Do you mind if we go to the mall another day?"

"That's fine," Jeff replied. "We can go on a real date. Dinner and a movie." "Sounds good," she agreed.

"You busy this weekend?" "Nope."

"Good," he said. "Then it's settled."

She laughed. *So smooth*, she thought. But a silence overcame them. They turned on to her street, walked up to her front lawn, and sat on the grass. Her shoulders drooped, feeling the weight from the events occurring last night and this morning. Her thoughts started to drift again to the scenes, when he squeezed her hand.

"Want to talk about it anymore?" Jeff asked.

"I might as well," she replied. "I didn't finish telling you everything that happened this morning."

"What did he tell you?"

Marisa exhaled a deep breath, looking off in the distance. "I asked him if he was really my father and why did he come back after ditching my mom, but he said he didn't ditch her," she said.

Jeff was silent for a while, thinking over her words. At last he said, "Seems like he's lying and trying to cover it up."

"That's exactly what I'm thinking," she agreed. "What else did he say?"

"He came back for the woman he loves and for his child," she replied, shrugging. "I left after that." She let out a deep sigh, running her hands through her hair.

Her eyes shifted to the ground, her thoughts racing to earlier, when her friends had asked, "Now what?" The question continued to stare her in the face, laughing and pointing, waiting for an answer. An answer she didn't have.

"Why come back? Why did he leave to begin with?"

"If he didn't ditch your mom, maybe you should ask what happened?" Jeff suggested.

Another silence washed over the two of them. Marisa buried her head in her hand, fuming. Her alleged father, who had made himself known yesterday. But then again, she did leave before he could say anything else.

"You only found out yesterday," Jeff pointed out. "Give it time. I'm sure he'll come around and talk to you."

"But what if I don't want him to?" Marisa met his eyes. "I had no desire to meet him."

"He's also your teacher," Jeff added. "You'll have to face him sooner or later. Maybe he has a good explanation."

"For leaving my mom when she was pregnant?" Marisa asked, raising an eyebrow.

Jeff made eye contact, seeming confused by the question. He studied her face, his eyes darting back and forth. "If you never had a desire to meet him, why dwell over him?"

She paused, thinking over his words carefully. "Because I never expected yesterday to occur. Now I'm so frustrated and angry with him. I have so many questions, but no answers."

"There's probably a reason he came back," Jeff said.

"That's what worries me," she said. "That reason could be good or bad." She released a deep breath, bending her legs. She brought them close to her body, wrapping her arms around her legs, resting her chin on her knees.

"Ah." Their eyes met. "That's what's bothering you? Why he chose now to come back?"

She thought over his words and slowly nodded. "We've done fine without him. What made him decide to come back? Realized his mistake and wants to fix it? Why?"

"Why are you so afraid?" Jeff pressed on. "There's nothing wrong with having your father in your life."

"I don't know him," she answered. "He's a stranger to me."

"You'll get to know him," he said. "It might be good for you and your mother."

"I don't know." She hesitated, glancing at the grass. "I guess I'm still shocked that he even came back. It's kind of surreal right now. I don't know what to think. That's what is making me so afraid."

"It sounds like you need to understand the situation better," he commented. "Maybe from his side to fully understand what happened between them. You know your mom's side, but not his side."

Again, she nodded. "I like how you put it into perspective."

"You need to hear his side eventually." He shrugged, stroking her idle hand that he had been holding this entire time.

She smiled. "I'm sorry for dumping all this on you."

"Don't be," Jeff said. "You're my girlfriend." He glanced up at the beautiful sky, where the sun stood directly over them. "Let's forget about him for the rest of the day and enjoy ourselves."

"OK," she said, smiling. "You know, you haven't finished telling me about yourself." "I like to play basketball," Jeff informed her.

Marisa laughed, shaking her head. *He's so cute*, she thought.

They continued talking the afternoon away. She extinguished a sigh of relief, her eyes fixed on Jeff. He entertained her with all types of stories about his life—his interests, his family, his childhood, the numerous jokes he would play on his siblings when they were younger.

She was lucky to be with him. They had only been a couple for a few days, yet it felt longer.

She had noticed in this short time that he didn't pressure her into anything, nor did he rush the stages of their relationship. Even though she sat alone with him in front of an empty house, there hadn't been a reason to worry, nor would there be any reason. She was safe with him.

I found a good man, she thought, studying his handsome face. *One who really cares about me.*

Together they watched the sun set on the horizon. Marisa stood up and swung her book bag onto her shoulder. The afternoons always flew when she was with Jeff. She kept him at her house longer than intended, but he didn't seem in any rush to leave. There was no one waiting for her either. What better way to pass the time than with her boyfriend?

"I'll call you," Jeff said. "See when we can go out this weekend." "That sounds good," she replied. "I'll see you later."

"Call me if anything else happens."

"OK, thanks for listening." She turned toward the house.

"Anytime. Bye."

Marisa unlocked and opened the door, entering the house while glancing back at Jeff one last time. He stood watching to make sure she entered safely. She waved to him before shutting and locking the door behind her. Her stomach growled; it was dinnertime. She made her way into the quiet and empty house, dropping her bag in her room before returning to the kitchen. Marisa heated up some leftovers to eat while simultaneously picking up around the kitchen. Pan goes here, plate there, cup over here.

Though she felt better, she still didn't know what to think. What was she supposed to think? She was so used to not having a father; therefore, she accepted it. Jenni and Patty had never mentioned him. When she first met them, they found out he left. She had been angry then, and she was angry now. With him back in the picture, she didn't know what to feel. It wasn't like she missed or longed for him.

She didn't know him. Several other kids had single parents as well. Why did she have all these mixed feelings about him now that she knew who he was? Now that he was back?

Should I open up to him and accept him? she thought. *Am I ready to let him in my life? Should I let him in my life?*

Her mom hadn't really said much about him after yesterday. She didn't expect her to either, since all this happened so suddenly. She also didn't know what to expect now. *If I let him into my life, will everything change or will it stay the same?* Jeff had made a good point, though. If she hated him because he left, forcing her mom to work nonstop, why was she so afraid of him, when the thing she hated could be undone? *If that's what my mom wants.*

It was late by the time she ate dinner, but her mom wouldn't be home for some time.

Picking up the remote, she switched on the television to a random channel to create some noise in the house. Marisa walked around the house, straightening up a bit. When the house was decent, she collapsed on the couch to unwind.

Maybe I can talk to her, she thought. *If she's not too tired. No, wait. She's off for the next two days. I'll take my time and approach the subject delicately. This couch is so comfortable. I think I'll lie down and rest for a little bit ...*

Marisa awoke with a start, feeling disoriented from the quiet, pitch-black surroundings. After blinking several times, she discovered that all the lights were off, the television was turned off, a blanket was covering her, and her mom's bedroom door was closed. Yawning, she rubbed her eyes and saw it was after midnight. Throwing the covers off her, she tiptoed back to her room and collapsed on the bed.

CHAPTER 10

"Hey, Marisa. Do you want to go to One Shop with me?" her mom asked.

It was early Saturday morning, and she finished eating a late but favorite breakfast with her mom—chorizo, potato, and egg tacos, covered with cheese and hot sauce.

"Sure," she replied. Her spirits lifted upon seeing her mother in a good mood this morning. For the next two days, she would have her mom to herself and relished the idea of spending time with her. She always jumped at the opportunity. Feeling like her old self again, she helped clean up the kitchen. "What do we need to get?"

"Some toiletries, and I want to look at the kitchen appliances," her mom answered. Marisa changed, dismissing the past few days. Her mom was happy, so she was happy.

Once dressed, she joined her mom waiting in the living room when Jeff popped into her mind.

He said he would call so they could go out. She hadn't heard from him yet but didn't know if he called last night when she fell asleep. *We can always go out later*, she thought.

"Ready?"

"Yeah."

They exited the house together and climbed into the sedan. Her mom started the engine and backed out of the driveway, heading over to One Shop. The convenient store was closely located, selling groceries, toiletries, household items, clothes, toys, outdoor equipment, and entertainment, a little bit of everything. Her mom pulled into a parking spot, and they piled out of the car. As they entered the store, Marisa grabbed a basket, and her mom pulled out a list.

"Let's see here," her mom said. "We need toilet paper."

She pushed the basket, following her mom to the grocery section, who grabbed a package off the shelves and placed it in the basket. "What else?"

"Let's hit the toiletries aisle," her mom replied. "Then we'll look at the appliances." "What about shampoo?" she asked. "We're running low."

"It's on the list."

They turned around and walked over to the toiletries. Her mom grabbed the various items they needed, setting them in the cart.

"Can I look at the makeup?" she asked, eyeing the aisle next to her.

Her mom also looked over at the next aisle before glancing at her watch. "I'll tell you what," she said, "I'll run over to the appliances and meet you in the makeup aisle. Sound good?"

"Are we in a rush?" Marisa asked, pulling the basket aside to allow the other people room to walk by.

"Danny's coming by to fix your toilet."

"Danny, as in Danny the handyman?" She raised her eyebrows.

Her mom rolled her eyes. Danny went to high school with her mom. He was a repairman now, and her mom called him whenever they needed something fixed. He used to come over regularly these past few years, but not as much anymore. He was all right—a little weird at times, but seemed harmless. He was handy, so there were advantages to her mom knowing him. Every time she called him, he always came over in remarkable timing and fixed anything they needed—at a reasonable price too.

When he came over, he would talk about the past with her mom. But as long as he could fix the problem, her mother didn't mind talking to him and putting up with his endless chatter, though she once admitted to not remembering him. Apparently, he dropped out of high school because he was a troublemaker. But he claimed to change his ways.

Sometimes Marisa listened in on their conversations, during which she discovered his weirdness. He would always brag about how he could fix anything, how he could cook and clean, how he wanted a wife and family, how he wanted a big house, how he made a good living off his job. How he only had a GED, yet he knew several trades.

Or rather a jack-of-all-trades, a master of none, Marisa thought after one visit.

But after hearing Danny converse with her mom, she found the insistence of what he wanted strange. Too strange of a topic to keep talking about, at least. Why he kept mentioning these factors, she didn't know. He was always working, so he made decent money.

"I didn't know he was coming over," Marisa said.

"I called him last night," her mom informed her.

"Oh." He was coming over today? "He works on the weekends?"

"Yes," her mom replied. "But not through the company. He charges a flat rate. The company charges just to come out and take a look at what's wrong."

"So it's on the side?"

"Yes." Her mom approached the basket. "I'll meet you back here." She tried to move Marisa's hands out of the way.

"Forget the makeup," she said. "I'll stay with you. Go—I got this."

Her mom rolled her eyes and continued walking to the appliance section.

"But I get to rummage through your makeup bag later," Marisa called out. Her mom looked back, throwing the look. She giggled, pushing the basket, and following her mom's footsteps.

They reached the section, and Marisa stopped. Her mom looked around the cooking utensils, searching and comparing them.

"You need to get this now?"

"You broke the other one," her mom replied.

"Are you making a special lunch for a certain someone?"

Her mom threw her another look. "No …" She smiled. "You're making lunch." "Whatever," Marisa said. "Mom, do you like Danny?"

"Why do you ask that?" her mom asked, frowning.

"Because you always call him," she stated. "I don't know how you put up with him. He always wants to talk."

"True, but he has his uses," her mom answered.

"I thought he was a troublemaker in high school."

"I didn't really know him in high school." Her mom picked up a spatula and two cooking spoons, throwing them into the basket.

"How do you know he's changed?"

"He claimed to be a troublemaker." Her mom shrugged. "I don't remember him at all.

But people change all the time. They mature and settle down." "I see," Marisa said. "Then you do like him?"

"He's OK, but he's not someone I'd settle down with." She nodded. Her mom picked up a pan and placed it in the basket. Marisa raised an eyebrow. "You scratched the other one."

"Sure, blame it on the kid," she remarked.

Her mother pretended to choke her, then continued looking around the aisle. She laughed and watched for a while, thinking back to the response. *Uses*? she thought, tilting her head to the side. *Hmm …*

Suddenly Marisa heard a noise behind her and turned around. No one was there. That was odd. She could have sworn she heard a strange noise. She faced forward and watched her mom again. A few seconds later, she began to feel eyes on her. She quickly glanced over her shoulder, but saw nothing.

"Here it is," her mom announced, grabbing a timer and joined Marisa, where she set it in the cart.

"What else?"

"I think we're good," her mom replied. "Can you think of anything else while we're here?"

"Nope."

She pushed the basket, following her mom toward the checkout line. Between the two of them, they found a line that wasn't too crowded. As they stood waiting, Marisa felt eyes staring at her again. She casually turned around and pretended to look at the magazines that were at the front of the registers. She scanned the area for anything out of the ordinary. Wait. Something caught her eye—or rather someone. The back form of someone stood close to the other side, looking over the aisle. She glanced around it and saw Mr. Dolton eyeing her mom.

Marisa tiptoed back to the line and whispered in her mom's ear, "Mr. Dolton's following us. He's in the next aisle, staring at you."

Her mom frowned and gazed over to the next aisle, shaking her head. Marisa kept her eye on him. He never moved, only stared at her mom, while pretending to look at the items.

After they checked out, they quickly left the building. The bags kept bouncing off Marisa's legs, the sharp edges of the items jutted out the top opening of the bags, digging into the sides of her thighs. Marisa's fingers twisted from the handle turning every which way. Her calves burned from the exertion of racing across the parking lot. They finally reached the car. Hastily throwing the bags in the trunk, she jumped in the sedan. Her mom gunned the engine to life and raced out of the parking lot.

On the way home, Marisa looked in the rearview mirror to make sure Mr. Dolton wasn't following them. A black Mustang was behind them. The driver wore dark clothes, and the windows were tinted. Her mom moved over to the turning lane and kept her signal on to turn left onto a street. They waited at a red light. The black Mustang moved over to where they were behind them again. Their turn signal came on.

"Mom, are we being followed?"

"I don't know." Her mom looked in the rear-view mirror. "Why?"

"That black mustang has switched lanes and is also turning," she replied. "Only one way to find out," her mom said. "Hang on."

The light changed to the green arrow, and her mom sped forward, veering to the right lane in front of oncoming cars trying to turn left and passing through the intersection at the last minute. The black Mustang also sped up and swerved to the right, narrowly missing the cars that stopped for her mom. The Mustang straightened out the car, speeding to catch up with them. Her mom stepped harder on the gas pedal. The Mustang also sped up, staying right behind them. Marisa turned around in her seat and looked closely, trying to see who it was, but she couldn't tell. Her mom made a sharp unprotected left turn at the next light in front of several cars that stopped and honked. The Mustang tried to make the turn but was stopped by oncoming cars venturing forward. It waited at the light, gunning its engine.

"They're stuck back there," Marisa announced. "Go, go, go!" She turned around and sat face forward, holding on to the seat. Her mom swerved to avoid hitting a car. *What's going on around here?*

Her mom made the left turn, raced down the street, made a sharp right, and pulled into their driveway. Marisa jumped out of the sedan, running around the front end as the engine was cut. "We'll get the stuff later!" her mom shouted, dropping the keys in her purse. "Go!"

"Mom!" Marisa yelled, throwing her hands up. "Your keys."

Her mom's face turned from blank to shock. "Oh, crap!" she shouted. She dug in her purse while simultaneously pushing

Marisa up the front steps. They stood on the porch by the front door. "Where are they? I just had them."

Marisa patted her own pockets, but to no avail. She hadn't bothered bringing anything with her. "Hurry up," she shrieked, glancing around.

The keys were retrieved when the Mustang turned onto their street and pulled up along the front of their house, stopping parallel to the sidewalk and within view of the front door. It roared at them, the figure watching, the engine gunning louder and louder. Suddenly the Mustang peeled off from the road and raced down the street until out of sight. Black tire marks were left behind where it had sat only moments ago.

"Talk about rudeness," her mom said, unlocking the door. "Come on, let's get the bags."

Marisa wondered whether that really was Mr. Dolton, since they saw him at One Stop. If so, why did he do it?

* * *

The dark abandoned warehouse was over forty feet tall, with rusted windows covered by shingles falling apart, making it appear old and run-down. The place seemed unused for a long time, filled with junk, dust, and mold. Bookcases, filing cabinets, and desks littered the room. Some furniture stood upright, and some pieces were on their sides. Some lay in piles like they had been thrown there, never to be bothered with again.

On the inside of the large room was a door, revealing a staircase that led down to a basement. A big group of guys filled the basement, all in their late twenties. Most of them were built, and some were big enough to pass as bodyguards. Only one light was on. The room was empty except for some chairs and a table placed in the center where the guys sat around.

Danny—tall, built, and short-tempered—looked up at the sound of approaching footsteps on the staircase.

Being darkened by the outdoors, he had brown hair and brown eyes. A deep scar marked one side of his cheek.

"Hey, Danny, John's trying to make a comeback on Lisa," Ben announced, entering the room.

"What?" Danny roared. *John's trying to get back with Lisa?* he thought. *That cannot happen.*

"He was at One Shop, following her," Ben said. "When they left, I followed Lisa all the way to her house, giving her the scare of her life. She thinks it was John."

"Good," Danny said, rubbing his scar.

Danny's fumes raced with anger. He hadn't heard anything from Lisa in a while, and he wondered what was going on. Surely, she couldn't be too busy for him to stop by. No sir. He wouldn't allow that to happen. Lisa was too hot, and she had been taken away from him once already. Anything he wanted was his for the taking.

He learned the hard way from letting Lisa slip away from him, but then he found her again three years ago. He had been practicing with her ever since. The only drawback was he had to be patient and slowly work at her. Danny hated being patient. It drove him crazy and usually never worked out for him, especially in the past. First, he was kicked out of high school for misbehaving. Stupid teachers. What did they know? Then he served jail time here and there for drunk driving, unpaid tickets, attempted robbery, possession of cocaine, domestic abuse from his former common-law slut, and the list went on and on. Danny moved around a bit, escaping law enforcers searching for him. He settled back in his home city, but in a new subdivision. He came here intending to stay only a few days and crashed at a buddy's house, laying low for a while, when he saw Lisa out shopping by chance. After following her around that one fine day, he discovered where she lived.

He decided to live here again and get a common job that allowed him to be close to her again. It worked out in the end. No one knew he was back here. He couldn't understand why the police were always after him anyway. It was all a matter of being in the wrong place at the wrong time. Getting a new but lousy job, he seized the call when it came in and got to visit Lisa at her house. She looked even hotter now, with those long luscious legs and those come-get-me thighs. Oh yes, she had filled out nicely from drinking her milk like a good girl.

Everything seemed to be going in his favor. He had nothing but time to kill on his hands. He figured if he couldn't get Lisa, he would simply use other forces. But Lisa had a kid and he didn't want things to get too messy. The kid began resembling Lisa more and more each time he visited.

When too much time had flown by without her calling, he drove by her house to do a little checking up. And what did he discover? She was home. She was home and she still hadn't called him. Probably just her and the kid too. Not like they were doing anything. The house was quiet. Surely, she could have called him. He knew a few ways to keep her busy. Give her a workout. Have her screaming his name.

Lisa had no other relatives here and as far as he knew, she was too busy to socialize with friends, let alone make them. He himself was only invited over occasionally to fix one thing or another. A mutual agreement at best. He gets to see her and chat for a little bit; she gets her garbage disposal fixed. But he had to take it slow this time around. He couldn't screw up and let her get away. Not again. It would only be a matter of time before she came running into his arms.

Now John was back in town. Probably trying to get back with Lisa. Either that or check up on that kid of his. The kid who should have been Danny's. John coming back didn't help at all; it only ruined Danny's perfect plan. This was something he worked very hard at, trying not to slip or get impatient.

Trying to stay clean enough to avoid scaring Lisa. Now this drew the line. He would have to take matters into his own hands. He had to be careful, but he had to work fast to win Lisa. It was all about timing.

Or he could simply get rid of John so he would be out of the picture. Hmmm … Oh, Johnny boy, you pushed it too far this time. It's payback.

Ben approached him as he stood up, turning over new plans in his head. "What are you going to do?"

Danny remained silent, thinking for a while on what to do about the delicate situation. Remembering his appointment today with Lisa, he glanced at his watch. He still had plenty of time to shower, change, and get ready. "I'm going to do what I've always done," he answered. The noise in the room ceased. He raised his voice louder, turning toward them. "I'm going to continue seeing Lisa, but maybe I need to keep an eye on John too."

The other guys nodded.

"Who's John?" Tom asked, the biggest and tallest of them all, counting his money.

"You know John," Danny barked, getting impatient. "The basketball player. Stole Lisa from me. And the captain's position from you."

"Oh yeah, I remember now," Tom said, eyeing Danny, a malicious grin forming. He stood up, allowing his stocky legs to stretch, and flexed his muscles, showing off. With a face scarred from bad acne and a tattoo showing on his upper arm, he made one hand into a fist and punched it into his other hand. "I still have a few words for him too."

"Now, now," Danny said, "let's not get too hasty. Don't worry, though. You'll get your chance. For now, I say simply keep an eye on him." No one said anything for a while, and slowly murmurs of agreement came from around the room. "Then it's settled."

Danny moved to the center of the room. His friends waited eagerly for him to continue.

He smiled, realizing how loyal his friends were. Always kept in touch with each other throughout the years. Eventually meeting up again some years back before running into Lisa. They were good to him. They wouldn't allow anything to slip by, especially with Lisa back in the picture. They all checked up on her, tracking her every move. Made sure the coast stayed clear for Danny. They each kept tabs on their girls. It was the well-known rule, unspoken, but always done without question.

Bros before hoes, Danny thought, smiling. "I want all of you to be following Lisa and John around. Hell, let's keep track of her kid while we're at it."

"Yeah!" the guys shouted in unison.

"I'll keep an eye on the girl," Ben volunteered, causing smirks to emerge. "In a few years, she'll be nice and ripe like Lisa."

The room exploded into laughter. Each guy made an obscene gesture.

Danny snorted, letting the guys joke around a bit. He took another glance at his watch. "I'm heading out," he announced. "Time to pay her a visit."

* * *

"Mom, where did you put the rice?" Marisa asked, raising her voice over the noise she made digging through the cabinets.

It was early Sunday evening, and she was preparing to make supper. Marisa never made it to the movies or dinner with Jeff the night before. After their little scare from shopping, she stayed home that evening with her mom. She told Jeff what had happened on the phone—from seeing Mr. Dolton at the store to the Mustang chasing them to their house, though she still wasn't sure if it was him behind the wheel.

Jeff expressed his doubt to her. "He wouldn't do something careless like that," he said. "Not to his daughter and the mother of his child."

Either way, Jeff understood and agreed that she stay home for the evening. There was always tomorrow. They agreed to go out in the early afternoon the next day. She hung up feeling better and went in search of her mother.

Her mom decided on having a girl's night in for the two of them. They rented some movies and made popcorn. Most of it ended up on the floor as they tried to catch it in their mouths. Getting hungry for a real snack, they decided to make something sweet and fattening. Marisa stayed up all night baking homemade chocolate-chip cookies with her mom, which they covered with ice cream before eating.

She eventually rummaged through her mom's makeup bag in the late hours of the night. They applied different colors and shades to her face. Marisa laughed the night away, knowing she was being a total goof but didn't care. She was having too much fun. Her mom was game too, carefree and letting her hair down.

They slept in late this morning, resting from their craziness the night before. After a late breakfast, Marisa spent the early afternoon walking around the mall with Jeff like she promised. Her mom gave her a weird look when she first mentioned it, but eventually agreed to her request.

Holding hands, Marisa and Jeff window-shopped at every store, discussing what they like and didn't like. They talked about what kind of house they would buy and how they would decorate it on the inside and the outside. How Jeff would buy nothing but designer clothes for her to wear. Marisa simply laughed and let him talk, eventually nodding to his words.

Jeff bought them blizzards to cool off and enjoy. They sat in the food court, chatting away while savoring the ice cream. Marisa always loved hanging out at the mall. It was close enough to walk to, and they ended up seeing several kids they knew from their school. A few kids stopped by their table to say hello before heading off.

After the mall they walked around the neighborhood park, working off their blizzards, since the day was beautiful, and they were having too much fun. Many people from the surrounding cities took advantage of the day as well. Families, large groups of friends, and couples; walking, jogging, running, bike riding, skating, skateboarding, and playing basketball on the outdoor court. Other folks were having a picnic on tables. Couples young and old were sitting on the benches, talking or lying on a blanket. As usual, the weekend flew by too fast, and she would be back in school tomorrow.

"Marisa, I'm on the phone," her mom shouted, jarring her thoughts.

She looked over her shoulder. Closing the cabinets, she walked over to the dinner table and sat on a chair to listen. Her mom must be talking to someone she didn't like. She rarely ever yelled, since Marisa never gave her any reason to raise her voice.

"No, I cannot have a conference today," her mom said firmly, but she quickly rose to yelling. "Yes, I know she's been to detention and lunch detention. So what?"

It was Mr. Dolton. He sure kept calling and appearing wherever they were. She was surprised her mom even talked to him after what happened yesterday and during the past week. If it was him yesterday. Remember what Jeff said.

"What do you mean why not?" her mom asked. "Because I can't. I have stuff to do. Look, bud, I don't have to tell you what I need to do. It's my business and my personal life. I can tell you right now that you're a sorry teacher, and you'll get fired if you keep on bugging your students' parents … Well, maybe if you would quit making the classes so boring, Marisa would behave." Her mom clicked the phone off.

"Go, Mom," Marisa said, smiling. "I don't see why he has to have a conference in the first place."

"Probably so he can make up with me." Her mom shook her head. "Mom, if he ditched you a long time ago, why did he come back?"

They had yet to talk about Mr. Dolton and their situation. At first Marisa figured her mom was upset about him coming back; then she couldn't find a time to bring it up delicately. But a few days passed, and her mom never mentioned him. Like nothing ever occurred. Now she wondered why.

They needed to talk about him sooner or later. He couldn't be ignored forever.

Marisa waited.

Her mom stood by the counter, staring at the floor, fidgeting with her hands. The silence seemed to expand throughout the house. At last she replied, "Probably wanted to see how you were doing."

"Oh."

CHAPTER II

The murmurs of students talking and laughing filled Marisa's ears upon entering the front doors. Approaching her locker, she found her friends chatting away and getting their books for class. They instantly surrounded her, since she was the last to arrive. Jeff stood by her locker waiting and she smiled at him.

"Hey, guys." Marisa glanced at Jeff. "Hey." "How are you, beautiful?" He winked.

She shook her head and rolled her eyes.

"Is everything better at your house?" Jenni asked.

She glanced at Jenni, raising an eyebrow, and then changed her books. Why would she ask? Did she know something? They knew Mr. Dolton was her father, but not what happened over the weekend. Her eyes darted briefly at Jeff. He met her gaze unflinching. No, he wouldn't tell them anything without her permission. Then she remembered her distant mood on Friday.

"Oh yeah." She shrugged. "I guess. He called yesterday requesting a conference, but my mom hung up on him after chewing him out."

"Dang," Patty said. "I wish she was my mom."

"No kidding," Sean added. "I could use her to tell off all my teachers." Laughter erupted within the group.

"I say party at your place next weekend," Mark interjected. "Your mom sounds cool." The warning bell rang, making groans erupt among them.

"I'll see you guys later," Marisa called out to Sean, Mark and Jenni. They parted in separate ways down the halls.

Jeff gave her hand a quick squeeze. "I'll see you in a bit."

"All right." She watched him take off running to catch up with Sean, her eyes admiring him from head to toe. Very nice.

"Stop checking out your boyfriend," Patty shouted. "We're going to be late."

"Sorry." She giggled, running to catch up with her halfway down the hall. "I can't help it".

"He's so hot."

"Yeah, yeah."

They briskly walked over to their Math classroom, taking their seats. They passed notes back and forth during class, where Marisa filled Patty in on what occurred Saturday. Patty was shocked to find out, but she agreed with Jeff that it couldn't have been Mr. Dolton.

"Then who is it?" Marisa wrote, passing it back. Who could have done that?

Patty read the note, glanced over at Marisa, and shrugged. When class ended, they headed over to computer class.

"Jeff said the same thing," Marisa told her.

"It's been one thing after another with you," Patty said.

"No kidding."

She followed Patty into the room. It had been one thing or another in her life. Ever since Mr. Dolton arrived too. Her eyes met his when she passed the front desk. She broke the contact, averting her gaze to the back of the room. She walked over to her seat and sat down, smiling at Jeff, who checked her out longingly this time, making her laugh.

"Tell Jenni what happened Saturday," Patty said to her.

"What?" Jenni asked, looking over at them.

"I'll tell you in a second."

Mr. Dolton stood up. He passed out a worksheet to each row and told the students to spend the class time completing it. When he approached the back row, Marisa stared at her blank computer, waiting for him to leave. Once he made his way to the front of the classroom, Marisa leaned over Patty and told Jenni what happened.

"That's crazy," Jenni remarked.

Mark leaned back in his seat and tapped his fingers on their table, making them look up to find Mr. Dolton staring at them. The entire class was quiet, waiting. She turned her attention to the lecture, hoping no one heard anything.

"As I was saying…" Mr. Dolton continued. She glanced around the class, noticing the female students following his every move. He walked up and down the middle aisle between the four rows on either side of the room, explaining the instructions. "Get to work," he said. "It's due at the end of the period."

The class became quiet again. Students were soon busy, bent on the task before them. The only noise was the sounds of pens scratching over paper or students asking Mr. Dolton a question. Gradually, a soft murmur developed among the students struggling to complete the work. Marisa completed about half of the worksheet before giving up. She exhaled deeply by her little progress, but wasn't about to give Mr. Dolton a reason to talk to her.

"This is so boring," Marisa whispered, tapping her long fingernails against the table. "I hate this class," Jenni said.

"No kidding. We still have thirty minutes left," Patty announced. They all groaned, and Jenni raised her hand.

"Don't bring him over here," Patti declared. She and Marisa shot Jenni a look. "Oops, sorry." Jenni shrugged.

Mr. Dolton approached their row, and Marisa kept her eyes on the worksheet to avoid eye contact. Her peripheral vision showed Jeff scooting his chair back toward her.

"Hey, did you have fun yesterday?" he whispered. "Of course." She smiled.

"When do we get to play on the computers?" she heard Jenni ask Mr. Dolton. "Soon," he said.

Patty jabbed her in the ribs, making her grunt. She glanced over to find Mr. Dolton staring at her and Jeff. He reluctantly turned around and moved his chair back into place.

When Mr. Dolton finally left the row, Jenni whispered, "He's always staring at you." Marisa looked up, realizing she was talking to her. "Me?"

"Yes," Jenni replied. "Every chance he gets."

"I noticed that too," Patty added softly, nodding. "He has always stared at you, but ever since you found out, he does it even more."

Suddenly it occurred to Marisa the reason why. She was his daughter. He had known it this entire time. She didn't know how, but his behavior toward her became clear. But exactly how long had he known? She shrugged. "You know why, though."

"But no one else does," Jenni whispered back.

They had a point. She noticed the stares numerous times, but she thought it was only her. If her friends had noticed it, surely the other students would notice it. They already watched his every movement.

Once class finally ended, Marisa grabbed on to Jeff's arm, and they walked to study hall together. She smiled, seeing Patty with Sean in front of them, next to Jenni and Mark. It felt good to have so many friends. Not only her best friends but also their boyfriends were also cool. She considered the guys to be her friends. They merged into a big group easily. *They really help me get through the day*, she thought.

"I tried calling you last night," Jeff said, breaking her thoughts.

Her brows scrunched over. Patty glanced over her shoulder at them, making Marisa's gaze shift over to her.

"You trying out for the team?" Patty asked him.

"Yeah," Jeff said. "They start at three thirty, right?"

"Yep," Mark replied, glancing over his shoulder.

"What tryouts?" Marisa asked.

"Basketball," Sean answered.

"That's why I called," Jeff commented.

She nodded. They followed their friends into study hall, where they found an empty table and sat down. "That's cool."

"All of us are trying out," Mark said, putting his arm around Jenni.

"We're going to state this year," Sean said, jumping out of his seat. He pulled Patty up from her chair. "My babe too."

"You too, Patty," Jenni exclaimed. Patty nodded, laughing and dancing around. "That'll be cool."

"Can we watch the tryouts?" Marisa asked Jeff, who nodded.

She smiled, watching Sean twirl Patty while hollering. Mark and Jeff joined in cheering, while Jenni and Marisa laughed. Soon the teacher told them to sit down and stop making so much noise. The six of them spent the rest of study hall talking and laughing.

When school let out, Marisa wished her friends good luck and watched the four of them race to the gymnasium.

"I'm going to the restroom real quick," Jenni told her. "I'll meet you in the gym."

"OK."

Marisa walked over to her locker to change her books, figuring she had a few minutes before tryouts began. Suddenly someone appeared next to her. The last person she wanted to see right now—Mr. Dolton. Her shoulders drooped; her eyes sharpened. He wouldn't leave her alone. She needed some answers from him, but not at this moment.

I'm getting tired of him always appearing when I least expect it, she thought, folding her arms over her chest. *He always picks the wrong time to approach me.*

"Marisa, can I take you home?"

Her eyes widen. Did she hear right? "What?"

"Can I take you home?" he repeated slower, stepping closer to her.

"Why?"

"Because you're my daughter, and I want to take you home," he said.

"I'm not ready to go home yet," she replied. "I do have a life."

"It'll give us a chance to talk more in private," he added. "Maybe we can grab a bite to eat."

Marisa hesitated, seeing he had a point. They do need to talk. She just wished his timing were a little better. She looked around for Jenni but didn't see her anywhere. And her other friends were at the gym. She wouldn't get to tell Jenni where she was going. She sighed. "Fine."

She reluctantly followed him out the school building. Several students stared at them. Great, now more students would notice. First the stares, now they were seen leaving the school together. She ignored the looks, shrugging it off. She couldn't do anything about it. He led her to a blue sedan and stopped walking.

"This is your car?" It wasn't him.

"Yep."

They climbed into the car. He started the engine and took off, exiting the parking lot, but he turned in the opposite direction of her house.

"Hey, you're going the wrong way." She turned around in her seat to look at the direction he should have gone. "My house is that way." He didn't say anything. Marisa looked over at Mr. Dolton. He didn't even ask where she lived. She should never have gotten into his car in the first place. What was I thinking? "Where are you taking me?"

"Somewhere."

She stared out the window, watching the route he took. She may need to know later. They passed the high school. They crossed an intersection and entered a subdivision. He pulled into the driveway of a one-story house that was definitely not her house. This house looked older than her house, as well as the neighborhood, though it seemed well kept. "Whose house is this?"

"Mine."

She climbed out of the car, straightening the book bag on her shoulders, and looked around the neighborhood, trying to remember how he came here. She glanced in the direction that led out of the subdivision and toward her house. Mr. Dolton headed up the walkway that led to the front door and stopped in his tracks, seeing that Marisa stayed rooted to the spot next to the car. She couldn't believe he brought her to his house. He wasn't doing a good job of trying to make an impression on her.

He looked back at her. "Come on."

"You said you would take me home," she pointed out. "This is not my house. Now take me home right now." She debated whether or not to walk home, though she wasn't familiar with this area. The neighborhood was fairly established; the houses seemed to have been there awhile now. She had seen this area before and knew it had existed for some time, but didn't know her way around. It shouldn't be too hard to get out of here. Just go back the way he came. *Why did I get into his car in the first place?*

"Get inside," Mr. Dolton said firmly.

"I'm not going in there." Marisa turned away from him. She looked around the street, deciding she would find her way home by walking. They were on the other side of the high school. Her house was right beyond it. She could simply head toward the school. The sun pounded relentless and sweat formed on her back from simply standing there. *It's OK*, she thought, adjusting the bag on her shoulders. *Rain or shine, you can walk the distance.*

Mr. Dolton suddenly appeared in front of her. "Marisa, come on. We can get pizza or nachos or ice cream—whatever you want. And we can talk."

Marisa glared at him, angry that he tricked her into going to his house. They needed to talk but now she no longer wanted to talk. She was too angry with him for using her. Now she couldn't trust him. She hesitated. But if she stays with him, she can call her mom to come get her and tell her what happened. She grunted then followed him up the driveway. He approached the front door and unlocked it. He opened the door and stepped aside, so she could enter first. He closed the door behind him, and she headed straight to a couch where she sat down. She clenched her fists, digging them into the cushions.

"Make yourself at home."

"Why am I here?" she asked.

"Because I'm your father," he replied, dropping his workbag on an armchair.

"And that gives you the right to take me to your house any time you want?" she shot back.

Ignoring her, Mr. Dolton walked over to the couch where she sat and picked up a cordless phone off the coffee table in front of her. She noticed the phone too late. He dialed a number. Crossing her arms over her chest, Marisa glared at him. She couldn't believe he was doing this.

"Lisa, this is John. Marisa is at my house. I live at 1633 Mabieu Street, on the other side of the high school next to your old subdivision." He clicked off the phone.

What has gotten into him? She continued to see different sides of him emerging that surprised her. But then again, she hardly knew him. "Can you please tell me why I'm here?"

"So I can talk to your mom," Mr. Dolton replied. "I thought we were going to talk."

"I'll wait until she comes," he added.

"You could have taken me home and waited at my house," she said. "And get kicked out?" he shot back. "I don't think so."

"She's not going to like you by doing this," Marisa said. "I don't like that you lied to me and tricked me into coming here."

"I don't like being ignored, avoided, walked out on, and hung up on." His voice rose and shook. He paused and took a deep breath, but she could tell he was angry. "And frankly, I'm tired of it."

"Maybe if you approached it differently—"

"Maybe if you and your mom would simply talk to me in a civil manner, I wouldn't have to do this," he said firmly.

"Maybe if you'd quit bugging us every day." Her voice also rose. "Bugging you?" He crossed his arms over his chest.

"Yes." She stood up. The book bag slid off her shoulders and fell on the couch. Marisa faced Mr. Dolton. He remained on the other side of the coffee table. They stood glaring at one another, sizing each other up. She crossed her arms over her chest.

"I try talking to you—"

"You bug me every day at school, and you know it," she shouted. "You ask me to stay after school or after class. You're always freaking staring at me. With my mom, you kept asking for a conference. You follow us at the store. You trick me into coming here. You call her on the phone and now she has to come here to get me."

"You're absolutely right." He nodded his head slowly. "Excuse me for 'bugging' my daughter, whom I have never seen until last week."

Marisa hesitated, her eyes lowered, seeing his point. She knew exactly where he was going. Her cheeks burned.

"I didn't even know if I had a son or a daughter," he continued.

Wait, what? Marisa thought, raising an eyebrow.

"And excuse me for 'bugging' your mother whom I've been separated from for the last thirteen years," he added.

Her eyes glanced up sharply at him upon hearing those words. "Don't you mean who you ditched?"

"I did not ditch your mother!" he yelled, his voice echoed throughout the house. He paused again, rubbing his forehead with his hand. Taking a deep breath, he lowered his hand and met her gaze.

Marisa sank on to the couch, giving up. She may as well rest. They weren't going to get anywhere with this conversation. Although he had a point, he still didn't provide her with any answers. He just kept denying what happened. *I'll wait until my mom gets here*, she thought. *Maybe between the two of them I can get some straight answers.*

Mr. Dolton watched her silently, rubbing his temple again. He hesitated, appearing upset. His mouth opened a few times to say something, only to shut after glancing at her. He paced back and forth in front of the coffee table like a caged animal. "I'm sorry for yelling," he said, returning to his original spot. "I didn't mean to lose my temper."

She rolled her eyes, letting out a deep breath. "You know my mom works late," she said. "It'll be awhile before she gets here."

"That's fine," he said, waving his hand. She snorted, seeing he missed her point.

"Are you hungry? Thirsty?" he asked. "I can make you something. Or order something".

"What do you feel like eating?"

"I'm fine, thanks." Picking up her book bag, she opened it and grabbed some books to work on her assignments. Since her mom works over ten hours a day, Marisa knew it would be late before she came over. Might as well get some work done to pass the time.

She could feel Mr. Dolton's eyes watching her. She arranged her books and paper on the table, fishing out a pen to write with. He disappeared from the room and returned a few seconds later with a soda, which he placed on the table next to her without saying a word. She glanced at it and smiled. It was her favorite kind. She mumbled thanks and returned her attention to the assignments, intent on attacking the workload.

The time passed slowly for Marisa. Mr. Dolton occupied himself by disappearing and reappearing every few moments. She could hear him walking around the house, but she never looked up when he entered the room. She didn't know what he did. The house became quiet. The only noise was her pen scratching over paper and his footsteps shuffling back and forth. He picked things up around the house here and there. She kept checking the time on her watch and looking out the windows for any sign of her mom. After a couple of hours of doing that, she gave up. She did all her homework, and her mom still hadn't come by. She began to get worried, wondering if her mom would ever think of checking the messages.

Since she still had nothing to do, Marisa looked around in the living room. The furniture was simple and comfortable, yet kind of outdated. The house appeared older, but still nice and clean. There was one dark-green couch, a love seat, a matching armchair, a brown coffee table, and a television set.

She looked on the walls and saw several family photos, recognizing Mr. Dolton right away. He looked the same in the pictures, only a younger version of him. The biggest one was of him at a younger age with his parents. All the photos consisted of him and his parents. Why did he only have those pictures? Marisa expected to see more of his extended family or even friends of his family. There were also pictures of Mr. Dolton playing different sports, mainly basketball. But there were not a lot of recent photos. She spotted some small ones, one of him in a military uniform, and another of him with his parents.

He was in the military? she thought. He sure didn't look like it. His hair was much shorter in those days. This must have been a while ago, but she didn't know the branches. She couldn't tell which one.

"Are you hungry?" he asked.

She nearly jumped. She was so caught up in looking at the pictures that she didn't hear him walk in. "No." She was starving.

"Are you sure? It's almost eight. I can make you anything you want. What do you like to eat?"

"I'm—"

Suddenly there was a loud, angry, and impatient knock on the front door. Marisa started to run toward it, but Mr. Dolton pulled her back. "I'll get it," he said.

She followed him and stood on tiptoe to see over his shoulder. He opened the door and there stood her mom looking furious, exhausted, worried, and anxious, with puffy red eyes. She had been crying. Who knew how long her mom tried to figure out where she was?

"I really appreciate you taking my daughter without my permission, John," her mom said, stepping inside. Marisa walked around Mr. Dolton until she stood between them and off to one side.

"Correction—our daughter," Mr. Dolton informed her.

"Don't start that," her mom said. "You were in military school for four years, and I was the only person at her birth. Your name is not on her birth certificate."

She looked over at her mom. Military school? She never mentioned that before.

"Well, if you hadn't sent me away, I would've been there," Mr. Dolton said. "And since we're on the subject, I never received any contact from you. Not once during these thirteen years."

Marisa turned her head up at Mr. Dolton, unbelieving. Her jaw opened and shut, but she remained quiet.

Her mom caught the looks Marisa threw back and forth between them. Throwing her hands up in the air, her mom shook her head. "I don't want to hear it." She turned to Marisa. "Let's go."

CHAPTER 12

Silent and perfectly still, Marisa stood glued to the floor in shock after hearing both her mom and Mr. Dolton. *Military school?* she thought. *What was Mom talking about? She told me Mr. Dolton ditched her. What was he talking about? Why do I keep hearing different stories?* The more she heard about their situation, the more confused she felt.

Before she could reply, Mr. Dolton said, "No, don't leave. I need to talk to you." He dashed forward and quickly closed the door. "It's not about Marisa's behavior."

"Then what is it?" Her mom folded her arms across her chest. "Lisa, I want you to give me another chance."

"Why?"

"Because I love you," he replied, stepping closer to her. He grabbed her mom's hand, but she pulled away and stepped back.

"Love is one thing, taking advantage of me is another," her mom said.

"I didn't take advantage of you!" Mr. Dolton yelled, taking another step closer to her.

"Then what did you do? Get me pregnant?" Her mom stepped toward him; her hands perched on her hips.

"I would have been there for you if I wasn't sent away." He held her gaze. "And I never heard back from you.

Not once. Do you have any idea how that has been for me these thirteen years?"

"Well it's been a rough time for me too." Her mom turned toward Marisa. "Let's go."

She continued standing there in shock, watching them fight. She couldn't believe what she heard.

"Marisa."

"Wait a minute," she paused, trying to sort everything out. "Mom, you told me he ditched you when you were pregnant with me. Now you're saying he was in military school."

"Oh, not only did you make it hard for me to find both of you but you're also telling her lies about me!" Mr. Dolton yelled, stepping even closer to her mom. They stood nose to nose. "So this is where she heard that story."

"You were in military school?" she asked Mr. Dolton.

"Yes," he replied, glancing over at her briefly, then returned his attention to her mother.

My mom lied! Marisa thought. "Mom! Why did you lie to me?" They had always been honest with each other, whether they were big or small issues. She had been so narrow-minded with what her mom told her about Mr. Dolton, she didn't even give him a chance. Now Marisa really felt bad about the way she treated him. All because of what her mom had said.

"For your protection," her mom replied, stepping away from Mr. Dolton and toward the door. "Now let's go."

"I'm not done talking to you," he said.

"I am. Goodbye." Her mom opened the door, glancing back over her shoulder at Marisa.

The look thrown made all thoughts vanish. Her legs finally moved from the spot. She quickly grabbed her bag from the couch and followed her mom out the door, leaving Mr. Dolton alone.

It was already dark when they went outside. The moon was shining and the night was cooling off. The whole day had come and gone.

* * *

Danny waited until the car sped out of sight. He started his own car, made a quick U-turn, and headed over to his apartment. During the drive his thoughts raced over what he had witnessed. Following the three around turned out not to be hard at all. He only had to follow one, really, or two, and the others were surely to surface.

But it was tonight's encounter that left him feeling giddy.

Lisa didn't even see him or his car when she came outside. She probably didn't see anything. She seemed too caught up in her own thoughts. Both she and the kid looked angry, shocked, surprised—even confused.

He couldn't hear what was being said inside the house. But he didn't need to. Her face said the meeting hadn't been a good one. She was fuming. He could almost feel the anger rolling off her with each stride she took to her car. Her movements were jerky and impatient, forceful and hurried as she climbed into her vehicle. Even the kid seemed the same way, wanting to get away from the house quickly.

He was glad too. He had almost sneaked through the yard to hear them conversing. But he didn't want to chance anything. All he needed was a reason like trespassing for the police to be called, and they would haul him off to jail.

Maybe he wouldn't have to do anything to John or them after all. His fingers drummed the steering wheel. The fact that John was back didn't really mean anything. Lisa showed signs of disgust after talking to him. *Maybe I still have a chance. I'll keep an eye on them for now. If Lisa remains angry with John, then I'm still in the clear.*

Danny thought back to his recent encounter with Lisa over the weekend. He didn't accomplish as much as he would have liked, but he remained a steady contact with her. They only talked for a little bit after he fixed the toilet in the kid's bathroom. He felt an awkward change in Lisa when he had overstayed his visit, trying to chat and asking for something to drink. He almost invited himself to stay for dinner, complaining how he was alone and lonely, longed for company and a decent home cooked meal. He made the comment jokingly, though he was only half joking. But he quickly realized it was time to go. Her face changed instantly. She struggled to smile and to remain polite, but her lips were strained thinly. The kid exchanged silent looks with her mom questioningly.

That kid of hers. His eyebrows furrowed. She was a handful like her mother. Danny knew he would have to be careful and patient around her. He would have to eventually win her over, too, if he wanted to get Lisa. There was something fishy about that kid. Something he could not quite place his finger on. What was it? Oh yes, her eyes.

The way she had looked over at her mother. The way she stood there silently, moving from room to room, watching his every move. Almost like a shadow. Never speaking, only watching. It was damn near nerve wrecking. He didn't like it one bit. But he couldn't do anything about it. Certainly couldn't say anything to her. Not without upsetting Lisa. He couldn't chance that.

He let it go. Trying to block her out when the change occurred. Her face became frightened almost instantly. Her eyes grew wide. He didn't know why the kid got scared all of a sudden, but he saw it the same time Lisa did.

And he bolted. He fled like a scared little kid. Afraid of someone calling the cops on him or yelling for help. He fled with his head down and his tail between his legs, making some excuse to leave, and ran for his van, never looking back.

Later, he promised to do better. He simply needed to remain calm and patient. *All in good time,* he thought. *She will be mine.*

* * *

On the way home, Marisa and her mom sat in an awkward silence. She tried to think out everything her mom and Mr. Dolton had talked about. If her mom had been honest, she wouldn't have been so rude to Mr. Dolton. Her mind raced back to the conversation, struggling to put the pieces together.

He never ditched my mom, she thought. *He had been in military school for four years and never heard from us these thirteen years. My mom lied! She lied to me all my life.* It was devastating to discover her mom had lied to her, especially about her father. She thought they were close enough to never do that to each other.

At last her mom spoke. "Marisa, I know you're probably upset with me for lying, but you have to realize where I'm coming from. When I was fourteen, I got pregnant. I really liked him, but I wasn't too happy with the situation. I was so scared. My parents, who were extremely upset, took him to court and had him sentenced to military school. When I had you, I was given a choice to either keep you or put you up for adoption."

"I'm glad you didn't have an abortion," she interrupted.

"I didn't believe in it; therefore, I went ahead and had you. Anyway," her mom continued, "I wanted to keep you, so I quit high school and took up a job. My parents didn't give me any money or support, because they said it was my fault for becoming pregnant. They convinced me how much of a jerk he was, making me so narrow-minded that I did it to you. I apologize for that. I know what he did to me was thirteen years ago, but I'm still mad. I went through a lot raising you on my own. I also wasn't expecting him to come back. If you were in my position, you would still be mad too."

"What about those lies you told me?" she asked. "You said he ditched you. Because of that, I've been really mean to him. I've never had any desire to meet him."

"I know," her mom said. "I guess I was ashamed to tell you the truth when you asked about him and where he was. What was I supposed to tell you? He took advantage of me at a young age and that is not a very good example for you, now is it?"

"He took advantage of you?" Marisa asked. She glanced over at her mom. If he took advantage of her, then that was a different story all together. "You could have just told me."

Her mom hesitated, her eyes darting between the road and Marisa. "I know that I should have."

"But he mentioned that he never heard from you all these years," she said.

"I don't know what he's talking about," her mom said. "I never heard from him either. He was sent away." She looked over at her mom and their gazes met. "I wanted to protect you, to move on with my life. I never expected to see him again. I only wanted what was best for you."

"I understand." She hesitated. "I'm angry that you lied to me, though. I prefer that you stay honest with me. That's what I thought we always had between us."

Her mom nodded. "I'm sorry for lying. It won't happen again." "No matter what?"

"No matter what," her mom responded. "Doesn't matter if it's bad news or good news, no matter how painful the truth may be. I won't ever lie to you again."

"Good."

"That means you can't lie to me either." Her mom threw Marisa a look. "Ever." "Deal."

Her mom pulled into the driveway of the house and cut the engine. Marisa climbed out of the car and followed her mom inside. She felt the weariness of the long day take a hold on her. Saying good night, she entered her room and closed the door, relishing the peace and quiet that welcomed her. Exhausted, she dropped her book bag by her desk and collapsed on the bed.

Suddenly she realized how much she missed out on today. Her stomach growled on cue, reminding her that she didn't eat dinner—all because of her stubborn and relentless insistence toward Mr. Dolton. But it was too late, and she was too tired to move. She had also missed the basketball tryouts. Hopefully her friends wouldn't be worrying about her unexpected disappearance. Slowly her mind drifted back to the evening at Mr. Dolton's house.

The more Marisa thought about it, the more she realized her mom was trying to help. Her mom had been afraid she would go through the kind of feelings she had been experiencing. But the situation wasn't finished. Now that she knew Mr. Dolton was her dad and didn't ditch her mom, she wasn't mad at him anymore. But she also figured it would take some time to get use to him. She felt bad about how she had treated him. He went through so much, and all he cared about was getting them back. But what was going to happen now?

* * *

Marisa approached the lockers. Her friends surrounded her immediately, seeming worried and apprehensive. She stopped in her tracks, looking at them. They formed a circle around her.

Jeff was the first to reach her side. "Are you OK?" he asked. "You disappeared," Jenni said.

"What happened?" Patty demanded. "Where did you go?" Mark questioned.

"We searched everywhere for you," Sean added.

"Ahhh," Marisa called out, throwing her hands in the air. Her friends stopped firing questions at her. They still appeared troubled, though relieved to see her. "I know; I'm sorry," she said. "Aw, you guys do care." She pretended to wipe away a tear.

Patty punched her in the arm, making her friends laugh.

"Oww. OK, OK, OK." She held up her hands, surrendering. Where to begin? She took a deep breath, and quickly glanced around the hallway. Her friends scooted closer. "Mr. Dolton took me to his house yesterday to talk." Her eyebrows scrunched over. "But we mostly fought." Silence greeted her. Her friends shifted from exchanging glances with one another to staring at her.

"What?"

"He took you to his house?" Jeff's eyebrow rose. "To talk?"

"You're kidding, right?" Jenni exclaimed.

"Can he do that?" Mark asked.

"Yes." She nodded. "I mean, no. Wait. Ah." She paused, taking a deep breath. "He wanted to talk with my mom and me. But I ended up arguing with him, then when my mom picked me up late last night, they ended up fighting for a bit." The warning bell rang, making them all groan. "I'll tell you guys the rest later."

"You better," Sean said.

"I will; I promise." Her friends started to part ways and she glanced over at Jeff.

He grabbed her hand and held her gaze. "Are you sure you're OK?" he asked. "You don't seem angry."

"Yeah, I'm fine." She forced a smile. "It's because of what I found out that puts a whole new perspective on things." A new thought occurred to her, making her eyes light up. "Sorry I missed your tryouts. He wanted to talk, and I couldn't exactly say no. I tried, but he wasn't having any of it. I found out more about what happened, though. But I'll tell you everything later."

He raised both eyebrows this time. "OK." He released her hand. "I'm sorry," she said, throwing it in the air. "I'm rambling."

Jeff smiled and stroked her cheek. "I'll see you in a bit."

"All right." She turned to Patty, who waited. Jeff took off down the halls in the opposite direction and Marisa fell into stride with Patty. They ran to their first class, sitting down right as the final bell rang.

"I swear," Patty whispered. "You're going to give us a heart attack one of these days." "It's not my fault." She giggled.

Marisa welcomed the relief from last night's events. She felt touched by how concerned her friends were. *They really care*, she thought. *My mom has been fighting nonstop with Mr. Dolton since he entered our lives, but my friends have kept me sane.* She paused, realizing how she rarely thought of or referred to Mr. Dolton as her father, even though he was her father.

When math class ended, she left the room and walked with Patty to the computer room. Her pace slackened. They approached the room, she trailing behind Patty in an effort to blend in and walk past his desk unnoticed. Which was what Mr. Dolton had pointed out yesterday. She had been ignoring and avoiding him. *I have to face him sooner or later*, she thought, pausing outside the room. *So why am I hesitant? He didn't ditch my mother. Maybe it's because I see him all the time now, more than my mom.*

Patty had started to enter the room but stopped and doubled back to where Marisa stood, unmoving. "Are you OK?" she asked.

"Yeah." She exhaled. "I don't know how to act around him now." "He's also your teacher," Patty pointed out.

"I know, but all this stuff has been happening so fast," she said. "I see him before anything gets fully resolved. I don't know what to say or how to act."

"Look, class is about to start and you're his student," Patty said. "No one else knows anything about the situation. Don't bring these personal issues into class."

She nodded, seeing Patty's point. Feeling reassured, she followed Patty into the room at the same time Mr. Dolton looked up from his desk. Their gazes met. She passed his desk, tearing her eyes away and continued walking toward her seat. Her vision drifted over to her friends, whom were already seated. Jeff caught her gaze and smiled, lifting her spirits. Her other friends also threw her encouraging smiles. She followed Patty to their row and sat down. Mr. Dolton stood up to begin class. She fished out her book, flipping it open to the page they were currently discussing.

Next period I can finish telling them what happened, she thought. Her thoughts drifted though her eyes focused on the front of the class, hearing Mr. Dolton but not listening to his words. She glanced around the room, seeing that female students continued to follow his every move. She rolled her eyes as the girls pant away. *I can't believe I thought my own father was cute.* She shook her head, though that was before she found out he was her dad.

Mr. Dolton stopped at their row, forcing Marisa to pay attention to the readings. She pretended to study the open book that lay before her. Jenni and Patty also sat up straight, becoming quiet, staring at their books. Mr. Dolton called on Jeff to continue reading. Glancing to the row in front of her, she saw Mark and Sean turn quiet. They also gazed at their books while Jeff read a page. Her peripheral vision showed Mr. Dolton looking at her. Her eyes darted over to his face briefly, where he threw her a small smile, then asked the class a question.

He didn't ditch her, she thought. Her eyes followed him moving away from their row. *But my mom said he took advantage of her. That's why her parents took him to court and sent him off, but he hadn't heard from her all these years.* Now that she had heard more of the situation, she understood her mom's reasoning for the action taken.

But she also saw his side.

In spite of it all, he did come back. She frowned, still not knowing what would happen next. It was noble of Mr. Dolton to come back. But then again, he took advantage of her mom. That didn't help his situation. Ugh, too many things were happening so fast.

I'm adjusting, she thought. *It will take time.* The same question continued to appear in her mind. *Now what? What will happen next?*

Her mom had never talked about it any further last night.

He wanted another chance with her, she thought. *Is she going to take him back? They could start over and work things out. Make it right. It might be nice to have my father around. I see him every day as it is. Should I open up and accept him? I need to at least get to know him. But how? I only see him at school or when he pops up out of nowhere. Maybe on a Saturday.*

Ultimately, it came down to her mom.

I wouldn't leave her for anything, she thought. *It would have to be her decision.*

"Marisa," Patty whispered, jarring her thoughts.

She shook her head and looked over at Patty, seeing that Jenni also stared at her. Marisa scanned the room, noticing the silence. All the students were glancing back at her. "What?" she whispered back.

"Can you please continue reading?" Mr. Dolton asked from the front of the room.

Her gaze shifted over to him, then to the book in front of her. She had no idea where they were, since she had stopped paying attention some time ago. Seeing the problem, Patty pointed to a paragraph on the page. Marisa nodded and started reading until Mr. Dolton stopped her to ask the class a question. He called on someone else to read. Jeff glanced back at her when she finished, meeting her gaze, and she shrugged. He smiled, shaking his head.

When class ended, Marisa gathered her things to leave. She wanted out of the room and time to herself to think. Shifting the bag on her shoulder, she and Patty waited as Jenni continued packing her bag in between talking to Mark.

"Woman, let's go," Patty called out. "I'm hurrying," Jenni replied.

"Any day now," she remarked, gazing over at Jeff. He stood behind Sean, waiting for Mark to move.

"They're too busy flirting," Jeff added.

"Man, hurry up," Sean told Mark. "She's already your girl, so you don't need to impress her anymore."

Mark punched Sean and the group laughed. "You know you're jealous."

Jenni and Mark left the rows and started walking toward the front of the classroom. Marisa smiled, watching her friends pile out and pair up together before heading out. She followed Patty out of the row, about to turn to Jeff who stood waiting for her, when she saw Mr. Dolton stopped by the row. He stepped in front of the aisle, forcing her to stop in her tracks, blocking her from exiting the row. He shifted, turning his back to the class, shielding the view from the students piling out of the room.

"Can I talk to you for a minute?" Mr. Dolton asked quietly.

She hesitated, glancing around him at Jeff, who waited. Jeff's face turned anxious for a second, and she shook her head. He nodded and turned around, heading out the door. Her peripheral vision showed he took his time, glancing back at them every few steps. Her group of friends also lingered around the door, looking at them. The rest of the classroom was now empty.

Mr. Dolton saw them waiting. "Class is over."

Throwing her one last glance, her friends left the room, leaving them alone. Marisa extinguished a deep breath, waiting on Mr. Dolton. The sudden silence and stillness of the room filled her ears. She hesitated, not knowing what to say. *I'm never going to finish telling them what happened.*

"Let's take a walk," he suggested. Her eyes opened wide. "What?"

"Come on," he said, turning toward the front of the room.

Shrugging, Marisa shifted the book bag on her shoulders and followed Mr. Dolton out the classroom. *As long as we stay on school grounds, I'll be fine*, she thought, entering the hallway. *He can't take me off campus while school is going on, so it's not like he can take me to his house again.* Mr. Dolton slowed his steps until Marisa fell into stride next to him. Their footsteps echoed along the quiet, empty hallways, where classes continued all around them.

"What did you want to talk about?" she asked, breaking the silence between them.

"You tell me."

"What?"

Glancing over at her, he said, "You've been really quiet and out of it today. I wanted to make sure everything's all right."

She narrowed her eyes at him. "Are you kidding?"

"No." He shook his head and motioned to the right where the cafeteria stood. "Let's go this way."

They turned and entered the cafeteria side by side. No one else was around, thankfully, so their pace was slow and relaxed. Their voices were soft enough so wandering ears couldn't hear what was spoken.

"You thought I was out of it because I lost our place during the readings?" she asked, raising an eyebrow.

"Marisa." He shot her a look this time. "You've been quiet after I had a confrontation with your mother. This was never my intention."

Her gaze shifted to the floor, feeling her face turn hot. How was she supposed to respond? *Of course I'm going to be out of it*, she felt like saying, while wringing his neck to knock some sense into him. *You two are always fighting, you're always bugging me, and I'm slowly finding out the truth though never getting any straight answers. What's a matter with you? Are you blind?*

But instead, she bit her tongue and followed his lead. They stopped by the vending machines. How could she tell him anything without hurting his feelings?

I understand you didn't ditch my mom, her thoughts continued. *But you did take advantage of her, which was why her parents took you to court and sent you off to military school. Granted, you did come back. That was mighty noble of you. She lied about you, but you did a naughty thing. I don't know you, so I'm going to be a little awkward around you. But you're my father, so I must accept you and let you in my life ...*

No, that wouldn't work either. Marisa kept silent.

"I know there are some unresolved issues still lingering in the air between your mom and I," he went on. "Last night didn't go like I had wanted, or the other day for that matter. But I want you to know that you can talk to me anytime. You can ask me anything."

"I had questions for you the other day, but you didn't have any answers," she pointed out.

"I'm not saying I'll have all the answers either," he added. "But my talks with your mother have been about us and the past. I want to hear your feelings about all this too. If there's any way I can help, I will. I don't want you to feel like you have to avoid or ignore me, because you feel awkward about the situation."

She hesitated before letting out a deep breath. He had seen right through her, hitting the nail on the head. Just like he noticed she had been ignoring him. But what else could she do? How was she supposed to act around him, especially when she was still adjusting, still discovering the whole story for herself.

Mr. Dolton put some money in the machine and bought two sodas, handing one to her.

She took it automatically, realizing again he never asked what she liked to drink. He did the same thing last night, too.

"I just…I mean I know now that you didn't ditch her," she began. "But it's like you said, everything has been happening so suddenly. Yet I see you again before anything is resolved. It seems like I see you more than my mom at times." She shook her head. "Regardless, it's going to take some time for me to accept what I've been told and to accept you as my father. I mean I'm not trying to be rude, I just…" She shrugged. "I don't know you." Marisa finally made eye contact, trying to gauge his reaction.

He simply nodded. "I understand," he told her. "I know it's going to take time." He opened his soda, took a drink, and turned around to head back out of the cafeteria. She followed.

"Remember, my door will always be open for you." He glanced over at her. "However, I don't want this to affect your schoolwork."

She nodded. "OK."

"You have study hall now, right?" "Yeah."

"I'll walk you over there, so you won't get in trouble." He rolled his eyes, and she smiled.

They turned the corner, exiting the cafeteria and heading toward her study hall classroom. Marisa felt relieved by their small talk. Now maybe she wouldn't feel so apprehensive about seeing him during class. No more excuses.

He's making an effort, she thought. *I can take my time getting to know him. Put the past behind us and move forward. But is my mom willing to move on? Open up and accept him?*

They reached the classroom, and Mr. Dolton paused, turning toward her before she could open the door. "All I ask is a chance to make up for all the years I missed out on as your father," he whispered, catching her gaze.

She nodded. "OK."

"All right," he said. "Like I said—any time you want to talk, I'm free."

"Sounds good." She held up the soda. "Thanks for the drink."

He smiled. "I'll see you later."

Marisa opened the door and entered the quiet room, spotting her friends at a nearby table. They instantly stopped talking upon seeing her and looked over. Jeff pulled out the empty chair next to him and she collapsed into it, her back landing on top of the book bag still perched on her shoulders. She grimaced but was too lazy to move it, rather grateful to be with her friends. They leaned in toward her expectantly, whereas she opened her soda and took a long drink.

"What did he say?" Jenni asked.

"Are you all right?" Jeff placed a comforting hand on her shoulder.

"I'm fine," she said, waving her hand in the air. "He wanted to make sure I was all right. He said I was a little out of it from last night."

"Where's my soda?" Sean asked.

"The same place you left it," Mark answered. The group laughed.

"Finish telling us what happened from last night," Patty said. "Oh yeah."

The bell rang, and Marisa rolled her eyes. The group groaned, reluctant to move. She grabbed onto the hand Jeff held out for her and he pulled her out of the chair. Standing up, she smiled and leached onto his arm.

"We're never going to hear the whole story," Jenni remarked.

The group scooted their chairs under the table and grabbed their book bags. "I'll finish it during lunch," she said.

"If it wasn't for school…" Sean added, shaking his head. They laughed, heading out of the room.

CHAPTER 13

"You were saying?" Patty said.

It was lunchtime, and Marisa sat with her friends in the cafeteria. They looked at her eagerly, making her laugh. She took a deep breath, her entire demeanor changing to serious. Now how to begin explaining the recent events that occurred.

"Mr. Dolton didn't ditch my mom," she replied. The table became silent, eyebrows rose, and glances were exchanged between one another. She told them everything that happened yesterday and last night, as well as what she discovered about Mr. Dolton and her mom. She gazed around the table, seeing her friends appear to be in disbelief, shock, and surprise. "Welcome to my world."

"He took advantage of your mother!" Jenni exclaimed a little too loud. "Shh," Jeff said.

Marisa looked around her but didn't think anyone heard. The cafeteria was already noisy to begin with. "Well…" She shrugged. "That's how she had me."

"He also came back," Patty added.

Her friends nodded, murmuring in agreement upon seeing the two points. If it wasn't for Mr. Dolton, she wouldn't be here. Yet despite the fact that he was sent away to military school, he came back for the two of them.

"I'm finding everything out for myself," she said. "I don't know the whole story."

"Dang." Sean shook his head.

"What now?" Mark asked. "Are they getting back together?"

She shrugged again. "I don't know," she replied. "They fought when she picked me up and we just left. I don't know what's going to happen. I know he wants another chance."

"To be with your mom?" Jeff asked.

"And to be my father."

They nodded, while Jeff caught her eye at that last remark, remembering their conversation last week. Her friends began casting glances from Mr. Dolton to her. She looked over her shoulder, following their gazes until spotting him at the teacher's table. Several teachers sat with him, but he wasn't really talking to anyone, nor was he eating.

"He looks sad," Jenni remarked.

"That's exactly what I was thinking," Patty said.

"Ah, poor thing," Sean uttered. The group laughed and Patty smacked him on the arm. When the final bell rang, Marisa met her friends at the lockers. She wished Jeff, Patty, Mark, and Sean good luck. They raced to the gymnasium amid the crowded hallways and noisy students, chatting away, pushing and dodging a path through the chaos. Basketball tryouts were going on for the entire week. She watched them leave with Jenni by her side. They had a few minutes to spare before the tryouts began.

"I need to change my books," she told Jenni. "Same here," Jenni said.

Marisa quickly changed out her books and shut the locker, hoisting the book bag on her shoulders. She waited for Jenni to finish, anxious to see her man in action.

"That'll be so cool if they make the team," she said. "You know they will," Jenni said.

"What do you want to do to kill time?"

"I'm going wherever you're going." Jenni shut her locker. "I'm not about to have a repeat of yesterday."

She laughed before realizing it was exactly twenty-four hours ago when Mr. Dolton had approached her. Though after their talk today, it was unlikely he would do it again. But who knew. She glanced around the hallways, making Jenni laugh.

"You do make a valid point." She nodded her head toward the hallways. "Let's go." They walked down the hall, pushing their way toward the gymnasium. Seeing no sign of Mr. Dolton, she raced through the crowds until reaching their destination. They entered the gymnasium and sat on the bleachers, located off to the left side. The students were filing out of the locker room and warming up for the tryouts. The coast was clear, letting Marisa drop her guard. She sat back to enjoy herself.

It was late by the time tryouts ended. Marisa felt tired, her stomach growled, and she wanted to be off school grounds already. The coach had gone a little over the time, drilling the kids hard. But she had enjoyed watching her man, seeing his defined muscles, perfectly trim and hard body race up and down the court, until he glistened with sweat. Patty had done really well for the girls' team, proving to be one of the best offensive players. Several students had stayed and watched, cheering on some of the kids. She and Jenni had joined in cheering for their friends, drooling for their men and shouting when one made a basket, until the coach finally blew the whistle.

When her friends were released, Marisa stood up and stretched her limbs. Grabbing her bag, she ran down the bleachers with Jenni right next to her. Their friends had retreated back to the locker room to shower and grab their things. They came out with their stuff after a few minutes, whereupon Marisa and Jenni joined them. The group exited the gymnasium together, commenting about the tryouts, laughing here and there. Each couple paired up, making their way out of the school building. Marisa grabbed onto Jeff's arm, exiting the front doors.

"Bye, you guys," Marisa called out to her friends. The three couples headed in different directions. "Bye."

"See you tomorrow."

"Don't let her out of your sight."

"I won't; I promise."

"We'll hold you to your word."

"Yeah, yeah," she said amid the laughter echoing down the street.

Marisa faced forward and proceeded walking across the parking lot. Jeff grabbed her hand, glancing over at her, and she smiled. The sun was lower on the horizon, offering some relief. The noise around them soon ceased, allowing a stillness to take place. A calming silence developed. They walked along, enjoying the moment. Within minutes, her house loomed into view.

"Thanks for listening," she broke the silence, meeting his gaze. "You've been a big help throughout this whole mess."

"Anytime."

They reached her front lawn and stopped, gazing at one another with their hands locked. She knew it was time for him to leave, since they had been out later than usual on a school day. But she didn't want the moment to end. She had found herself looking forward to their time spent alone, even if only for a little while. It allowed her the time she need to unwind, relax, think, and be herself. To get away from everything yet remain with her man. He also gave a fresh perspective and some clarity to her thoughts amid all the confusion, fights, and chaos.

Right on cue, he said, "If you open up, get to know him and form a relationship with him, you gain your father back."

It would not hurt to have a father finally. "That's true," she said. "I guess I'll have to wait and see what happens between them."

"You mentioned before that you feel bad because your mom is always working," he continued. "If they get back together, she wouldn't have to work as much."

"Yeah."

Jeff smiled, taking a step closer to her and stroking her cheek. "Did I ever mention how beautiful you look today?"

Marisa also smiled. His finger tickled and caressed her skin ever so gently, making her cheeks turn hot. *He is so good*, she thought, eyeing him. Her eyes met his gaze. She couldn't stop herself from blushing by his simple touch, yet her knees felt weak. They were standing close to one another, all alone in front of a beautiful sunset. No other person could be seen; no other sound could be heard. Her heartbeat pounded in her ears. He grabbed her other hand, clasping both of her hands against his chest.

The sun started to set on the horizon, making their surroundings appear darker suddenly.

She blinked a few times to adjust her eyesight.

"I should get going," he commented, though he didn't make a move.

"Yeah," she added after a few moments of silence.

"I'll see you tomorrow."

"OK." She reluctantly let go of his hands. "Bye."

Marisa turned and walked up her front porch, fishing her key out of the book bag.

Unlocking the front door, she entered and turned to glance at Jeff one last time. He stood in the same spot watching her. She waved goodbye, and he waved back, smiling. As she closed and locked the door, she leaned against it, waiting for her heart to slow down. A flush of heat passed through her face. She released her breath, not realizing she had been holding it in.

He is so hot, she thought, smiling and fanning herself with both hands, *teasing me like that*. Once her knees regained their strength, she picked herself off the door. For a moment she thought he would kiss her. *That's what made me so weak.*

And she had wanted to kiss him too. They had a perfect setting, but the moment had pass. *No*, she thought, finally willing her legs to move. *I don't want to rush it. Everything is going great between us. I have all the time in the world to get to know him.*

Entering her room, Marisa dropped her bag near the desk and headed to the kitchen. Her stomach was really growling now. But she stopped short in the hallway, thinking. When was the last time she brought in the mail? A couple of days, at least. She turned, ran to the front door, and opened it. Racing outside to the mailbox, she glanced around, but Jeff was long gone by now. She opened the overstuffed mailbox and emptied its contents. She dashed back inside the house and locked the door. She dumped the mail on the coffee table and retreated back to the kitchen to make dinner.

By the time she was fed and her homework was complete, her mom arrived. It was after eight when she entered the house, closing the door while balancing several bags on both arms.

"Hey, mom," Marisa said, rushing forward. She grabbed the bags off one arm and set them on the floor. She lifted the remaining bags and all but dropped them, straining under the weight.

"Hey," her mom replied. Tired lines etched the corners of her eyes. She stifled a yawn. "Thanks, sweetie."

"How was work?"

"Oh…" Her mom headed straight for the couch and collapsed on it, though sitting up this time. She struggled with her shoes until they were off her feet and nestled comfortably against the cushions. "Now I'm better."

"Long day?" she guessed, sitting in the armchair.

"Yes," her mom said, shuffling through the mail. "My boss is demanding. He always…" Her voice drifted off in mid-sentence, lifting a letter out of the stack. Her eyebrows scrunched over. She turned the letter over and quickly ripped it open. Unfolding the sheet inside, her eyes skimmed over the contents, widening. Her face instantly distorted to outrage.

"What is it?" Marisa questioned.

"Damn it!" her mom yelled, standing up from the couch. "What?"

She jumped off the armchair and scurried forward, trying to read the letter. But her mom brushed her aside and snatched up the cordless phone off the coffee table. Marisa stepped back a few steps and watched her mom dial a number, clutching the letter so tight her knuckles turned white. She sat down, waiting. Now what? Could it possibly get any worse?

Things can always get worse, she thought and shook her head, shushing the voice.

"What gives you the right to do this?" her mom yelled.

Marisa's eyes widened; her eyebrows rose. Since she couldn't see the letter and didn't know who her mom was talking to, she waited. Her stomach turned to knots. Bad news was coming. *This isn't good*, she thought. Her palms turned sweaty.

Her mom clicked off the phone and threw it on the floor, smashing it. Marisa jump back in the armchair, looking at the pieces. A perfectly good phone. Oh, wait. It wasn't broken. The back cover and batteries fell out. That was all. She bent over to fix it, when the sound of tears reached her. She glanced up to find her mom crying.

"Mom, what's wrong?" Marisa leaped from the armchair and sat on the couch. *Now what's going on*? She thought, placing a comforting hand on her mom's shoulder.

"Your father," she began, wiping some tears away, "is taking me to court Friday afternoon to claim you."

Marisa blinked a few times before registering the words. The hand slid off her mom's shoulder and landed in her lap. Her eyes widened, her eyebrows rose, her jaw dropped open and shut as the words slowly sunk in. He's claiming me. It felt like the breath had been knocked out of her. This was the last thing she had expected to hear—the last thing she had expected him to do. She never even saw it coming, never even thought about the possibility. He simply said he wanted another chance as a father. He never mentioned claiming her. "What?"

"Don't worry," her mom said. "I have a good lawyer. He won't win." But the look on her face said she wasn't entirely confident.

She couldn't believe it. Mr. Dolton wanted to claim custody rights despite what she told him. He knew she was still adjusting, that she needed time. The shock of the news slowly dissipated, the numbness disappeared off her body in waves. Her face grew hard; her cheeks burned. She was outraged. The nerve of that man! He told her only today she could talk to him anytime. He knew how she felt about him, about the whole situation. He saw how it affected her life. Now he wanted to take her from her home and her mom. She barely knew him.

"Marisa," her mom said, a little hesitant, cautious.

Though she heard her mom speak, she didn't answer. "How can he claim me if he was sent to military school?" she asked instead. "Doesn't that look bad on a person's record?"

"It's not on his record," her mom replied. "It wasn't considered a felony. Plus he never terminated his parental rights when you were born."

"Huh?"

"He's still entitled to custody rights."

Marisa no longer knew what to say or do. Everything had happened quickly; it was one continuous shock after another.

"Honey, look," her mom said, "I know you're upset, but don't worry about it."

"Mom, I do have to worry about it!" She jumped up from the couch, pacing back and forth through the living room. "What if he wins? I'll have to live with him. I don't know him!"

"I know, I know," her mom said, also standing up. She stepped in front of Marisa, blocking the path to keep her from pacing. "That's why Friday I'm going to try my hardest so you won't have to live with him." The tears subsided, but her nose began to run a little.

"Thanks, Mom." Closing her eyes, Marisa buried her face in her mom's hair, who hugged her tightly, holding on as if she would never let go or let anything happen to her. Marisa savored the embrace. Mr. Dolton couldn't win. He *would* not win!

* * *

The rest of the week remained the same routine for Marisa. She went to her classes, accompanied by her boyfriend and friends. After school ended, she went to the gymnasium with Jenni to watch the basketball tryouts. When the tryouts ended for the day, she walked home with Jeff by her side. They would talk for a little bit before saying good-bye. She ate dinner and did her homework in an empty house, staying up every night and waiting for her mom to get home from work. Her mom arrived late, past the usual hour Marisa retired for the night. But she stayed up to chat, even if it was only for a few moments to say hello.

Her mom always appeared tired, stressed, fretting about her job. Claiming to have a demanding boss whose whole life revolved around their career. Who always found more work for her once she had finished for the day. She brought up the idea of fewer hours; the boss laughed and scoffed at the mere thought.

The only thing that changed for Marisa was her behavior toward Mr. Dolton. She avoided eye contact with him, talking to him—she avoided him entirely. He continued to teach computer, though noticing the change in her attitude. He approached her numerous times, cornered her in trying to talk to him, asked her to stay after class or after school, offered to drive her home from school. But Marisa gave him the cold shoulder. She ignored him. Wouldn't even look at him. Whether during class or in the hallways, it didn't matter. She paid attention during class so he couldn't find a reason to get her in trouble. But whenever he did approach her, she brushed past him and kept walking. Like he didn't exist. Like she had never seen him. If he managed to catch her before she left class or left the school building, she walked around him and continued on her way. He stopped in front of her numerous times, blocking her path, but she refused to acknowledge him and managed to escape.

Marisa told her friends what happened, much to their astonishment. They agreed to assist her in avoiding him. If Mr. Dolton managed to trap her, one of them would distract him with a question long enough so she could slip by unnoticed. The few moments she was alone in the hallways, he would appear out of a side door or from the opposite side of the hallway. When this happened, she turned around and took another path.

CHAPTER 14

It was only once Mr. Dolton almost succeeded in cornering her, on Friday morning after their Computer class ended. The day they were due in court. He rushed to her row as she gathered her things together. Her friends exchanged glances with each other, waiting until all six of them were ready to leave. Marisa met Jeff's gaze, but stood at an angle to where she could watch what occurred out of her peripheral vision.

Once her friends were ready, Jenni, Patty, Mark, and Sean piled out of the row together and crowded around Mr. Dolton. They fired question after meaningless question, circling him. Between the four of them, he was bombarded left and right, trying to answer the questions while keeping an eye on Marisa. Her friends continued to advance on him, simultaneously asking questions, forcing him to step back until cornered against a table. He was boxed in. Seeing an opening, she darted out of the row and turned to Jeff. They dashed out of the room, where a few moments later, her friends caught up with them.

And so she had escaped again. Choosing to stay away from him, for she was too angry to face him. She decided to wait until the court session, where things would be worked out and she could continue her life as before. After more time passed for her to calm down, she would talk to him. But not now. She feared her anger would get the best of her.

Why claim her? What would be the advantage? They barely knew each other. She understood if he wanted to spend time to get to know her outside of class. They really didn't have time to talk during school hours. But she could have saved a Saturday for that. However, she was outraged by his sly and sudden approach to matters. Rather than taking more time to work it out, he quickly claims her.

She noticed subtle changes in Mr. Dolton's behavior toward her, when he was around long enough before she sprinted away. His tone was softer…quiet. Almost shy. His actions were rushed, trying to approach her before she took off. Or he was nice, patient, but she often saw something deeper in his eyes. A sad, yet frustrated look. He was constantly searching for her, always seeking her out amid the crowds.

Marisa also knew her mom was angry with him for other reasons. They talked it over one night. Her mom wasn't sure if she wanted to take him back yet. She had no time to really think about it before the custody claim appeared. Now she was angry that he wanted to take Marisa away.

By the time Friday afternoon arrived, Marisa reported to the office to check out. The court hearing would begin very soon. Her future would be decided in a few hours. She felt her life hanging by a string. She hoped Mr. Dolton would drop the case and leave them alone. Give them more time to think and talk or something other than this route. There were a lot of unanswered questions and doubts about their situation. But no such luck came. Apparently, he had other ideas about what to do and didn't want to leave her alone.

Checking the hallways carefully, Marisa and her mom left the school grounds and headed to the hearing. The courthouse was located in downtown Saint Elois, a good thirty-minute drive.

The trip was quiet, each lost in their thoughts. Her mind drifted between what could happen and what she wanted to happen. Her mom had worked later these past few days since she spent much time on the phone discussing the case with her lawyer. But Marisa never asked about it, fearing the response.

Before she knew it, they arrived at Saint Elois Municipal Courthouse. Right on time too.

Once they passed security and located the room, they found their lawyer waiting outside the door for them. He hurried them inside the courtroom, stating their case should be heard any minute.

Marisa entered, spotting Mr. Dolton seated at a table on the right side, in front of the rows of seats, and nearest to the empty jury box. To the left of him sat a man who she presumed to be his lawyer. But this was all she could take in. Their lawyer ushered them forward. He motioned for Marisa to sit in the row directly behind the front two tables, leading her mom through the gate and to the empty table on the left.

She sat down. Mr. Dolton turned in his seat, looking over at them. She averted her eyes, looking straight ahead, pretending to be interested in the layout of the courtroom. Her peripheral vision showed his gaze following her mom. The lawyer sat at the end of the table, obstructing his view and putting more distance between them. He tried to meet her mom's gaze but soon gave up and waited for the trial to begin. Marisa smiled.

Since her mom was occupied with the lawyer, she glanced around to kill time. There were clusters of people seated behind her, and in the rows on her right. Probably waiting for their case to be tried. Her attention was called to the front as an officer came out and told them to rise, announcing the judge. A few moments later, the judge appeared and sat down, beginning the trial.

The case seemed to drag on for a while, both sides arguing back and forth. At first Marisa thought everything was going well. Now she wasn't so sure. She didn't think a custody case would last so long, but it seemed to take a different turn somewhere. She felt helpless. Two lawyers argued and questioned Mr. Dolton, trying to determine who should have custody over her. Here she sat watching all of it without being able to say anything. Her whole life was on the line here and she had no part in the decision. But from listening to everything being said, it seemed like the actual case revolved more around her mom and Mr. Dolton. Not on custody.

"Your Honor, I would like to call Lisa Perez to the witness stand," the prosecuting lawyer announced.

Marisa looked at her mom, who stood up, walked over to the stand, and sat in the chair. Trying to appear reserved, her mom seemed every bit as nervous as she was. Mr. Dolton's gaze fixed on her mom, who stared at the attorney. After swearing to tell the truth, the whole truth, and nothing but the truth, so help her—*win custody, please!*—the prosecuting attorney approached the stand.

"Ms. Perez, how old are you?" the prosecuting lawyer asked.

Marisa's eyebrow rose. She shot a glance at him. *What kind of question is that?* she thought. *It's a custody hearing; let's get on with it already.* Her gaze shifted back to her mom.

"Twenty-seven."

"As my client previously mentioned, after the car accident, when it was discovered you were pregnant thirteen years ago, he was sent off to military school," the prosecuting lawyer stated. "Is this correct?"

"Yes."

"Why was he sent off?"

Her mom blinked a few times. Her eyebrows rose. "Because he got me pregnant." "But how does that justify sending him off?" the prosecuting lawyer asked.

Her mom blinked again before letting out a deep breath. Marisa could feel the annoyance pouring out. This hearing would take a while. "He took advantage of me."

"Took advantage of you," the lawyer repeated. He paced back and forth in front of her mom. "Weren't you in a relationship with my client?"

"Yes," her mom said softly, lowering her eyes.

"Let me see if I understand correctly," he continued. His voice rose throughout the courtroom. "You were in a relationship with my client, and you became pregnant. Is that correct so far?"

"Yes."

"If you're in a relationship with my client, and he became the father of your child, how is that taking advantage of you?" The lawyer stepped toward the witness stand, stopping right in front of her mom. Marisa looked at him. His questions were redundant. What does this have to do with custody?

"My parents were upset, and they took him to court," her mom replied. She met his hard, unwavering gaze.

"Ah, so then it was your parents who were upset over this ordeal," the lawyer remarked.

"They told you he took advantage of you, didn't they? Just like it was their decision to take him to court. Not yours. Isn't that what really happened? You never had any disagreement because my client was your boyfriend. It was mutual consent between you two. Your parents were angry, weren't they?"

Marisa looked back and forth from the prosecuting attorney, her mom, and their defending lawyer. Her cheeks burned. The lawyer shouted and paced, only to stop in front of her mom. He braced his hands on the stand, fixing her with a piercing and accusing glare. Something needed to be done already.

"Objection, Your Honor!" The defending lawyer jumped up from his chair. "He is harassing my client."

It's about time, she thought.

"Overruled." The judge turned to her mom. "Ms. Perez, answer the question."

"Your Honor," the defending lawyer continued, "he is turning the events around, putting words in my client's mouth. He has no proof that it was mutual consent on my client's part. Both the prosecutor and the defendant were minors when this encounter occurred. The defendant's parents had to take action for justice to be served."

"Overruled."

"Thank you, Your Honor," the prosecuting lawyer said. He shot a glance at their lawyer. "And thanks for bringing up the topic of justice. Let's examine that for a moment, since there is quite a bit of proof." He turned to her mom. "If your *parents* wanted justice so bad for my client's actions, why didn't they go after him for child support? Prolong the sentence? Why didn't you? You were a legal adult when my client finished military school. Four years doesn't seem like much compared to eighteen years for raising a child as a single parent. But you made no contact with my client. And he tried contacting you numerous times. But you never did—not when he was released and not when you two became adults. Neither did your parents. Why?"

Marisa's gaze shifted to her mom, who was silent. Her eyes lowered. The whole courtroom became silent, waiting for an answer, but her mom didn't speak. She tried to remember all the questions the lawyer asked, but there were too many of them to keep straight. What does this have to do with custody? Why would her mom prolong the term? Mr. Dolton did his time, so what difference did it make?

"Ms. Perez, answer the question," the judge demanded.

Her mom looked up and blinked at the attorney. "You asked too many questions. I don't know which one to answer first."

"Ms. Perez, weren't you the one who became pregnant?" "Yes."

"Weren't you the reason for sending my client to military school?" "Yes."

"Wasn't it because my client—and I quote—'took advantage of you?'" "Yes!"

"Weren't your parents upset? Didn't they want justice?" Her mom exhaled a sigh. "Yes and yes."

She rolled her head back and forth, feeling tired from these tedious questions. This hearing needed to be over with already. She glanced over at Mr. Dolton. His gaze remained on her mom.

"If your parents wanted justice because my client took advantage of you when you were in a relationship with him," the prosecuting lawyer continued, pacing back and forth before stopping a few feet in front of her, "why didn't they seek further justice when he finished military school?"

"I don't know."

"You never asked them why?" the lawyer asked. "No."

"Why not?" "Because I didn't." "Why?"

"I wasn't living with them anymore," her mom replied. "Why not?"

"Because I was an adult," her mom's voice rose. "I had already moved out."

"But surely you still spoke to them?" the lawyer pressed on. "They're your parents".

"Didn't you maintain contact with them?"

Where is this going? Marisa thought. *Why is he asking these questions*? She had a hard time following the conversation, but it didn't sound good for them. Between the lawyer spewing out questions one right after another and pacing around nonstop, it was hard to concentrate.

"No."

"Why not?"

"That's irrelevant." Her mom's cheeks became red.

"I think it's very relevant," the prosecuting attorney said. "Your parents sent your boyfriend off to military school while you're stuck pregnant and alone. Surely you needed to maintain contact with them since you had no assistance from the father of your child. Remember, he was off serving a term. Why didn't you maintain contact with your parents?"

Her mom hesitated, staring at the ground again.

"Why didn't you maintain contact with your parents?" the lawyer repeated. "Need I remind you, Ms. Perez, you're under oath."

"Answer the question, Ms. Perez," the judge demanded.

"Because I was kicked out of the house!" her mom yelled.

Marisa's mouth dropped to the floor. She never told me that. Her grandparents were never mentioned. Neither was her mom's childhood. Her grandparents moved away years ago. She had yet to meet them, had never spoken to them. She didn't even know if they were alive. Before Mr. Dolton entered her life, she never knew any other family member.

"Your parents kicked their young, single, and pregnant daughter out of the house!" the prosecuting attorney exclaimed, slowly stepping toward her mom with each word uttered.

"Yes!"

"Why?"

"Objection, Your Honor," the defending lawyer yelled, shooting out of his seat. "These questions are irrelevant. My client's personal life and relationship with her parents have nothing to do with a custody case. The prosecution is harassing my client."

"Overruled," the judge stated. "Ms. Perez, answer the question." "Your Honor—"

"Overruled," the judge said firmly. He banged the gavel on the bench, looking at the defending lawyer. "Counsel, the defense has yet to answer all the questions posed by the prosecution." Their lawyer sat down again. "Now, Ms. Perez," he said, glancing down at her mom, "answer the question."

"Why did your parents kick you out of the house?" the prosecuting attorney repeated. "I had a disagreement with them," her mom stated through clenched teeth.

"And just like that, they kicked you out?" "Yes."

"What was the disagreement?" "I don't remember."

Marisa's jaw opened and shut. Her eyebrows rose, then furrowed. Was that why she never mentioned them? Because they kicked her out of the house and moved to another state? She let out a sigh. There was a lot she didn't know about her mom's past.

The prosecuting attorney stopped pacing. He stood in front of her mom, his arms crossed over his chest, peering intently at her. "Ms. Perez, I find this hard to believe."

"It's the truth."

"I don't agree," he continued. "I think you're lying. Your whole story is a lie. None of it makes sense."

Her mom didn't respond but continued to stare at the ground. Marisa shot a glance at the defending lawyer, sitting at the table in front of her. Why wasn't he helping her out? This wasn't turning out good at all.

"Ms. Perez, why not tell us the truth for once?" the prosecuting attorney asked. "You're lying now like your parents lied for you thirteen years ago."

Her mom didn't say anything. She stared back and an eyebrow rose.

"But I can tell you what really happened," the lawyer said. His voice rose. "Your parents lied about my client taking advantage of you. It was mutual consent. That's why you never contacted him after he was released. Or should I say after the hospital. That's why you never pressed further charges. That's why your parents never pressed further charges. That's why your parents kicked you out, because they lied in court. That's what the disagreement was about, wasn't it? And that's why you no longer speak to them. You wanted no part of the hearing to happen thirteen years ago. That's what really happened, isn't it?"

Her mom's eyes closed briefly. Marisa looked over at their lawyer, who continued to sit in front of her silently. His head bowed, letting out a deep breath. *Why isn't he doing anything?* she thought. *He's letting the man harass me.*

"All right!" her mom suddenly shouted. "It's true." Tears formed in her eyes. "My parents were the ones who took him to court and brought the charges against him. It was all them."

CHAPTER 15

Oh, crap, she thought. My mom's parents took Mr. Dolton to court and sent him away. My own grandparents! The courtroom fell into an eerie silence for several moments.

The attorney had a point there—a very good point. But why was that important? Mr. Dolton still took advantage of her mom. How could they overlook that aspect?

"Then my client never took advantage of you," the prosecuting attorney said. "It was mutual consent. Is that correct?"

Marisa held her breath. "Yes," her mom whispered.

Her mouth dropped to the floor. She couldn't believe it. Mr. Dolton never took advantage of her. Her cheeks became flushed. Her mom lied to her again. She told Marisa on the way home from his house he took advantage of her. *Damn it*, she thought, shifting her gaze to the ground. The revelation pierced her skin like needles, informing her to wake up. She said she wouldn't lie. Yet she never told me the whole truth to begin with. Damn it!

Marisa's gaze rose back to her mom. Tears streamed out the corners of her eyes, leaving a marked trail on both cheeks. She averted her gaze, angry with her mom and angry with herself for the way she treated Mr. Dolton this entire time. One part of her felt bad about her behavior toward him, but another part was still mad at him for claiming her so soon. She told him she needed more time to adjust. She glanced over to the right, only to have his eyes meet hers. He held Marisa's gaze for several seconds, before shifting his vision back to her mom. She continued staring at his side profile, trying to read his facial expression, but couldn't. He sat unmoving, his face set like a stone, his expression hidden to all eyes.

Giving up, Marisa returned her attention to her mom, who sat silently except for an occasional sniff. She tried to stop the tears from forming, but they continued to trail down her face.

The prosecuting attorney glared at her mom. He stood in front of her, not speaking for a few moments as though wanting her words to have a lasting effect. "No further questions, Your Honor." He returned to his seat next to Mr. Dolton.

"Counsel, your defense," the judge announced.

"No questions, Your Honor," their lawyer said, standing up and sitting right back down.

She extinguished a deep breath and looked at their lawyer, feeling frustrated and annoyed. Wasn't the man even going to try to defend her mom?

"Thank you, Ms. Perez," the judge said. "You may step down."

Her mom jumped out of the witness stand and returned to her seat, keeping her eyes to the ground, wiping away tears.

The judge extinguished a deep breath, peering at her mom. "Ms. Perez, you do realize that this was an act of misrepresentation on your parent's part and charges can be pressed for wrongfully sending the defendant to military school?"

Marisa's eyebrows rose, her eyes widened in surprise. Oh, crap. This isn't good. She held her breath, gazing at her mom.

"Yes," her mom answered.

"Counsel, do you wish to press charges?"

"No, Your Honor." The attorney stood up. "The prosecution wishes to waive the charges and only be granted joint-custody rights."

"Very well," the judge said.

Marisa extinguished a deep breath and rubbed her sweaty palms over her clothes.

"In light of these new findings, as the court has witnessed," the judge continued, "I find the defendant, Lisa Perez, was not taken advantage of and indeed gave valid consent. The plaintiff, John Dolton, is hereby granted joint-custody rights of the child, Marisa Perez.

"However, custody rights will remain intact for only one year, due to the child's age. Since the child is attending school, it is in their best interest that she alternates living quarters with each parent for two-week intervals. At age fourteen, the child is entitled to a preference and may choose who she wishes to live with full time, resulting to weekend privileges for the other parent. The child must move in with the plaintiff by Monday. The court is adjourned." The judge banged the gavel, and the officer told them to rise.

Marisa stood up, though her limbs felt numb, her mouth dry. *Damn it.* Her eyes gazed over the surroundings where simultaneously the judge exited the room, people began moving all around her, their lawyer turned to her mom and started talking, the noise level rose to a slight murmur, feet shifted and shuffled through the middle aisle, the door opened and shut behind her, and someone stood on her left side trying to get out of the row. *Damn it! I have to live with Mr. Dolton now.*

"Marisa," her mom said, facing her. She met her gaze. "Come over here."

Willing her limbs to move, she exited the row and stood near the gate, allowing other people to move around her. The lawyer spoke with her mom quietly. But Marisa didn't see anything particular or hear any of the words spoken around her. *Mr. Dolton didn't take advantage of my mom,* she thought. *But my mom's parents lied in court and sent him to military school—my grandparents!*

Marisa looked at her mom. Their lawyer tried to comfort her, but could tell nothing would work. He also saw this, shook her hand and promised to call before taking off. She sighed and didn't say anything. Her mom met her gaze and averted her eyes to the ground briefly. Her body shook and her face distorted. *It wasn't fair*! She thought. She just found out who her father was, and now she had to live with him. How could he take her from her mom?

Right when her mom reached the gate, Mr. Dolton approached both of them at the same time. Marisa looked at the ground to avoid saying anything sarcastic or rude. He didn't say anything either. Her peripheral vision showed him staring at both of them. But neither met his gaze.

"Come on," her mom said, "let's go."

She turned on her heels and bolted out of the room, hearing her mom's heels clicking rapidly behind her. They left the courthouse in silence and drove the long ride home, neither of them bothering to say anything. The silence grew awkward after a while. But Marisa didn't care. They sat, each left to their own thoughts. The sky was dark blue, with hardly any clouds. There was a strong wind today. At times it stopped, and everything around them became quiet. Eerily quiet. Marisa looked over at her mom and realized how angry she still felt.

When they arrived at the house, she followed her mom into the living room, who sat down on the couch. She threw her book bag on the armchair and stood in front of her, waiting. Her mom stayed unmoving for a long time before noticing Marisa and finally looked up to meet her gaze.

"Now I'm angry." She crossed her arms over her chest. "Why?" Her mom rubbed the corners of her eyes.

"First you tell me my father ditched you." She paced around the living room. "Then you say he took advantage of you. But in court you said he didn't. Your parents lied so he would be sent away for getting you pregnant. Did he or didn't he take advantage of you?" She stopped in front of her.

"Marisa, they already lied once, and I wasn't about to do it again." Her mom stood up from the couch and started walking toward the kitchen.

"You didn't answer my question."

Her mom abruptly stopped and turned around, her face quickly changing to anger. "Don't you get smart with me, young lady. I'm still your mother."

"Sorry," she said, backing up a few steps. She had no intentions of appearing that way; she only wanted some answers already.

"Like I said, I didn't want to lie again."

"But you lied to me," she stated. "Even after you promised not to. You never told me the entire truth."

Her mom hesitated, looking at the floor briefly. "It was too complicated to explain."

Too complicated, Marisa thought, taking a deep breath. *What kind of answer was that? I wished my mom would talk to me more.* The confusion, the anger, the mixed feelings, and the different stories she kept hearing—everything kept boiling up. All she wanted was some straight answers already. She would be living with her recently discovered father in a couple of days. Someone needed to start talking soon. "But now I have to live with him and I don't know him."

"Only until you turn fourteen, then you can choose whom you want to live with," her mom responded.

"I just turned thirteen."

"It could have been longer," her mom said.

"All right." She threw her hands in the air. "But why didn't you lie again? It worked the first time, so why not go along with it."

"Because I will not have it on my conscience!" her mom yelled.

"On your conscience." Her eyebrows rose. "You still have feelings for him, don't you?" She couldn't believe it. Her mom still cared for Mr. Dolton. And he loved her too. They already knew that. After all these years, they had feelings for each other.

Her mom, who began taking off her shoes, quickly looked up and Marisa recognized the flushed face. She took a deep breath, knowing what her mom would say and waited to hear it. "I don't want to talk about it anymore."

"You said you wouldn't lie to me," she whispered, struggling to hold the tears forming. "He didn't take advantage of you, did he?"

"It doesn't matter what happened!" her mom shouted, meeting her gaze.

"It matters to me."

Her mom stared at her, then collapsed on the couch, resting her head in her open hands, which she perched on her elbows and balanced on her knees. "It doesn't matter what happened or how it happened," her mom said softly. "Don't you get it? If none of this had happened, you wouldn't be here. But it did. And I have you, Marisa. I have you."

Tears trailed down the corners of Marisa's eyes. She felt like an idiot for screaming.

What could she say? Her mom had a point. She picked up on it when talking with her friends the other day. It didn't really matter what happened, because she was here now. Now her mom had no choice but to send Marisa to live with the father. And what did she do in return? She attacked her by trying to find out what happened. Her own mother! Come Monday, she had to move in with Mr. Dolton. None of this seemed fair.

She hates that I'm going to live with Mr. Dolton too, Marisa thought. But with her out of the house came another question: *Who would take care of my mom? I am all she has. Without me, the house will fall apart.* Marisa knelt beside her mom and laid her head on her lap. Her mom burst into tears, leaning over to hug her.

* * *

Since the weekend was the last two days with her mom for the next two weeks, they decided to make the most of it while they still could. They ate a late brunch at the local diner and drove to the mall in Saint Elois afterward to spend some quality time together. The ride over wasn't too long, but her mom took the back scenic route, since they weren't in any rush. They spent the time talking about different things going on, being careful not to mention Mr. Dolton. Her mom hoped to make a good impression on her new boss, in order to get fewer hours. She had been saving what money she could and was caught up with paying the bills. While they had money problems, they no longer had to struggle as much as in the past.

Her mom had the weekends off already but wanted to work set hours, like an eight to five shift or seven thirty to four thirty shift, if allowed. Not ten to twelve hour shifts. They were wearing on her, and she knew she would burn out if continuing to work so many hours for such a long period of time.

Marisa longed to have her mom around more in the evenings when she came home from school. She noticed that during the week, her mom was stressed and cranky, always tired and working. But over the weekends, she was fine. Carefree, fun, and lovely to be around.

Marisa knew her job was stressful, and being a single parent had its toll on her. She only hoped things would change soon for the better. Right now, she wasn't sure about the future.

Especially since she had to leave. No one would be there to help her mom with the house chores or fix the meals. No one would be there when she gets home from work. Even if the moon was out, the house wasn't empty.

These thoughts were pushed to the back of Marisa's mind. She filled her mom in on Jeff's background and family. Her mom added to be careful and not to rush anything. They had plenty of time.

"I don't want you guys to get too serious and then something happens to..." her mom's voice faded, looking at Marisa. Their gazes met. Her mom seemed at a loss for words. Her head tilted to the side, studying Marisa. She smiled and patted her arm.

Once again, Mr. Dolton was brought up and they both knew it.

"Do... do you..." Marisa began and hesitated, not knowing how to ask the delicate question. She always wondered if she was simply a mistake, a regret, an accident, or like Jeff had phrased it, an "oops" baby, but never had the courage to ask. She didn't necessarily want to stay on the subject but figured now was the best time to ask. She had to know. "Do you ... have any regrets about me?"

"None whatsoever."

"Really?"

"I know I complain and gripe sometimes," her mom said. "And this situation occurring right now doesn't help, but I wouldn't trade you for the world. You're my whole life."

Marisa smiled. The last thing she wanted was to be a burden, especially to her mom. She could never imagine having a child at her age, but that was exactly what happened to her mom. Her dreams were put aside to raise a child by herself. At least her mom was taking the responsibility for it. She admired her mom's bravery and courage to remain strong and independent.

The day turned out better than yesterday. Despite all the clouds in the sky, the sun shined and the temperature was still high. They arrived at the mall and spent the whole day there. The place was packed with sounds of laughter from children, families shopping, teenagers roaming in large groups, girls gossiping as they strolled by guys and couples enjoying a day by themselves. Marisa and her mom hit the stores, window shopping, browsing and trying on clothes and accessories, looking at furniture, knickknacks, and daydreaming away. It had been awhile since the last time they came here together. She felt like a little kid again, playing some video games and escaping from life's troubles.

Her mom was in good spirits. After exploring all levels of the mall, they decided to grab a bite from the food court, to rest their tired feet from all the walking and their arms from carrying all the packages. As they stood in line, realization came screeching back, hitting her mom first. Marisa saw her gazing at a couple holding hands and occasionally stealing kisses from each other. They appeared deeply in love and she knew her mom envied them. Her love life was nonexistent since she already had a child to care for. But she was sure her mom longed for one at times.

The custody battle didn't help matters. Her mom would once again be alone, thanks to Mr. Dolton. Marisa closed her eyes for a moment, trying to clear her thoughts. Why am I so angry with him? He's my father, but he's also taking me away from my mom. Or maybe because I barely know him, and everything is happening so fast.

"Marisa," her mom said. "You all right?" She smiled. "Yeah, I was just thinking."

Her mom shot her a look and rolled her eyes, making them laugh.

The ride back home was relaxing. Her body felt tired, but she was happy. Resting their weary feet for a few minutes, they rode in a comfortable silence, enjoying the scenic drive again. The view kept changing back and forth from open farmlands and busy streets, to highways and intersections, to more open lands until reaching their subdivision. Marisa loved how they could see a little bit of everything in Rorertown. The small cities were spread out enough to give a country feel but close enough to Saint Elois for anything they could need.

When they arrived at the house and unloaded all the shopping bags, it was already late in the afternoon and the sun was at its most fierce time, right before sunset. They decided to have another girl's night in, playing some board games together and making ice cream sundaes after eating a light dinner. Once nighttime approached, they stayed up late watching some movies on television until falling asleep.

Marisa woke up late the next day, her last day to spend time with her mom. She entered the kitchen and found her mom. They ate breakfast and decided to stay in and rest today, taking it easy. She started packing her things together since she procrastinated about it too long already. Only half of her clothes and things were packed since she wasn't going to live at Mr. Dolton's house permanently. When she finished, she decided to call Jeff to let him know what happened. She knew her friends would be dying to know, yet she neglected to call any of them all weekend. Marisa picked up the phone and dialed his number.

"Hello."

"Jeff, it's Marisa." She had a lot to say, but didn't think it could be said over the phone.

She needed to spend some time with him. "Can you come over? I need to talk to you."

"Sure. I'll be right over."

Marisa clicked off the phone and smiled. It felt good knowing Jeff was always there for her. She walked over to the living room to wait for him, sitting on the couch near her mom who occupied the armchair. She looked up from reading a book.

"What are you doing?"

"I'm waiting for Jeff to come over," she replied. "Jeff." Her mom smiled, stretching her limbs.

"I told him that Mr. Dolton is my dad," she explained. "I'm going to fill him in on what happened Friday."

"OK, but I get to meet him first," her mom pointed out. "Remember."

Marisa rolled her eyes, remembering their conversation from yesterday, after discussing Jeff. She promised to introduce him at the first opportunity. "All right." She smiled. "If you must."

The doorbell rang, causing her to jump off the couch. She placed the phone on the coffee table, ran to the door, opened it, and smiled at her man. Oh my.

"Hey, beautiful," he said, making her blush.

"Hey." She closed the door after him. "Come in." He followed her to the living room. "Mom, this is Jeff."

"Hello."

"Hi, Ms. Perez." He shook her hand. "Nice to meet you."

A silence formed throughout the house with them staring at each other. She hesitated, wondering if her mom would leave and give them some privacy or were they supposed to talk in front of her? Since her mom didn't appear to leave anytime soon, Marisa met Jeff's gaze and nodded toward her room, where the door stood open. He nodded and went in that direction while she remained behind. Once he reached her room, she turned back to her mom and leaned over the armchair.

"We're going to be in my room," she said softly in her ear.

Her mom, who had been watching the entire time quietly, dropped the book in her lap and threw her a look. That comment didn't help.

"Just to talk," she reassured her. "My door is open. You can see my room from here." "It better stay open." Her mom's eyes widen.

"It will." She nodded. "Unless you want to give us the living room?"

"I'm staying right here where I can watch you two," her mom said firmly. "All right."

Retreating back to her room, Marisa realized another issue would surface very soon.

Boys and dating. It was fine right now, since she and Jeff had only gone out a couple of times, but she knew sooner or later, the topic would come up, especially because of the manner in which her mom became pregnant. Though she didn't know all the details, it had probably started out innocent enough.

Shaking her head, she entered the room to find Jeff standing in the middle. He looked around the small, but comfortable bedroom.

"I like your room," Jeff announced. His eyes rested on the suitcases in a row against the wall and next to her nightstand. "Why are all these suitcases here?" He turned, eyeing her.

"Mr. Dolton won the custody battle."

She nodded.

He shook his head, his eyes lowering to the floor. "When do you have to move in by?" "Monday." She sat on the edge of her bed. "I have to live with him for two weeks. And every other two weeks after that."

"How long?" He sat on the opposite side at the end of the bed, facing her to make it easier to talk.

"One year," she replied. "When I'm fourteen, I can choose who I want to live with." "It's only a year."

"That's not even half of it."

His eyebrows scrunched over. Marisa told him everything she found out Friday during the court hearing. His mouth dropped open, shut, open, and shut again for several seconds without saying a word. She smirked upon seeing his reaction, allowing some time for the news to sink in.

"OK," he said, throwing his hand in the air. His eyes darted back and forth. She could see his mind struggling to sort through the jumbled news and make some sense of it. "He never took advantage of your mother?"

"That's what it sounds like." She shrugged.

"Your mom's parents lied in court and he was sent off," he finished.

"Yeah."

He paused. "Do they still have feelings for each other?"

"I don't know." She shook her head. "It sounds like they do, but I know my mom is angry over the custody hearing." Her mom admitted caring for him. Not directly, but indirectly. While Mr. Dolton already confessed that he loved her mom.

"And you?" he asked. "How do you feel?"

Marisa's eyes lowered to the floor briefly. "I was angry at both of them. Now I'm mad at him."

"Your mom too?"

"Well..." She hesitated. "Because she never told me the truth to begin with. I mean, I understand her reasoning for it, but I just wished she kept it real with me."

Jeff nodded. "Would've been easier." "There was no reason to lie."

"Maybe she was protecting you," he suggested. "She never expected him to come back."

"And your father?" he asked. "You've been angry at him since the hearing notice."

"I'm angry because he's taking me away from my mother," she answered. "He knew how I felt about the matter."

"He wanted a second chance," he said softly.

"But he didn't have to take us to court," she said firmly.

He paused again, glancing at the floor briefly. "Remember when you found out about the hearing?" He began and she nodded. "He talked with you during school. Everything seemed fine between you two. Not as bad as before."

"Yes," she exclaimed, standing up. "That's why I'm angry. He knew that I was having trouble adjusting. He said I could talk with him any time. But he goes behind my back and files a custody hearing. I found out about it that night."

"Bad timing?"

She hesitated. How long had the letter been waiting for them? A few days passed before she even brought the mail in. Maybe it was bad timing. Mr. Dolton would have had to file the hearing way in advance. No, it wasn't just the timing. It was his decision to claim custody in the first place. He must have claimed it weeks ago, but never bothered to mention it. Instead he waited until they received the notice. I wish he had waited and allowed more time for us to get to know each other. To work things out for all three of us. "He didn't have to go this route," she answered. "I never expected him to take me from my mom. I don't even know him."

He shrugged a shoulder. "Now you'll get to know him."

Marisa extinguished a deep breath, not knowing how to respond. Jeff had a point, but what about her mother. "But did he have to take me away from my mom?" she questioned. "Was that really necessary?"

Jeff didn't reply. He glanced at his hands, which lay idly in his lap. A silence fell upon them, each in their own thoughts. The remainder of the house was quiet. So quiet, Marisa glanced out of the open doorway and into the living room. She forgot all about her mom. She couldn't see her, but figured she was still on the armchair since no noise emerged.

Another realization came to her. Can she hear us talking? Marisa didn't think they were conversing too loud, but then again, her mom wasn't making any noise. The house was peaceful and quiet except for her room. She shook her head, returning her attention back to Jeff, who sat waiting patiently and silently.

"It's just…" She ran a hand through her hair. "Everything has been moving too fast. I have no problem getting to know him, but I have a problem with him taking me from my mom."

"What are you going to do?"

She shrugged a shoulder. "What can I do? I have to live with him now." "You going to give him a chance?"

Her eyebrows burrowed. "Should I?" "You could get to know him."

She paused, before her eyes sharpened upon him. "I thought you didn't like him." He shrugged his shoulders. "I don't want your life to be a nightmare."

Marisa's eyes lowered to the floor. Jeff had another good point. But another thought kept lingering. "What about my mom?" She met his gaze. "She's working all the time, and now she'll come home to an empty house." She started pacing.

Jeff also stood up from the bed, slowly coming toward her until she stopped in her tracks.

She slowly rubbed her temples. "Marisa," he said quietly. "You all right?"

Should she open up and give Mr. Dolton a chance? Accept him into her life? She pondered over this question for days. Now she had no choice since he took matters into his own hands. She was forced into sharing a part of her life with him. That factor made her angry. Not what happened between them. He went behind her back and took her from her mom.

"Marisa." Jeff placed his hands on her cheeks.

She met his gaze. "I don't know what to do." She lowered her hands until they rested on his arms. "I was considering talking to him and giving him a chance. I really was. But then my mom opened that letter and..." her voice shook. "He didn't have to take me from my mom."

Jeff stroked her cheek caressingly. "I know." He pulled her into his arms, pressing her tightly against his hard chest. Marisa closed her eyes, leaning her head on his shoulder, her hands firmly planted on his chest. She inhaled deeply, taking in his musky scent, becoming lost in the moment. His head moved along the side of her face until his lips grazed her ear. "Take one day at a time," he whispered. "See how it goes. Focus on the first two weeks. It might work out between you two, or even between him and your mom. You never know."

She nodded, lifting her head off his shoulder. Meeting his eyes, she extinguished a deep breath and smiled, feeling relieved after venting.

"There's that beautiful smile," Jeff said. "Let's go outside. Weather's nice." "OK."

They walked out of the room, through the living room where her mom sat reading, out the back door and onto the backyard porch. The sun was high in the sky, though the temperature dropped to a tolerable degree with a nice breeze in the air. They sat on the patio furniture, gazing out over the lawn and the surrounding neighbors' lawns. It was so peaceful and comforting. The sun continued to set, giving them a breathtaking view.

A new thought occurred to her. She tore her eyes away from the backyard and gazed over at her man.

Basketball tryouts ended Friday afternoon. She didn't know if he made the team. Or if any of her friends did. She had been caught up with the endless drama occurring in her life, forgetting about her boyfriend and friends. He met her glance and held it.

"Did you make the team?" she asked.

"Yep," he replied, beaming. "So did Patty, Mark, and Sean."

"Oh, good," she said. "When's the first game?"

"Friday."

They spent the rest of the evening talking, and soon she forgot all about Mr. Dolton and having to move in with him tomorrow.

CHAPTER 16

When Marisa awoke the next day, the events from the past several days came screeching back to her. The weekend flew by, as today was the day she dreaded. Today she moved in with Mr. Dolton. She knew it would be a very long and interesting day. Hopefully it wouldn't be stressful. Like Jeff had suggested, she would try to survive these next two weeks. That was all she could hope for. Take one day at a time. She still didn't know what else to do. Should she give him a chance? These matters took time, but she gave Mr. Dolton the cold shoulder for the last few days, not even speaking to him. She couldn't do that forever. I just have to see how it goes, she thought.

She arrived at school and entered through the front doors, heading straight to her lockers where her friends stood waiting. Upon spotting her, they crowded around until forming a circle to keep other students away from hearing anything.

"Hey."

"What happened during the hearing on Friday?" Jenni asked.

Marisa glanced over at Jeff, who shrugged. Since he arrived before her, she expected her friends to already know everything. She smiled, realizing she could trust him.

Even though she confided in him, he never repeated anything. It was her business. He placed a comforting hand on her shoulder as she told her friends about having to live with Mr. Dolton.

"Really?" Sean shook his head.

"I wish I knew what to tell you, but I don't," Patty said. "I don't blame you."

"You move in today?" Jenni asked.

"Yeah," she replied. "After school he's taking me to get my stuff, and then it's off to his house." She found this out when he called last night.

"That was fast," Mark remarked.

"No kidding," Jeff added.

"True, but it's also a little late for that," Patty pointed out. "Now you have two options: you can either put up with him or cause him trouble."

Marisa nodded. That option never occurred to her. "That's not a bad idea," she said. "But I don't need to give him trouble. I need to live with my mom."

"You need to or want to?" Jenni asked.

"Well…" She paused, glancing among the group. The questions only confused her even more. "I guess I don't need to. I want to. Well, no… wait. I do need to because it's hard on her to do everything by herself. There's no one to look after her." Silence greeted her. "What?"

"You sound like a mother," Sean said.

She shrugged, changing out her books. "I don't know, OK."

"First off, answer this question," Jenni jumped in. "Do you want to give him a chance?"

Jeff met her gaze. He had asked the same thing, too. Did she want to give Mr. Dolton a chance? Should she? The real question was why? He didn't ditch her mom or take advantage of her after all. But he claimed her without caring about how they felt, after she told him it would take time to accept him.

Though he did come back after all these years. She rubbed her forehead. Damn it! I still don't know what to do.

"Should I?" Marisa inquired. "I don't know. Will it help drop the custody claim or will it only hinder the situation?"

The first bell rang.

"It's up to you," Jenni said. "I'll see you guys in class." "Bye." She shut her locker.

Mark and Jenni took off in one direction. Sean and Patty stepped off to the side waiting, while Jeff grabbed her hand. He gave it a quick squeeze and their gazes met.

"Just take it a day at a time," he whispered, and she nodded. "I'll see you in a bit."

"OK." She smiled.

He took off racing down the hall with Sean to their first class. Marisa joined Patty and they ran through the opposite hall toward their room. They arrived and sat in their seats right when class began.

During computer class, she didn't pay attention, which wasn't hard since Mr. Dolton's class was always boring. Instead, she messed around with the computers to stay awake. Her friends kept throwing faint smiles since they didn't really know what else to say. They tried to keep her mind off it by talking about other things, though it only worked momentarily. As the day wore on, she became more and more apprehensive about moving in with Mr. Dolton. The next thing she knew, the final bell rang and school was dismissed.

"Call me tonight when you get a chance," Jeff said.

"Don't you mean if I survive?" she remarked, and he smiled faintly. "I'll see you later." She waved bye to Patty and the guys who headed toward the gym for practice.

Jenni started walking in the same direction, but stopped and doubled back when Marisa made no move. "Can't you stay for practice?"

Marisa shook her head no. "I don't think I can. We have to get my stuff from my house." "Surely you can do that after?"

"I don't know what's going to happen," she replied. "I haven't even spoken to him today."

"You need to talk to him eventually," Jenni pointed out. "I'm sure if you tell him your plans, he'll let you."

"I know." Marisa released a sigh. "Probably not today, though, since I have to get situated. Time to get this over with. I'll see you tomorrow."

"All right, bye."

Marisa turned around and walked over to Mr. Dolton's room. Students pushed past her in all directions. When she reached his classroom, she stood by the open door waiting silently. She peered into the room, seeing he sat at his desk, intent at his work. He didn't bug her at all today. She never spoke to him or looked at him during class.

He looked up at last, meeting her eyes and smiled. "Are you ready?"

She didn't reply. He stood up and gathered his things together. She stayed by the door, gazing at the floor until he exited the room. They walked out the school building together, heading to his car. The majority of the students already left the school premises. There were a few students here and there, who threw them questioning looks. Marisa ignored the stares, keeping quiet and climbed into his car. He started the engine and left the school, heading to her house.

During the car ride, Mr. Dolton tried to talk to her. Asking how her day went, how school was going for her this semester, whether her studies were too hard or too easy. She only heard about half of the questions. He kept talking and talking. But she remained silent, staring out the window and refusing to make the transition easy for him. Even though the drive was only two minutes, it felt like forever.

When they arrived at her house, Marisa extinguished a sigh of relief at seeing her mom's car. Her mom came home early to see her off, but would have to return to work. Probably took a late lunch or something. Marisa entered the house with Mr. Dolton right on her heels, to find her mom pacing in the living room. She stopped upon seeing them.

Mr. Dolton walked right over to her, and Marisa went to her room. She lifted up some of the suitcases and carried them through the living room, where she saw Mr. Dolton trying to talk to her mom, who wouldn't respond either. Giving up, he took the suitcases from Marisa and headed out the front door.

She retreated back to her room and grabbed the remaining suitcases. She carried them to the front hallway and placed them next to the door. She turned around and approached her mom, who watched silently. "Bye, Mom," she said. "I'll see you in two weeks."

"Bye, honey," her mom said, hugging her tightly. "Marisa, let's go," Mr. Dolton called out.

Marisa and her mom unlocked their embrace and looked over at the sound of his voice.

He stood in the doorway, watching them.

"Excuse me," her mom said firmly, "I'm not done saying goodbye to *my* daughter. Now go wait in your car, and I'll send her out when I'm finished."

Looking a little frustrated, Mr. Dolton glanced at the ground and sighed. He turned around and exited the house without saying another word.

"Marisa, listen to me," her mom said, holding onto her shoulders. She turned back to her mom. "If he tries anything on you or hits you, you call me immediately, and I'll come get you, OK?"

"Uh … OK." Her eyes widen briefly, but she brushed off the comment, figuring her mom was preparing her just in case. Marisa kissed her on the cheek and walked outside, where Mr. Dolton waited in the car. Reluctantly, she climbed in, and he exited the subdivision, driving toward his house. Once again, she fell silent during the entire ride. She simply stared out the passenger side window, focusing on how to get to his house from hers.

The drive lasted probably five minutes. He lived rather close after seeing the route again. It didn't seem too hard to remember now. She climbed out of the car and walked around to the trunk, where together they took out her suitcases. She slowly followed him inside the house. Glancing around, she passed the living room, kitchen, and bathroom. They continued on to the back of the house where she figured the bedrooms were located. They passed one room that she couldn't see into since the door was closed. Maybe a bathroom. He stopped in front of another room to open the door. Marisa saw that a third room stood further off to the side. Probably his room.

"Here it is," Mr. Dolton announced.

She entered behind him, where he placed the suitcases on the floor. The room had one full size bed with a blue bedspread on it, brown Chester drawers, a matching nightstand, a medium-sized desk, and a closet. She set her bags on the floor and waited for Mr. Dolton to leave. He took a couple of steps toward the door, but stopped and looked over at her.

"Did you need any help?" he asked.

He waited for her to answer and when Marisa didn't, he finally left the room. Heaving a deep sigh, Marisa started unpacking her stuff. She began to hang up posters and pinups on the walls so they wouldn't look plain. She placed a picture of her mom and herself on the Chester drawers. As she began unpacking, she wondered how Mr. Dolton could afford a place like this. From what she saw, the house looked about the size of theirs. She wasn't too sure about how many bedrooms or bathrooms, but it seemed a decent size. She guessed three bedrooms and two bathrooms. But he seemed like the only occupant; however, Marisa also knew that teachers didn't get paid very well.

How does he afford this place?

After she finished unpacking, Mr. Dolton entered the room again. He paused inside the open doorway, which he never closed earlier, and she forgot to shut. As he glanced around the room and her progress, Marisa stayed on the other side of the room by her nightstand. *When will he leave me alone?* she thought, glaring at him. *Why does he keep trying to talk to me? I wonder if there's a lock on the door.*

"Are you an early riser?" he asked.

Her eyebrows rose. She hadn't expected that. She hesitated, but the question couldn't be ignored. "Why?"

"We have to get to school by seven."

"Seven!" she exclaimed. "I wake up at seven."

"Sorry, but you'll have to wake up earlier." He started to leave.

"What do you mean we?" Marisa asked, stopping him. "I'm not getting up early just so you can go to school at seven."

"And why not?" He crossed his arms over his chest.

"You can go by yourself," she said. "I'll walk to school."

"You will not walk," he said firmly. "You—"

"I walk all the time."

His eyebrows rose briefly, and he shook his head. "Not anymore. You will get up early and come to school with me."

"And just what am I going to do until school starts?"

"Straighten your attitude." He turned and left the room.

She sighed, and her shoulders drooped. She closed the door only to discover it had no lock. *What is his problem?* she thought. *It's going to be a long two weeks. How can I live with him? He's already getting on my nerves.*

Having nothing else to do, Marisa started her homework. She wanted to watch television, but she could hear Mr. Dolton moving around in the living room. Since she wasn't in the mood to see him, she stayed in her room. There was no other noise emerging in the house except for him, making the surroundings seem eerily quiet. Awkward. She could have called Jeff but didn't know where anything was in this house. It was too early to call him anyway. He probably wouldn't be home for another hour. She missed her mom, wondering how she was doing right now. If she went back to work as soon as she left, she would work even later tonight.

Getting angry, Marisa threw her pen across the room and stared off into space.

This is not fair, she thought. *I want to go home*! The door to her new room opened, and Mr. Dolton stuck his head in. Marisa rolled her eyes. "How about you knock first before barging in?" she demanded. "I could've been changing."

He looked a little shocked at first, then nodded. "Fair enough. Dinner's ready."

Oh boy. She slowly stood up from the desk and followed him into the kitchen, sitting down at the table. Right smack in the center laid a bowl of chocolate candy. *Mmm, chocolate.*

"Do I have to go to school at seven in the morning?"

"Marisa, you're going," Mr. Dolton said. "Now drop it."

She glanced to her left and bit her tongue. She was so mad, it was better to keep her mouth shut. But he made it difficult to repress the urge to strike. Instead, she watched him serve both of them a plate of spaghetti and garlic bread. He kept running back and forth between the counter and the table, to get something or another. She found it amusing after a while, how he sat down, only to remember something else needed, and jumped up from the chair. Was he nervous? He finally sat down next to her and started eating. She was starving but continued to stare at her plate. She missed her mom and her own house so much.

"Aren't you hungry?" Mr. Dolton asked, after eating a few bites. "No," she shot back.

"Why not?" "Because I'm not."

"Marisa, what is your problem?" He put his fork down. "Why are you being so sassy? You just arrived and already you're not even giving me a chance … Well?"

"I don't know."

Mr. Dolton looked over to his right, and she saw him roll his eyes. *Copycat*, she thought. Now he's starting to act like me.

"At least try to eat," he said.

She picked up her fork like a good, dutiful daughter and poked at the food, swirling it around the plate.

"Come on, Marisa." He ran a hand through his hair. "I know you miss your mom, but you're going to see her in two weeks. You're my daughter too."

Marisa shook her head. He had the gall to say that after what he kept putting them through. She didn't reply and stared at her plate. She couldn't believe she was here.

He must have noticed her face. "Can you at least give me a chance?"

Not being able to take it anymore, she stood up and left the kitchen table, heading toward her room. She stopped right outside her bedroom door, and doubled back to the table. He watched her every move silently. Glaring at him, she snatched up the candy bowl and retreated to her room, slamming the door. Placing the bowl on her desk, she picked up the picture off the Chester drawers and sat on the bed. She hugged the pillow, staring at the photo. A huge sob escaped her mouth. Tears crept to the crevices of her eyes.

I cannot believe he said that, she thought. Now Marisa knew the answer to Jenni's question. Why should I give him a chance when he takes me away from my mom, knowing she needs me? Instead, she figured she could give him a hard time. He wanted it this way so now he was going to get it. He knew the situation controlled her school work and social life. She told him she hadn't accepted him as her father yet, and he still takes her away.

I want to go home!

* * *

The next day Marisa woke up earlier than usual. This would be the only favor she would do for Mr. Dolton, since she was still very angry with him. The sun was barely visible on the horizon when they arrived at school. The morning breeze followed her inside the building. She lingered in the doorway, enjoying the cool wind. Sighing, she tagged along after him, moving like a zombie down the quiet, empty halls to his room since no one else was there, except some other faculty members. When the bright light clicked on, she blinked a few times before sitting behind the nearest computer.

She twiddled her thumbs, trying to kill time. He was already situated at his desk, bent over his work. She never knew exactly what he was doing, but she always saw him surrounded by papers. She never knew where the papers came from though. Her class didn't turn any assignments in yesterday. The clock on the wall read 7:05 a.m. She sighed. It would be another long day and a long week. It was so early in the morning and already she felt tired and cranky.

Marisa opened her mouth to say something but stopped. What should she call him? She would continue using Mr. Dolton for class, but he was her father. However, she didn't feel comfortable calling him this, especially not at the moment. What other name could she use then? Oh, what was his first name? It started with a J, and it was short like her mom's name—John. But John seemed too casual, and Mr. Dolton was too formal. So now what?

Should I just refer to him as, 'Hey, you?' She shook her head and figured to stick with what she always called him. "Mr. Dolton, can I visit my mom during these two weeks?" She yawned and laid her head on the table.

"I'm not sure," he said. "But you saw her yesterday."

"Well, hmm." Marisa lifted up her head to face him. "I might get lonely and miss her.

Besides, she happens to be my mother."

"You'll get to see her when the two weeks are up," he replied, eyes on his papers.

"Doesn't it ever occur to you that I have feelings about being alternated between you two?" She could not believe he was acting like this.

"Why does it bother you?" he asked, finally making eye contact.

"I told you how I felt about all this," she said firmly. "I'm the one that has to switch houses every two weeks.

Don't I get a say in this?" Her voice rose higher and higher until she yelled.

"Hey!" he shouted, standing up. "Keep your voice down or get out."

She grabbed her book bag and bolted out of the room, slamming the door shut on the way out.

* * *

John Dolton sat down, desperately trying to hold in his frustration. He could feel the anger rising throughout his body and slammed his fist on the desk. His office supplies rattled, and his pen bounced up in front of him. Grabbing it, he threw it across the room at the closed door. Cradling his head between his hands, he leaned over in his seat until resting his elbows on the desk. A tear rolled down his cheek and he didn't bother to wipe it away.

He was running out of ideas on how to win them over. First Lisa didn't want to give him a chance, now Marisa wasn't giving him one. He knew it would take some time, but he thought at least one of them would like him by now. How can I get her to like me? He asked himself.

What do I have to do?

Marisa didn't want to live with him. She wanted nothing to do with him, just like Lisa. It hadn't been twenty-four hours and already she complained. He wasn't sure which was worse: All the time he spent apart from them and wondering about them or the hard time he was having now? He didn't know what else to do either. It shouldn't be this hard. He stood up and paced around the room. *If she would just give me a chance to prove myself to her*, he thought, *everything would be all right. Lisa will see what a wonderful father I am and give me a chance. We will ...*

John stopped pacing. He was getting way ahead of himself. He needed to concentrate more on Marisa since she was staying at his house. They already had two fights. What he needed to do was become closer to her. He missed out on her first thirteen years of life. That could be the reason why it was taking a while for her to adapt. He approached the window and leaned his hands against the frame, staring out. There has to be a way...

* * *

At promptly 7:30 a.m., students finally started showing up. Marisa thought she would die of boredom. She had spent the rest of the morning in the cafeteria alone and drinking a soda. She walked over to her locker but simply stared at it, since she already had her books. Glancing up, she saw Jenni enter the school building. Spotting her, Jenni approached Marisa, opening her own locker to gather her books.

"Why are you here so early?" Jenni asked.

"Mr. Dolton made me get up early so he could be here at seven," she replied. "You've been here since seven!" Patty exclaimed, approaching them.

"Who's been here since seven?" Jeff asked, appearing next to Marisa. Sean and Mark also came up to them.

"I have, and I just had a fight with Mr. Dolton too." She glanced at Patty. "I've decided to give him trouble."

Her friends didn't say much after. She couldn't blame them either. Jeff caught her eye but kept quiet. The bell rang and she said bye. Her friends split up, heading in different directions throughout the hallways. Her thoughts were miles away, for the next thing she knew, Math class ended. They headed over to Computer class.

"I really don't feel like seeing him right now," she muttered to Patty. "We'll protect you," Patty said.

Jenni joined them before they entered the room. "Patty can take him."

She smiled. Her friends formed a barricade around Marisa, walking into the classroom. She entered and turned her attention to the back of the room, catching Jeff's gaze. He watched her walking down the aisle. Her cheeks blushed with his eyes looked over her longingly. She sat in her seat without even looking in Mr. Dolton's direction. Marisa spent the class messing with the computers rather than paying attention to pass the time during the lecture. Jeff glanced back every so often and kept her smiling.

When class finally ended, she filed out of the row and Mr. Dolton approached her, asking her to stay. She met his gaze, hesitating. He stood in front of her, blocking the aisle. She had let her guard down and was now separated from her friends, who were already on the other side of him.

"He sure does ask that girl to stay after class a lot," she heard one guy remark.

No kidding, she thought.

The classmates filed out of the room. Marisa stood on her tiptoes, looking over Mr. Dolton's shoulder, and shot her friends a "help me" look. Jeff lingered behind even more.

Mr. Dolton moved over, blocking her view. "Class is over." He turned around and moved forward, ushering her friends out. She glared at him, walking toward the front of the room.

Mr. Dolton waited until the classroom was empty before addressing her.

"If it's about this morning, I have nothing to say to you," she said.

"No, it's not about this morning," Mr. Dolton said.

"Then why do you keep asking me to stay?" she demanded. "This needs to stop. It's becoming a ritual with you."

"Why weren't you paying attention in class?" He crossed his arms over his chest.

"Don't get me started on that. OK?" She took a deep breath, trying not to get angry again. She couldn't believe he was bringing this up. "I have told you a thousand times why."

"That's still no excuse," he replied. "You need to pay attention if you want to pass the course."

"Is that all you wanted to talk about?" She shifted her feet back and forth. "Yes."

She walked around him, heading toward the door.

"Hey, where are you going?" He ran past her and stopped in front of the door, blocking her exit.

"To study hall," she replied.

"You don't need to go," he said. "You can stay here with me."

That remark drew the line. All he ever did was take Marisa away from everything important in her life. She decided to let him have it. "Stay with you!" she yelled. "Why? What is it with you? First you take me away from my family. Now you're trying to take me away from my friends."

"Does it ever occur to you that I'm part of your family?" Mr. Dolton shouted. He stepped close to her. So close she could feel the anger rising off him. "Thirteen years ago, I lost the woman I love. I spent four years in military school. It takes me nine years to find you and your mother since you two are the only family I have left. Your mom doesn't want to give me another chance, so I figured I could at least get to you. That's why I claimed you—so I could spend some time with you. But you have to attack me with everything I say. You're *my* daughter, Marisa. I have every right to be with you. Now how do you think I feel?"

Marisa hesitated, staring up at him. It never occurred to her until now how alike they were. They both had a moody side and could be stubborn yet outwardly spoken when angry. So that was the way it was. She had his personality and her mom's looks. But at this moment, she felt silenced, not knowing what to say since he had a point—a really good point. One she had never considered. Still, he didn't really care about her feelings to take her away from her mom. Rather he did everything for himself. "Look ..."

"Just go," Mr. Dolton said, moving out of the way. "Get out of here."

She left before he could change his mind and walked over to study hall. She joined her friends, collapsing into the seat Jeff had saved her and stayed quiet, lost in her thoughts.

She tried to calm down so she wouldn't take her anger out on her friends. She smiled at Jeff, who rubbed her arm before standing up.

"You think I should try out for the cheerleading team?" Jenni asked her. "I think she should," Patty replied.

"But I don't want to be thought of as a ditzy blonde."

"But everyone knows you're not," Patty argued.

"I don't know." Jenni turned back to her. "What do you think, Marisa?"

They looked at her, waiting for an answer. "Sure, why not?"

Jeff, who now stood behind her, placed his hands on her shoulders. He leaned over until his face perched near her ear, whispering, "Is something wrong?"

"I had another fight with Mr. Dolton," she replied. The whole table became quiet.

"What do you guys fight about?" Mark asked.

She shook her head. What do we fight about? Where to begin? Waking up early? Her mom? Staying with him during study hall? "It's always something different."

"How long have you been living with him?" Sean asked. His face turned slightly angry. "Not even a full day."

"And already you had two fights with him?" Jenni asked. "Three," she said. "We had one last night."

The entire table fell silent.

When school ended, Jeff waited for Marisa by her locker. She saw her other friends head off to the gymnasium, even Jenni, who had cheerleading tryouts. Marisa approached Jeff, a smile creeping to her face.

"Hey," she said. "Don't you need to get to practice?"

"Yeah, but I wanted to see if you were staying." He grabbed her hands. "I miss walking you home."

"Sure. I …" Her voice trailed off, remembering she lived at Mr. Dolton's house now. "Oh man. I don't know if I can stay or if I have to leave with him. I don't know how long he stays after school or if he stays at all. I know … nothing about him." She paused. The words rang in her mind.

She knew nothing about her father. "But I know how to get to his house. It's not much further."

"Go ask him," Jeff suggested. "I'll wait." "But won't you be late?"

"That's fine," he said. "Just hurry."

"OK, I'll be right back." She smiled and released his hands.

CHAPTER 17

She sprinted to Mr. Dolton's room, thinking there was no reason why she couldn't stay. He gave her a house key last night, and she knew how to get to his house. He probably had work to do anyway.

As Marisa approached the classroom, her pace slowed at the thought of seeing him. Her mind returned to what he said earlier. And to what she just realized. Now that she heard both sides of the story, she wasn't mad at him for that. She was mad because he took her away from her mom. His attitude wasn't helping much either. He wanted to spend time with her, but she would have saved her weekends for him. But then again, the weekends were the only time she spent with her mom.

Oh man, she thought. *If he hadn't claimed her, would she have had time for him?* After all, her mom needed her. She really didn't even know what her feelings were right now. But it was getting too much for her to handle. Marisa crept to Mr. Dolton's classroom but stayed by the door. He glanced up and shifted his attention back to his work.

"Nice to see you too."

"Don't start," he replied sharply, jerking his head up and narrowing his eyes at her.

"Sorry." She winced at the slip of her tongue. This wasn't helping. If she was going to get anywhere, she had to get on his good side. And quick too. She took a deep breath. "Um, I wanted to stay and watch the basketball practice. Jeff can walk me to your house afterward."

"That's fine," he said softly, his face relaxing. "I need to get some work done anyway." "OK."

"I'll see you tonight," she heard him call out, but she already left the room.

She sped through the hallways and hurried over to Jeff, grateful to spend more time with him. "Let's go."

"All right." Jeff grabbed her hand.

They ran to the gym together, laughing the entire time. She wished him luck before he dashed to the locker room to change. She entered the gym and found a seat on the bleachers, where she dropped her book bag and searched for her friends. The teams weren't on the court yet, so Jeff wasn't late. She watched Jenni, who stood in the middle of the gymnasium, surrounded by other female students. They performed a few cheers, their voices echoing off the walls. Marisa sat back to enjoy the practice. Soon her other friends piled out of the locker room, forcing the cheerleaders to move to a corner of the gym.

Marisa watched, enchanted. Jenni joined her later after tryouts, where they continued following their friends' practice. Patty was on one side of the gym with the girl's team, while Jeff, Mark, and Sean were on the other side practicing with the boy's team. They talked and laughed, keeping an eye on their friends' movements, who raced up and down the court.

Westchester had a junior varsity and varsity team for the boys and girls. The players would usually end practice with a game on both sides. When practice ended and her friends showered, she joined Jeff's side. She said bye as the group split up into the three couples, heading off in different directions.

"I don't know where he lives," Jeff said. "It's on Mabieu Street."

"Oh, I know where that is," he said. "You coming to our first game Friday?" "If I can." She shrugged.

"You must be there," he said, facing her. "I need you to cheer for me." "What am I? A cheerleader?"

"Yeah." He stepped in her path to stop her from walking. Grabbing her arms, he turned Marisa around, facing the other way. She began laughing, while he did little cheering motions with her arms. "Go me, go me." Jeff wrapped his arms around her waist, picked her up, and spun her around. She shrieked, her legs flew out in front of her, and the wind caressed her face. She almost forgot how good laughing felt. By the time Jeff set her down, she was happy again.

"You're glowing." They started walking, holding hands.

"That's because I'm with you."

They reached Mr. Dolton's house, but she didn't want to say goodbye, though it was getting late. Practice usually lasted two hours, meaning it was after 6 p.m. But she was having too much fun. Instead, they stood on the driveway, facing each other, where Jeff's smile faded away. "I wish I could help."

"I'm sick of fighting with him," she admitted. "That's the biggest problem at the moment." There were several problems and unanswered questions, but this was the most important right now.

"Talk it out with him," Jeff suggested. "Sit him down and tell him how you feel. How else will he know if you don't tell him?"

"Never thought of that," she said. "Worth a try."

"Did I ever tell you how glad I am that you asked me out?" She gazed into his eyes. His eyebrows scrunched over for a moment, and she closed her eyes briefly, realizing what she said. "I'm sorry." She shook her head. "That didn't come out right."

Jeff's face slowly broke into a smile before he started laughing silently. She smacked him on the arm, and he blocked it. Suddenly his laughing ceased. He wrapped his arms around her waist, pulling her close to him until they stood embraced in a hug. He pulled his head away and slowly lifted her chin with his hand to where they gazed into each other's eyes. He gently stroked her cheek, and her heart pounded. She planted her hands on his back.

"Did I ever tell you how beautiful you look today?" he whispered, making her smile.

Is he going to kiss me? Marisa thought, feeling her cheeks heat. *This is it!*

Jeff placed both hands on her cheeks, cupping them into his palms, and he leaned toward her.

Her eyes almost closed when her peripheral vision showed a car pulling into the driveway. She backed away from Jeff and looked over. The car stopped right in front of them. It was Mr. Dolton. She glanced over at Jeff, not too sure what to do since he didn't cut the engine or get out of the car. Instead, he simply watched them.

"We're standing in the way." Jeff cupped her elbow and led her off the driveway.

"He said he had to work late." She didn't know what time he would get home, but she hadn't counted on him arriving now.

Mr. Dolton eyed them sharply, before moving the car forward. He ruined the perfect moment.

"Call me later," Jeff said.

"All right, bye."

Jeff walked away, and she raced toward the front door. Of course, the timing had to be bad. Hearing Mr. Dolton get out of the car, she fished the key out of her book bag and unlocked the door. Hurrying inside, she shut the front door behind her, despite him yelling for her to wait. She ran to her room and shut the door, dropping the bag on the floor, and collapsed into the chair. If she was going to talk to Mr. Dolton, it had to be now. Although it didn't help he almost saw Jeff and her kissing.

His footsteps quickly approached her room. "What was that?" he asked, yanking open the door.

"What was what?" she shot back. "You arrived before anything happened." She took a deep breath, swiveling around in her chair. "Can we talk for a minute?"

He studied her face for a while. "All right. I'm not too happy with what I saw out there." "Nothing happened. I meant can we talk about us. Please?"

Gazing into her eyes, he nodded. "OK, but we'll finish this conversation another time."

Marisa gestured for him to enter and he sat on the edge of the bed, facing her. Her eyes fixed on him, noticing his mood and appearance for the first time. He looked a little pale, tired, anxious, and worn-out.

"Look, um," he began. "I wanted to apologize for my behavior this morning."

"You don't have to," she interrupted. Her eyes widen briefly. She had intended on doing all the talking, yet he said something first. Without even knowing what she wanted to talk about.

"No, really. I insist," he continued.

"I understand, but you have to see where I'm coming from," she pressed on. "All my life, I've been with my mother and was told a different story about you. Then suddenly you came and said you were my father. Just as I find out what really happened, you take me away from my mom before I can even adjust to the fact that you were my dad. All this stuff is happening too quickly. That's why I've been mad at you. I even told you this trying to hint at something."

Mr. Dolton didn't say anything. He looked kind of shocked. At least they weren't fighting. It wouldn't do any good. He wanted to spend some time with her and be given a chance. But she had to tell her story if they were going to get along. Jeff didn't have a bad idea after all. The timing wasn't right, but there probably would never be a perfect time. "I see," he said finally. "I guess I was kind of hard. I mean

I really love your mother. I've tried everything I can think of, but she doesn't want to give me another chance. I figured if I couldn't get to her, I could at least get you on my side. That's why I took your mother to court."

"You've tried everything?" she asked. "Are you sure?" While the situation was difficult, there were several different ways to approach it. Probably even better ones.

"I thought about it for days, but this was the only way where I could definitely talk to your mom," he replied. "And spend some time with you."

"Yeah that's understandable." She released a deep breath. "I'm glad we had this talk." "So am I," he said, looking relieved.

Standing up from the desk chair, she approached Mr. Dolton and hugged him, and he hugged her back.

* * *

Ever since their little talk, Mr. Dolton and Marisa started getting along better. They talked more, being open and honest with each other. Her routine continued on as before, but with less stress and smoother sailing now. She still accompanied him to school early every morning, using the quiet time to talk to him, do some homework, or study. Then she would join her friends before heading off to class. The day after they made up, she told her friends how the two of them were no longer fighting. Her friends were relieved and glad to see her happy and enjoying the time with him.

During the school days, Mr. Dolton no longer bugged her to stay after class or try to stop her in the hallways since there was no need. Sometimes she did stay to tell him something or see how his day was going. Usually, for a few minutes, she would chat with him before meeting up with her friends. She even paid attention and participated in his class.

Once school ended, she would head to the gym and watch her friends' practice. They worked hard preparing for their first game. She would also watch Jenni practice the routines.

When practice ended, Marisa would walk to Mr. Dolton's house, accompanied by Jeff. This arrangement allowed her to spend time with Jeff, while Mr. Dolton worked for a few hours at school. He usually arrived at the house the same time they did, whereas Jeff and Marisa would part ways. Then she would help Mr. Dolton fix dinner, and they would sit down together to eat as a family.

She had to admit; it was nice with him home at a decent time. She didn't have to stay up all night by herself waiting. She didn't have to eat dinner by herself or entertain herself until late at night, struggling to stay awake, night after night, just to say hello before going to bed. Or to say hello before her mom collapsed on the couch. Or to not fall asleep while she was talking to her mom, but too tired to fight it every night.

Once dinner was finished, she would usually do her homework, before staying up late to chat with Mr. Dolton. They would sit on the couch, watching television, talking about their day, retelling funny stories, eating a late snack, all depending on the time. Sometimes they stayed up so late, it was the next day before realizing the time. By then, she was wide awake. She paid for it at school, but it was good fun.

When Marisa didn't have homework during the week, and he didn't have work to do, they would play video games, watch a movie, play a board game, or watch television. She enjoyed the time after a long day. It made her days easier, having something relaxing and fun to look forward to. She made a point to stop procrastinating about her schoolwork. The more she accomplished at school, the more time she had in the evenings to kick back and chill with Mr. Dolton. If anything, she laughed more when she was with him. It felt good to smile and laugh at home rather than worrying. It felt good to see him laughing, rather than quiet and preoccupied. The time spent together reminded Marisa of her weekends with her mom, when she let her hair down and devote the whole time to her.

Her friends were also opening up and talking more to Mr. Dolton. He usually stopped by the cafeteria to give Marisa a soda during lunch. They would chat with him then or stay behind after class with her to talk to him, saying hi as he passed by in the hallways, hanging out in his room before the first bell rang, running to his room before practice to see if he could watch or check to see if he was still there after practice ended. Sometimes Mr. Dolton watched the practice with Marisa if his workload allowed him. Marisa really enjoyed being around him. He wasn't so bad after all.

Only her friends knew he was her father, since they never told anyone. She continued referring to him as Mr. Dolton on and off school premises. She had yet to call him father, but he hadn't called her daughter either.

Occasionally students would throw weird glances at Marisa when they saw her walking alongside Mr. Dolton and talking to him. But she brushed off the looks since it was no one else's business. They remained careful not to give anything away at school. Marisa always saw students who talked to teachers outside of class all the time, so she had no reason to worry. She knew people were going to stare and talk no matter what. Let them. She could care less.

To make up for all the time missed out as father and daughter, they spent their first weekend at the movies, the mall, and walking downtown. They visited museums and ate at fancy restaurants. Mr. Dolton also bought her several gifts: clothes, jewelry, music, movies, books, and decorations for her room. It was quickly adding up.

At one point she felt guilty. Every time they went out, he bought her something. Almost every time he came home, he brought her a present. She never knew when he found the time, but despite how much work he had—meetings after school or errands he had to run—he always managed to buy her something.

"Do you like it?" he asked.

The bags sat on the counter, filled with groceries waiting to be unloaded. To be opened and prepared for dinner. But Marisa hardly noticed. In her hands, she held a pair of heels. The very pair she had jokingly mentioned in passing when they were walking around the outlet stores that they would match the new dress he had bought her. She had been kidding because they were pricey. And now she owned them.

"If you don't like it, I can take it back."

Only then did she realize how much time had passed and still she hadn't answered him.

"Is it the wrong size or color?" he rushed on. "I thought this was the one you wanted—"

"I love it," she replied. "It's just ... you didn't have to."

He laughed, the tension releasing from his shoulders. "Don't be," he said simply. Like it settled all matters.

"But you're spending a lot on me ..."

"It took thirteen years to find you," he reminded her. "I could never make up for what I missed."

Marisa glanced downward, feeling her cheeks blush. His words were so true. It hit her suddenly. What he went through, how much time he spent looking for them, and the way she treated him when they first met. And yet she still hadn't called or thought of him as her father. Right now, she was getting to know him. She could feel him watching her, trying to make eye contact. When his hand came under her chin, she met his gaze. He looked anxious, his eyes darting everywhere. Her face must have said it all, because his eyes widen briefly.

"It wasn't your fault," he said firmly and reassuringly. "Don't ever think that. I want to do this. Let me dote."

Whether it was a loss of words or worrying her voice would crack, Marisa could only nod.

After talking more, she found out they had more in common than she thought. Along with what she already knew, they also liked a lot of the same movies, foods, interests, video games, books, and television shows. They even did some of the same actions or said the same words at the same time. As for sports, he loved to play basketball. She liked basketball but never played on a team before and didn't really know all the rules to it. She thought of her friends as the basketball players. She played during PE or sometimes after school, but more goofing off than playing.

One time, Mr. Dolton took Marisa to the park in the late afternoon and taught her how to play. She caught on quick, and he even showed her some good tricks he knew. Pretty soon they started challenging each other.

"You're good," she admitted when they stopped to take a breather. "Thanks."

"Did you ever think about becoming a professional basketball player?" she asked.

He looked over at her, shocked for a second, and smiled. "Your mother asked me the exact same question once."

"Oh really."

"Yeah," he muttered, softly. "But I wasn't really given the option."

"Oh." Marisa glanced at the ground briefly, remembering what he went through, feeling uncomfortable by accidentally bringing up the situation. He shrugged, disregarding the comment, since it wasn't intentional. No matter how hard she tried, the past always came up. "You just decided to teach instead."

"I knew a lot about computers, so I figured why not." He took a sip of water from the fountain.

"Cool."

"Ready for another round?" He picked up the basketball. "You bet." She smiled.

They spent the rest of the afternoon playing. When they were heading home, Marisa promised to try out for the team. This year's season already started so it wouldn't be until next year. This way, she could continue to practice with him and improve before trying out.

She called her mom every night to see how she was doing and make sure everything was all right. Sometimes her mom would work fewer hours and come home at a decent time if the workload wasn't too bad. Marisa worried whether she would be OK in the evenings by herself. She explained things were better between her and Mr. Dolton, which eased her mom.

The days were flying by now, faster than she anticipated. What she originally dreaded turned out perfectly fine after all. The second weekend was quickly approaching. She would return to her mom on the following Monday. But she didn't want to leave Mr. Dolton. Though she had to alternate back and forth for a year, she no longer wanted to. She didn't want to live with only one of them at a time. She wanted to live with both of her parents.

Soon, she thought. Her eyelids drifted down, opened slightly, then shut. Her head rolled to the side, nodding off. Her eyes slowly opened when she felt something move near her. Marisa glanced around. She must have fallen asleep. Her room was completely dark, the hallway light spilling into the room. Mr. Dolton placed the book she had been reading on the nightstand. He pulled the covers over her body, whereas she turned on her side into a fetal position facing him, nestling her head deeper in the pillow. "What time is it?" Her eyes closed again.

"Late," he replied. "Get some sleep."

"Night," she muffled into the pillow. Marisa felt his hand smooth away the hair from her face. His lips brushed her forehead.

"Good night," he whispered.

She heard his quiet footsteps retreat from the room. The door slowly closed, engulfing her in total darkness.

* * *

Lisa Perez tried to control her emotions. She sat on the couch in the empty house. She talked to Marisa on the phone earlier, who sounded very happy. Now Lisa found herself with free time on her hands. She was able to work less hours a few days here and there. But since Marisa left, she spent her time cleaning up the house, paying bills, and taking care of other neglected business. She caught up with everything a few days ago. Tonight she roamed, bored out of her mind. She was sick of reading, there was nothing good on television, and she didn't want to rent a movie without Marisa to enjoy it with. She realized how much her life revolved around Marisa, how much she loved and missed her. Her whole life had been about her daughter—raising her, supporting her, being there when needed emotionally.

But now Lisa wasn't needed as much. She always valued Marisa, knowing she could talk to her about whatever she wanted, whenever she felt like it. Except for her past. Marisa was right about that: she never told her daughter the whole truth, nor had she spoken about her own childhood. How could she revisit those long ago memories buried deep inside her?

Great, just what I need, she thought. Now Marisa will want to live with John permanently. She stood up again and stormed into her room.

Life hadn't been fair for Lisa. It had been hard and tragic. One thing after another kept happening. Her parents weren't the easiest in the world to please either. They wanted a strong family, a family who did well for themselves, especially her father. He was proud of his children and wanted them to be the best, since they had more opportunities than he did at their age. He wanted them to get an education and good jobs, become a manager of a company. He wanted to brag about them to his friends about how well the family was doing. Her mother was as hard as her father, demanding that they did well in school, get involved in activities, clubs, and sports—anything for a breathtaking resume.

"You never know who you'll meet," her mother often said.

They pushed her to do well in school. They questioned her about the future, antagonizing her with every little thing she did or didn't do. She always felt a heap of pressure on her shoulders to be the best in school with grades and social events. No matter how well she did, it wasn't good enough. They weren't satisfied until she made straight As or was in the top 10 percent of her class. When she made perfect honor roll, the pressure increased. She had to keep it up every semester, every year. Despite how hard the classes grew. Despite how tough the competition became.

As for career choice, she had an idea of what she wanted to do, which was similar to the job she had now. However, they wanted her to explore other career options. Fields she had no interest in. But Lisa didn't see herself as a social person, attending meaningless functions and meetings for organizations she never heard of or didn't understand what exactly they accomplished, let alone what they believe in and stood for. Nothing ever resulted from appearing at them either. These people weren't her friends. If only she could get her mom to see it. Once an interest was shown, they expected constant donations and volunteering. Always asking for participation. They never stopped, either. And it was all for what exactly? That was the part she couldn't figure out.

She wasn't the outspoken type who enjoyed attending events and youth gatherings. Her mother called it socializing, hoping Lisa would find a good boy and a future husband there. On other days it was networking, hoping Lisa could find a future job. Neither happened. Lisa considered socializing as hanging out with her friends. Between her parents nagging her about the future, the teachers telling her she can do better by applying more effort, and the daily fights with her former friends, she felt bombarded at home and school.

And she folded.

Lisa took the family photo off her dresser—the last one taken with all of them and the only one she had.

She sat on her bed and stared at the picture, gazing over them one by one. There was her dad, a strong man, the leader of the family; and her mom, considered the perfect wife and mother by the community, but controlling behind closed doors when it came to her children. Then there were her older brothers, Manuel and Joseph. Manuel was the oldest by one year and the closest to Lisa. Both of her brothers were in the upper levels at high school when Lisa was still in junior high school.

She often looked up to Manuel and admired him. He was the cool brother, the popular one at school, the one who protected her and made sure she was always happy. Whenever something bad happened, Lisa could always go to him for comfort. He made everything all right. He answered any questions she had and gave advice about life. Joseph, on the other hand, was the shy brother. Like Lisa, he was quieter and kept to himself most of the time. He enjoyed drawing and wanted to work on creating video games. But usually butted heads with her parents for allowing his studies to "fall behind," as her mother often said, since his grades didn't meet their standards.

After finishing high school, Manuel landed a promising job over the summer with an emerging business company and decided to stay instead of attending college. Oh, how he fought daily with her parents to prove he was doing well that way. And he was doing fine for a little while. He moved out of the house and into an apartment. Due to a decrease of sales in the economy, Manuel was laid off within the first year. Five months later and still jobless, he was borderline impoverished and became depressed. But he refused to give in. He didn't want to move back home, though he couldn't make ends meet. Seeing no other alternative, he ended his life. This deed shocked Lisa more than anything else. She never expected him to commit such an act.

She closed her eyes, remembering how sad and furious her parents were. Her father jeopardized the situation even more for Joseph, threatening his future education if he didn't make the grades. This was the reason why Manuel chose not to attend college, according to her parents. Joseph graduated from high school with good grades but not well enough for her father. He was no longer given the option to go to college, since the grades weren't high enough for a full-time scholarship. With all the competition, there weren't even high enough for part of a scholarship. But her father didn't see it that way and refused to get a loan for thousands of dollars. Joseph accepted a construction job for the time being. The call came a few months later, changing everything. A new worker was careless with the equipment, and Joseph was crushed to pieces.

Her parents were mournful but also shocked, outraged, and in disbelief. Two funerals for two of their children were heartbreaking. The goals and dreams they wanted were destroyed. But they became even harder on Lisa. Now all the weight was thrown on her shoulders. She would have to live up to her parents' standards and it wouldn't be easy. They were stricter than ever by the time she entered high school.

It was at that moment John entered her life. Lisa smiled, remembering how much she liked him. How handsome he was. She thought he looked even better now. How long she waited for him to notice and talk to her. He was popular back then and easy going. He could enter a room, seeming relaxed and friendly with everyone all at once. The guys would surround him, joke with him and slap him on the back. The girls stopped whatever they were doing and watched his every move, while whispering to their friends about him. Lisa loved watching his tall, lean, firm, and nicely built body race up and down the gymnasium. How he was always caught up in the precise moment, concentrating on the game.

John never seemed to have any problems making friends, for kids were always around him. But his popularity never seeped into his head. She found that aspect of him appealing. Lisa, on the other hand, was shy and had only a few close friends. Her controlling and demanding parents made her quiet around others. Many girls liked John, and she didn't think she stood a chance. She tried to act cool when he finally approached her. She was so excited when John asked her out on a date but knew her parents would never allow it. They considered her too young to be dating, stating she could date in two more years. Lisa had to make up a story for her parents to go out with him. He had been the one and only guy she ever dated.

She managed to get away with their first date, his game, saying she went with her best friends. She really did go with them to the game—she just didn't leave with them. If they were not so protective and nosy, she wouldn't have had to sneak around. But she knew each date would prove harder. That's when she decided he needed to meet her parents. She thought maybe if they met John, they would see what a great guy he was and would like him as well. Then maybe they would let them date.

Well, that didn't go as planned, she thought, remembering when he came over for dinner. They were not impressed with him. If anything, it became worse. Every night they bombarded her with several questions about where she was, who she was with, and what she did. They never believed her when she said she was with John.

"Doing what?" they asked. How long were they going to be out? When was she getting home?

Poor John, Lisa thought. She remembered when he would stop by unexpectedly or call her at night. How she had to get rid of him or get off the phone. She hated having to treat him that way—all because of her strict parents. But she knew they wouldn't let them hang out or talk on a school night. It wasn't even late either. But it was late to them.

Then the car accident happened—she discovered she was pregnant.

She had suspected but didn't get a chance to tell John first so they could figure it out and come up with a plan. Instead, everyone found out at the hospital.

Her parents were furious. They weren't going to let her screw up life like her brothers. Instead, they decide to discipline her. She wasn't allowed to see or talk to John. When she was recovering at her house, she saw him walking away through her bedroom window. Or she heard the phone ring several times unanswered. She knew it was him calling. But her parents wouldn't pick up.

Later she found out about the hearing.

How embarrassing and heartbreaking. Her own parents putting the only guy she ever liked in military school. Lisa knew she shouldn't be surprised by their actions, though. They turned coldhearted and ruthless over the years.

Lisa would never forget her father's chilling words when they came home from court that one terrible day.

"Pack your bags and get out of the house!"

Lisa was disowned at age fourteen. She never imagined life would be that way, but she had no choice, though she gladly accepted it. She was tired of being prisoner in her parent's house. She wanted to move far away hoping to start over, to never see her parents ever again. But they moved to a new place where no one knew them, meaning she didn't have to relocate. That demand was the last straw, and she no longer had any desire to see them. The plan sounded perfect, but it wasn't easy.

As the years passed, her feelings for John were ... well, she wasn't sure what they were. She thought they changed, but she no longer knew how she felt. She never expected him to track her down. One part of her liked him and cared for him deeply. Lisa smiled, remembering the few but remarkable times with him. These feelings came back when she saw him again. She couldn't believe they existed.

After all these years, he still looked good, Lisa thought. *The little tease.*

But another part of her was angry with him. She wasn't sure whose fault it was, but that didn't matter anymore. It could have been unconscious thinking or the heat of the moment, but either way it happened. That one time was somewhat blurry, but the events afterward were visibly clear enough. Getting kicked out of her house; raising a child on her own with no outside help; and no money, no job skills, no education, nothing.

Lisa's anger became the best of her when she finally saw him after all this time. She surprised herself by yelling at him, but those were her feelings. She never had a chance to speak with him alone after discovering she was pregnant. If anything, he had more reason to be angry with her. Her parents lied. Only he wasn't upset. And why not? That was the real question she needed to ask. Or better yet, why was she angry with him? She was the one whose parents lied.

She was the one whose parents sent him away.

Afterward she never thought about how she would react upon seeing him again. It didn't seem necessary. She was more shocked by his sudden appearance than anything else. No warning or anything. Now she didn't know how she felt or what to do about John. No, she wasn't being honest. With herself or with him. But that wasn't the whole issue. There was always more, always another side.

Then there was Marisa. Lisa went over in her mind the conversation they had earlier.

"Don't worry about me, Mom. I'll be just fine. Everything is getting better here. I'll see you soon."

Marisa had been good to Lisa and understood everything wasn't easy for her as a single mom. Lisa knew she wasn't the best mother, for work occupied most of her time. Even dating was out of the question for now. She wasn't worried about men right now. Marisa made life easier and Lisa wanted to concentrate on being a better mother. Everything was starting to get easier too. She received a pay raise and hoped to work fewer hours, spend more quality time with Marisa.

But with John returning, Lisa was unsure. She didn't want to lose Marisa.

Now her biggest battle was fighting over custody of Marisa. Lisa couldn't believe he won in court. His lawyer found the perfect angle. They would probably continue to see each other there for the moment. Lisa already asked for an appeal to the custody decision, but was in the waiting process.

That's all I need, Lisa thought, collapsing on her bed. *Something else to happen. How did I get in this situation?*

She stared at the ceiling, and John's face reappeared in her mind. How did she feel about him now? She was angry that he took Marisa away from her. That much she knew. But the more she thought about it, the more of a blank she drew. She couldn't hold onto the past forever.

Marisa was a blessing. If she wasn't angry because he impregnated her, then what else caused the anger? Was it really him, or was it her parents? Was he the easier target because her parents weren't here?

More importantly, how else did she feel about him?

"You still have feelings for him, don't you?" Marisa's words rang in her mind. Lisa hesitated before releasing a deep sigh. "Damn it! Yes, yes I do."

CHAPTER 18

Danny started the engine to his 1994 Ford Taurus and drove off from the side of the curb, exiting the subdivision and headed home. The night engulfed him and the quiet streets flew passed him. He shook his head roughly to wake himself, realizing he stayed later than intended. Few cars were out right now. The streetlights led the way toward his run-down apartment. It was nearly one in the morning, and the day's events caught up with him. More like the past week took a toll. Following Lisa, her kid, and John around was more work than he imagined. It filled his days and nights almost like a second job. Not that he had much else to do in his spare time, since they were constantly occupying his thoughts now.

It certainly beat anything else he would have done. Usually his nights were spent at strip clubs. For a bachelor like him, strip clubs had it all: free buffets, drinks, shows. He could smoke a cigar, play some poker, have a few drinks, and get a lap dance all at the same time. No cooking, no messes, no cleaning. After driving around all day in the sun, putting up with stupid people who were too helpless to fix anything on their own, he needed to unwind.

But he had to be careful. Once the waiters, bouncers, and girls knew him by face and what he ordered, it was time to find a new joint. The last thing he needed was for some dick to call the cops on him. Though the joint was better than some stupid hoe. They were getting too damn needy and too high-maintenance. One look at his place, and they bolted. He no longer needed them anymore. He had Lisa.

When he wasn't at a strip club, he would go to the warehouse. Tom bought it a year ago to go into business for himself. It was supposed to be a warehouse for groceries. After the plant prepared, cooked, and packaged the food, it would go to his warehouse. He would then ship out orders to stores all over the world. There was a big growth in the southeastern part, but no warehouse. Tom saw an opportunity to make some real dough. All his buddies were ready to quit their jobs and work for him. But there was some screw up. Another warehouse sprang up before the contract was signed—a temporary setback.

For now, it was their hangout. Danny could go there any time in exchange for a case of beer. He would always find at least one of his buddies there. The warehouse served many purposes. He could go at night, weekends, for a little break during the day, after work, or right before he clocked out. He learned to kill the few minutes before his shift ended rather than take on another job and get stuck working late. But he hadn't been there in a couple of weeks.

If anything, spying on John, Lisa, and the kid saved him money. He planned on following them around in the evenings after finishing up his jobs for the day. But he soon found himself keeping an eye on them all throughout the day, like a routine. He had to after discovering that he came over too late one evening to find Lisa's house completely empty. He didn't know what had happened, and it drove him crazy all night. But then he discovered the house empty the next night. He decided to drive by John's house, only to find the kid staying there.

He didn't know what to make of it since Lisa's routine never changed. He couldn't tell if it was good or bad news.

He was excited at first, thinking if the kid was gone, then Lisa would be alone in that house. Man, what he would do to get her all to himself. Oh, the endless opportunities.

The mere thought made him pant like a dog. How he would wait for the call to come over and have a home cooked meal ready to devour. How he would gather her into his arms and head over to the master bedroom. Oh yes, he already knew what he would do to her. He fantasized about it for days. But Lisa still hadn't called him. Instead, she came home late as usual each night to an empty house.

Maybe now she'll see how it feels, he thought, his bushy eyebrows furrowing.

Now he drove back and forth between their houses. Sometimes John and that kid didn't get home until late themselves. Over the weekend, the two of them were just as busy. Lisa was always leaving the house on her days off too. What were they doing? He almost entered the house when she was gone to break something and give her a reason to call him. But he chickened out. He didn't know where she went and when she would be back. If she came in to find him there, his plans would be ruined. He could only wait for now. Wait for something to happen so he could make his move. But he felt his patience running thin. Something must happen and soon.

Ben saw John and the kid the other day by chance. He nearly ran into John at the same store where he saw all three of them a few weeks ago. The first time, Ben saw them from a safe distance, allowing him the opportunity to follow Lisa and the kid. Last time he headed down an aisle only to find John with the kid. Luckily, John had his back to him. Ben quickly turned around and bolted, since he knew John would recognize him. Danny knew Lisa and the kid wouldn't recognize any of his buddies, only him. But John knew Ben and Tom. This factor could be a problem, since Danny and his buddies still looked the same after all these years. Even John.

Tom and Ben. Danny smiled at the thought of them. They used to hang out with John. But not anymore. He had them now and they turned out to be quite useful. He never learned anything about John—nothing he didn't already know, at least—but they proved their loyalty to him time and again.

Danny blew out hot air, shaking his drooping eyes. He jerked the car to keep from hitting the curb, cursing under his breath. He wasn't as young anymore as he used to be. Hell, that was why he wanted to settle down. Lisa had a nice house, all ready for him to move in. He made decent money since he worked every day, but there was no sense in spending it when he could simply move in with Lisa. That was the master plan. Now she was really alone. So why wasn't she running into his arms?

He sighed, pulling into a parking spot. He cut the engine, but made no move to get out. Instead, he remained seated in the dark, surrounded by the quiet night. He had had a long day today at his job, with stupid customers questioning his work, watching him constantly, afraid to leave him alone in their house, moving along with him in every room that he entered, or only allowing him to enter the area that needed fixing, studying him closely while each family member made excuses to be in the same room. But did anyone offer him a glass of water in this heat? No.

His boss rode his ass to get the jobs done and pick up some more. He could only sneak off in his work truck for a few minutes here and there to drive by their houses during the day, see if anything was occurring, but both houses were empty. Right after work, he changed and sped over to Lisa's house, hoping for a glimpse of that tight little body, which curved in all the right places as she walked, beckoning him.

He closed his eyes to keep himself from panting, the fantasies flooding his mind. He saw her hair spread out across the pillow, her lips pouting. She lay beneath him, pleading with her eyes for more. He knelt over her, admiring her smooth body from head to toe, before lowering himself on top of her. What he would do to her...

Danny's eyes opened again, and the vision faded.

His gaze shifted downward briefly. He would simply have to take care of that later. Right now, he should get his butt up to the cold, empty apartment that awaited him. He could always count on the stupid place to be there. With no food, no phone, no television, no furniture except an air mattress for a bed, nothing. He should get up there and crawl under the battered, worn sheets since he had a long day tomorrow.

But he lost track of time, and now he was fully awake. Between waiting for something to happen and waiting to get a glimpse of Lisa, his days were packed with running around only to wait some more. It was like she completely forgot all about him and everything he did for her. Surely, she could make time for him. She wasn't doing anything else besides working now. The kid wasn't there, so what was the deal?

He closed his eyes, and he slouched back into his seat, picturing her in his mind again. *Maybe I should stop by unexpectedly for a chat*, he thought. *No, I must remain patient. Don't want to scare her now. Oh well, first things first.* His hands slid off the wheel and landed on his lap, where he quickly took care of business.

* * *

One night, while Marisa watched television with Mr. Dolton in the living room, she started to miss her mom. Her two weeks were almost up, but now that she knew Mr. Dolton better, she didn't want to leave him. She wasn't use to having a father. This last week and a half showed her what she missed out on. What she really wanted was for him and her mom to get back together. Her mom still cared for him. She had to, after admitting her parents already lied once in court. *Maybe if they could get back together*, she thought, *the three of us could be one big happy family.*

"What's wrong?" Mr. Dolton asked. "I miss Mom."

"That makes two of us." He sighed. "Can I ask you something?"

"Sure."

"If you were ..." She paused. How to ask the question delicately? "If you were ... away for thirteen years and recently started working as a teacher here, how were you able to afford this place?"

"This house belonged to my parents," he replied. "They died a few months ago. I inherited this house, their money, and their assets."

"Oh." She never knew his parents were dead. Poor guy. That was why he wanted to get back with the two of them; they were the only family he had left. "Sorry to hear that."

"Everything is still the same way they had it." "Really?"

He nodded. "The house was left untouched. I moved back in, fixed it up, sorted out all their stuff, and started looking for a job."

"I see." He referred to the furniture in this house and the old pictures of his family on the walls. She glanced around the living room, taking in all the belongings. He kept everything the same. "How did your parents die?"

"Car accident." He glanced briefly at the floor. "Not sure what happened."

"Oh." Marisa became silent, not quite knowing how to respond. What was she supposed to say? He just lost his parents. Maybe it was better to change the subject. Find out other things about his life that she didn't know. "Do you have any siblings?"

"Nope."

"How old are you?" "Twenty-eight."

"Man, I'm half your age," she said. "That's crazy. No, that's right, because my mom will be turning twenty-eight soon." She paused. "How were you able to get a teaching job?"

"There was a job opening, and I applied." He shrugged. "I was lucky; I came at the right time."

Her eyebrows scrunched over. "But weren't you a substitute originally?" She remembered he substituted for another teacher before landing the job.

"Yes." He nodded. "Another teacher had to leave on short notice. They ended up moving a teacher to that subject and hired me."

"You mean Mrs. Saltinee left, and Mrs. Hager took her spot, whereas you took Mrs. Hager's spot."

"Exactly."

Another thought occurred to her. None of the other students knew they were related besides her friends. But what about the teachers or staff? "Does the principal or any of the teachers know that you're my father?"

"No," he said. "They didn't need to know either. Thought I'd wait to see if I could work it out with you two first."

That made sense. "You have never taught before?" she asked.

"Nope." He shrugged like it was no big deal.

"Have you always wanted to teach?"

"I never planned on teaching," he admitted. "But I enjoy it. I wanted to do something different since I got out of the air force. I have an IT background, so I thought I could try it."

Her eyebrows widened briefly. The more she talked to him, the more she discovered what she didn't know. "You were in the air force."

"I joined after military school." He took a sip of his soda. "I was able to go to college and work. I was relocated a few times. Got to travel and see the world."

"Oh wow!" she exclaimed. She couldn't believe how much he had accomplished at once. "Surprised you came back and settled down here."

"Well, my parents lived here so I would come visit when I could," he said. "But a part of me always wondered about you too. About where you were. If you were still here. I found I was always pulled back to this place. I just ... I had to know. I had to know about your mother and you. I didn't even know if I had a son or daughter. I just couldn't leave until I knew about you guys."

Her eyebrows scrunched over. "When you first came here, how did you know how to get to me and talk to my mom, and how did you know who your daughter was right away?" Ever since Mr. Dolton first saw Marisa, it seemed like he knew she was his daughter all along. He gave her a detention slip on his first day of teaching. After that he always wanted to talk to her mom. She was suspicious, but only for a little while, since everything happened fast.

Mr. Dolton smiled. "When you first entered my classroom, I knew it was you." "How?"

"You came out looking like your mom," he replied, getting up. He walked over to a closet, grabbed something off the top shelf, and then returned to the couch. He held what looked like an old yearbook. He opened it to a certain page and showed Marisa a picture of a young, beautiful teenage girl. "That's your mom."

"That's Mom!" she exclaimed. "Yes."

"She's gorgeous."

"And you look exactly like her." He studied the picture, and his brow furrowed. "Who is Ramirez? You and your mom go by Perez, but this year book says Ramirez."

"Ramirez is my mom's real last name," she said. "She told me that Perez is my grandma's maiden name. She changed both our names to Perez when I was born."

"Because of me?"

Marisa winced, hearing the hurt in his voice. "I honestly don't know." She shrugged. "She never told me why."

"How long have you been living here in Rorertown?"

"As long as I can remember," she answered. "I was born and raised here." "Hmm." He looked at the yearbook again.

"Huh?" She also gazed at it. The front cover said in bold letters, Rorertown High School. "That's the high school down the street. You two met there?"

He nodded. "You've lived here the entire time?"

"Yeah ... no." She paused. "We lived in an apartment for a little while when I was younger, but that was a couple of streets down."

"But you've lived in this area?" "Oh yeah."

"Well, that's how I knew it was you," Mr. Dolton said. "I wanted to talk to your mom and decided to get you in trouble."

Her mouth dropped open. "So you gave me that detention slip for nothing?" she asked. "And that's why you kept getting me in trouble."

He smiled. "Did you even look at the slip? I didn't write down why you received it. I never recorded it either, so you have nothing to worry about."

She buried her face into her hands. "You're kidding, right?" "Nope."

"You had everything planned out, huh?" She looked up at him and smiled.

"No." He shook his head. "There were a few times I went too far. I could tell you were suspicious. Trying to win you over took longer than I thought."

"Any kid would have been wary," she added. Quickly. Too quickly. Trying to cover how bad she felt for acting how she did. "You were acting a little weird, always staring at me, tracking me down, wanting to talk to me or wanting to talk to my mom."

"True," he said smiling. "I couldn't help it. You looked just like your mom. And I finally got to see you. I just wanted to talk to you and see how you were doing. And I wanted to see your mom and talk to her... or try to talk to her."

A silence washed over them. Marisa didn't know what to say, and Mr. Dolton frowned.

How could she reply to that comment? She couldn't defend her mom and take her side after hearing everything he told her. Both of their stories were complicated enough.

"Let me get this straight," she said. "Everything you have done after seeing me the first time has been connected with getting back with us?"

"Of course."

She looked at him, her eyebrows raised. He wanted to get back with her mom, yet he already gave up. What was the problem? "But if you want to talk to my mom, then how come you haven't?"

"I tried, but I don't know what else to do." He sighed, leaning back against the cushions on the couch.

"Ask her on a date," she suggested. "She'll say no."

"How do you know that?" she asked. "You haven't even asked."

"She won't even talk to me," he pointed out. "Why would she go on a date with me? I contacted her several times, but she always cuts me off."

"But I want you to get back with her," she said. "Don't get me wrong. I like living with you, but I also need to take care of my mom. I'm sure she's lonely right now. Besides, the two of you were in a relationship before. You belong together."

The comment lit up Mr. Dolton's eyes, looking happy and relieved. His face focused on the coffee table for a moment, before turning back to her.

"What?"

"If you can get us back together, I'll drop the joint-custody charges."

Nodding her head, she answered, "Deal." Marisa leaned over and kissed him on the cheek. He gave her a double look, appearing shocked at first. She wrapped her arms around him, her head resting on his shoulder. Then he smiled. Lowering his head, he kissed her on the forehead.

It felt incredible to have a father. Someone to hold and snuggle up to. Once she could get her parents back together, everything would be all right. It wouldn't be easy, but worth it. Whether or not her mom wanted to admit it, she still had feelings for Mr. Dolton. Otherwise she wouldn't have been with him in the first place. Her mom needed the feelings to be brought out, to see the side of him that Marisa saw the last two weeks, the side of him that she fell in love with originally.

It would be hard to see since so much had happened in the past, especially after Mr.Dolton reappeared when her mom least expected it. She needed to forget about what happened in the past and start a whole new relationship with him. And Marisa would be the one to make it happen.

CHAPTER 19

During lunch the next day, Marisa brought up the subject of her mom and Mr. Dolton to her friends since she needed some ideas. "I need to figure out how to get my mom and Mr. Dolton back together."

"I thought you liked living with him," Mark said, rubbing his eyes.

"I do," she said. "That's why I want them back together because I like living with both of them. They belong together." She paused. "Deep down inside, I know my mom likes him but doesn't want to admit it. She can't seem to forget the past."

"Tell them to go meet you someplace at the same time, and they'll run into each other," Patty suggested.

"That's perfect," Jenni agreed. "No, that won't work."

"Why not?" Sean draped his arm over Patty's shoulder.

"Because they don't need to run into each other," Marisa interjected. "They've run into each other plenty of times and it hasn't worked. They need to get back together like they were in the past."

"Didn't Mr. Dolton say he would drop the charges if you would get them back together?" Jeff asked.

"Yeah."

"There you have it," Jeff said. "Have your mom go on a date with him, and he'll drop the charges. Your mom would agree to get you back. One date should rekindle the relationship."

She thought about what Jeff said. She hadn't considered the option last night when Mr. Dolton mentioned it. Jeff was right: her mom would agree to one date so she could live with her again. "That might work."

"Did you ever have any doubt in me?" Jeff asked.

"Not anymore." She smiled, and he wrapped his arms around her.

After school Marisa stopped by Mr. Dolton's room to see if he could join her to watch the practice. He had work to do, but promised to be done by the time it ended. She agreed to meet him at the house and headed over to the gymnasium. She considered telling him the plan but decided to wait until tonight, when he had fewer distractions. She found a seat among the crowded bleachers right when her friends piled out of the locker room. Jenni stood off to one side with the other cheerleaders, practicing their routine.

Her friends began their warm-ups on the court. The teams won their first game. Now they were preparing for the next game. She smiled, drooling over her man race around the court. Jeff caught her watching a few times, smiling back and shaking his head. Jenni joined Marisa's side after the first hour, and they continued watching their friends. She longed to join the basketball team, studying their movements, but she knew it was too late. The season already started, and she recently learned how to play. Instead, she would practice on her own and try out next year.

Maybe we can get a basketball hoop, she thought. *My friends and I could practice together after school and during the summer in the off-season.*

When practice ended, she and Jenni joined their friends, piling out of the locker room refreshed. The six of them filed out of the gymnasium together, talking and laughing. As they exited the building, the big group split up into three pairs. Marisa said bye to her friends, and Jeff grabbed her hand, leading the way to Mr. Dolton's house.

"Have you told him yet?"

"Nope," she replied. "I'll wait until he gets home. He should be finished by now."

They crossed the street and she lifted her head high. A slight wind arrived that morning, making the air nice and cool, blowing through her hair. She glanced over at Jeff, realizing how much he meant to her. How much she cared for him. He walked her home every day, visited with her, and took her out on a few dates. He hung out at her other house once, but that was it. Yet during all this time, he had never been over for dinner. They were serious as a couple, together at least a month now.

He caught her gaze and held it, stopping in his tracks and squeezed her hand. She also stopped walking, facing him. They had reached the subdivision, but not Mr. Dolton's house. "What's up?"

"You've never stayed for dinner," she blurted out.

His eyebrows scrunched over for a moment before he broke out into a smile. "You're so cute."

"You've met my parents, but you've never stayed over for dinner," she repeated.

He didn't reply at first, but studied her face instead. Seeing that her expression remained unchanged, his smile slowly disappeared. "I know," he said softly. "That's fine. There's plenty of time. No need to rush."

She hesitated. How could he stay for dinner with one only parent? That wouldn't be fair or right, not to him or her mom and Mr. Dolton. They both knew him, though Mr. Dolton knew him better since he saw him more often. But neither her mom nor Mr. Dolton ever asked him to stay for dinner. Maybe it was better to wait until they were one happy family. "Maybe once they get back together."

Jeff nodded. "Sounds good. You still need to meet my parents too."

"Speaking of parents," Marisa said, spotting Mr. Dolton's car turn into the subdivision. He waved while driving by and pulled into the driveway.

"Come on." Jeff grabbed her hand again and they resumed walking toward the house. Mr. Dolton stepped out of the car. "Hey, Mr. D, I brought you a present."

She laughed. Jeff cupped her elbow, leading her up the front lawn. She smacked him on the arm and Mr. Dolton rolled his eyes. They stopped near the front porch, whereas Mr. Dolton remained by his car getting some things out. They turned away slightly for some privacy.

"Call me tonight," Jeff whispered in her ear. "I want to see if my brilliant plan works." "OK, bye," she said.

"Bye, Mister D."

"Bye, Jeff. See you tomorrow."

Marisa watched Jeff retreat from the front lawn and retrace his steps, heading out the subdivision. She smiled, feeling herself blush when a door closed behind her. She turned around to discover Mr. Dolton watching her. He approached the front porch. "Did you need any help?"

"No." His gaze never wavered. "What?"

"Nothing." He passed her and stopped outside the front door.

He was watching us, she thought.

Her face grew even hotter by the mere thought of Mr. Dolton seeing her with Jeff. They didn't do anything, and he already knew they were a couple. He read the note when Jeff asked her out. She released a deep breath, knowing it was another subject she would deal with eventually. Her boyfriend. Her mom still wanted to talk about the issue. Now Mr. Dolton would want to discuss it, too.

Oh man. She shook her head. They needed to get back together soon. I don't want this conversation twice. Marisa walked to the front door and stopped next to Mr. Dolton. He fished out the house key from his bag. "You like Jeff, right?"

Mr. Dolton smiled, unlocking the door and holding it open for her. "Yes, he's a good guy."

Releasing a deep breath, she entered the house and headed straight to her room. Dropping her bag on the desk chair, she heard him moving around the house. It was time to reveal the plan. But she wasn't sure how to approach it. Should she simply tell him straight up? She sat on the bed, thinking everything over. It was a school night and the two of them had a date to go on, though they didn't know yet. He would do anything right now to get back with her mom. This plan had to work for the three of them. If her mom agreed to the date and all went well …

Jumping up from the bed, she snatched up her book bag and dumped out the contents. She grabbed some clothes, toiletries, a book, and a magazine, stuffing them in there just in case. Satisfied that she was prepared, she picked up her bag and exited the room. Marisa entered the living room and threw the bag on the armchair near the front door. Hearing Mr. Dolton in the kitchen, she ventured that way.

"I know how to get you and mom back together," she announced upon entering the kitchen.

He had his back to her, holding the refrigerator door open. He turned around, facing her. "How?"

"Tell her if she goes on a date with you, you'll drop the custody charges," she replied. "She won't agree to that."

"Oh, I'm sure she would," she told him. "If she does, the rest is up to you." "OK." He shut the refrigerator door. "Let's go tell her!"

He grabbed her arm, cupping her elbow, and led her out of the kitchen. As they passed the living room, he snatched up his keys and wallet from the coffee table, never breaking his stride. She remembered her book bag on the armchair by the time he ushered her out the front door.

"Wait a second," she said, getting out of his grip. She turned around and reentered the house, grabbed her book bag, and dashed outside to find him already behind the wheel. *He sure was excited*, she thought, locking up.

Sprinting to the car, she climbed in and he took off. They practically flew to her house. On the way over, she could tell he was nervous because he kept asking how he looked. When they were close, she glanced at her watch. It was nearly seven. She hoped her mom was home by now.

They reached her house to find her mom's car parked in the driveway. Mr. Dolton parked next to it and cut the engine. Gripping her book bag, Marisa fished out her house key, and they approached the front door. She unlocked it and opened the door upon the quiet house. The hall and living room lights were on, though they remained unoccupied. Mr. Dolton stayed right at her heels. She entered the house, dropping the bag on the armchair near the door. She heard noises in the kitchen, seeing the light emerge from the bottom of the door. She looked over her shoulder and pressed a finger to her lips, informing Mr. Dolton to keep quiet. He nodded, closing the front door behind him softly. She tiptoed to the kitchen and swung the door open, discovering her mom standing near the oven with her back to them.

"Hey, Mom," she shouted.

Her mom nearly jumped at the noise, and she burst out laughing. Turning around, her mom's eyes gleamed at the sight of Marisa. She ran over and embraced her, holding her tightly for what seemed like an eternity. Soon Marisa found herself hugging her mom the same way. How she had missed her. "Marisa." Her mom pulled away. "I thought you weren't supposed to come back for three more days. Oh, don't tell me I lost track …" Her mom's voice trailed off upon seeing Mr. Dolton.

She looked over her shoulder to find him standing near the kitchen door, staring at the floor. He peeked at the two of them, seeming a little bit nervous and apprehensive. He opened his mouth a few times, only to shut it.

Now he acts shy. She rolled her eyes. She had to tell the plan if they wanted it to work. She glanced at her mom, who appeared uncomfortable, too. A silence washed over the house. Her mom and Mr. Dolton continued to sneak glances at each other while she watched them. Her mom started to say something to him, but she jumped in. "I know how to get Mr. Dolton to drop the charges."

"How?"

"Go on a date with him."

"Did he tell you that?" Her mom glared at him. "No, Mom," she said. "Just one date. Please."

Her mom hesitated, looking between Mr. Dolton and Marisa. She finally answered, "Oh, all right."

Yes, she thought, and quickly walked around to the other side of her mom. She had to act before anyone changed his or her mind. "I'll stay here." She ushered them out the kitchen. "You kids go out. Don't stay out too late. Don't drink and drive. Have fun, but not too much."

Her mom threw her the look. The three of them walked through the living room, Marisa's pace never slowing. She grabbed her mom's purse from the coffee table, motioning them forward with her hands. Thrusting the purse in her mom's hands, she continued crowding them until they reached the front door. Mr. Dolton opened it, and her mom stopped in her tracks. Marisa kept pushing them onward until her mom held onto the doorway with both hands, standing her ground. She looked up to find both of them peering at her, forcing her movements to cease. She smiled back.

"Will you be all right by yourself?" her mom asked. "I'll be fine."

"Bye," Mr. Dolton said. "Have fun."

Marisa held her breath, watching them exited the house side by side. When the front door closed, she released a sigh of relief. It was up to Mr. Dolton now.

* * *

Danny sat in his car, gripping the steering wheel so hard his white knuckles reflected in the moonlight. Breathe, damn it! Breathe. He took a deep breath and slowly released it. His fingers relaxed, uncoiling from the steering wheel. He continued watching John and Lisa from across the street. They were heading to John's car. A moment of panic seized him for an instant, but only an instant.

Remain calm, he thought, then ducked slightly in his seat. He focused his eyes on Lisa, noticing her facial expression. You might not have to react yet.

Her eyes seemed to dart around her, not really seeing anything. Like her thoughts preoccupied her mind. She didn't seem happy about leaving with John. Wherever they were going. No, not too happy at all. She remained indifferent, trying to be polite in her gestures. Danny's eyes moved to John, who was eager to please. John, who ran ahead to open the door for her, nearly stumbling over himself. Skinny, slim John, who tried to hide the ecstatic look on his face. He was happy; she was not. So where were they going?

Danny watched John now climb behind the driver's seat and start the engine. Panic seized him again, debating what to do. His hand moved to the ignition, where the key sat ready. Should I follow them? Quick, think. They're about to leave. His hand released the key, rested on the steering wheel. He watched the car reverse from the driveway and take off down the street. He looked back at the quiet house, seeing only a few lights on through the windows. This might be the moment I've been waiting for.

He knew the kid was inside alone, since he saw her enter with John. Like before, he didn't know what had been said. But he could easily guess with John's goofy grin and Lisa's pissed off controlled look. John was probably trying to win her over. Take her out on a nice date somewhere. Make up for old times.

Danny slammed the steering wheel with his fist, hard and fast, but lucky enough to miss the horn. All his waiting, all his efforts in following them around, all his work for Lisa. And for what? To have his plans crumble before his eyes? He reached his boiling point, his patience no longer intact. He had *had* enough. This wasn't the way it should have worked out. He was tired of waiting around. It was time to take matters into his hands.

This wasn't good. He opened the car door and snatched out the key. *Oh, Johnny boy. This wasn't good at all, especially for you. Things were going too well. You were better off leaving her alone and just worrying about that kid. Now I get to have a little fun.* Danny stepped out of the car quietly and closed the door. He glanced up and down the street until satisfied that all was quiet around him. All indeed.

No one was in sight. Houses stood silent, lights dim and few in between. The neighbors were inside minding their own business like they should be. He made his way up the front lawn, careful to avoid the streetlights, staying in the shadow. Calm and collected, his mind raced on the possibilities. Oh, the possibilities were endless. He would take his time too. They barely left, which meant a couple of hours to kill, passing the time with the kid.

He stopped in his tracks, perched on the front porch, hidden in the dark corner. He contemplated how he would make his grand entrance. How he would appear with the kid when the two parents came home. Should he call his buddies for help? They could meet at the warehouse in twenty minutes. Show up together and ambush the kid.

Nah, he thought. He could handle this just fine. He could handle the three of them perfectly. Oh, what a pleasure it would be too. He could take on all three of them easily. John was fast on his feet—that was all Danny knew. But Danny had years on him. Danny had experience from doing time, doing jobs, and doing the fighting. Always doing the fighting.

Danny had the weight and the muscles on his side. Slim, perfect John would be too occupied trying to win Lisa and caught off guard.

This will be fun indeed.

*　*　*

Marisa locked the door and jumped up and down, cheering. She couldn't believe the plan worked. Her parents were going on a date! She stopped in her tracks, realizing how she thought of them. Her parents. Should she start calling Mr. Dolton her dad, since he was her dad? Maybe it was time she did. She knew him better now and liked him a lot. He earned the title.

Strolling into the kitchen, she approached the oven to see what her mom started cooking. Since she wasn't hungry, she turned off the appliances, sampling bits of food here and there. She left the kitchen and entered her old room, shutting the door behind her and flopping on the bed. It was good to be back in her room again. Everything was the way she left it, so she started rummaging around for something to do.

Oh, I need to call Jeff, she thought, but decided to call him after her parents returned so she could tell him all the details. She turned on some background music, picked up a magazine from her desk and flopped back on her bed. She started to flip through it when a noise came from the living room. She paused in her movements, listening for it again, but didn't hear anything.

I must have been imagining it, she thought. She continued browsing through the pages and heard the noise again. It sounded like a footstep. She leaned over the bed and lowered the music.

Creak.

There it was again. It was a footstep. *Is someone in the house? It couldn't be my parents. It better not be them*, she thought. *They just left. So who is it?* Dropping the magazine,

Marisa stood up quietly and walked up to her door. Who could that be?

She opened it slowly in order not to make any noise. Peering into the living room, she scanned the surroundings carefully but didn't see anything. She tiptoed over to the kitchen doorway and opened it while looking inside. Nothing. That was weird. She could have sworn she heard something. Maybe it was just my imagination.

Marisa turned around to reenter her room, when something grabbed her from behind, making her cry out.

CHAPTER 20

John and Lisa were officially on their date. John decided where to take her for a romantic evening and headed toward Saint Elois. "You hungry?" he asked, gazing over at her.

"Yes."

They became silent for a little while. John took a deep breath, trying not to be nervous. "Is Romano's OK?"

"It's fine."

Another silence washed over them. He looked over at Lisa studying her. She stared straight ahead. Feeling his gaze, she glanced down and turned her attention out the side window. John fixed his eyes back on the road, sighing. He didn't know what to do or say, since the restaurant was a good twenty-minute drive. But he wanted to take her somewhere special for just the two of them, and this was the closest fancy restaurant he could think of. There were other choices, of course, but he didn't know what her favorite restaurant was. He doubted she would be any help. Now that he thought about it, he didn't know much about Lisa. He never had the chance to learn. Too much time passed between them. He loved her, but he also knew they were practically strangers to each other. They had much to catch up on to make up for the lost time.

He peeked at her again. She stared out the window the same way Marisa did the day she moved in with him. John swallowed, seeing the resemblance between Lisa and his daughter clearly. He opened his mouth, shut it, opened it, and shut it again. There was so much he wanted to say, so much he held on to, but he didn't know where to begin. *Great, how am I going to make conversation when we sit down if I'm having trouble already?* John thought.

He stepped on the gas.

They arrived at the restaurant, and he pulled into a parking spot. As soon as the engine cut, Lisa opened the door and stepped out of the vehicle. John jumped out of the car, sprinting to keep up with her pace. By the time he fell into stride with her, they entered the restaurant and were seated in a booth right away. They had some small talk, mostly about the weather and scenery, so the ride didn't turn out too bad. But there was still some ice to break. And he had to do it.

"What have you been up to lately?" he asked.

"Mostly work," Lisa replied. She picked up a menu and held it up to where it blocked her face.

"Marisa says you're an executive assistant," John said to the menu. "Yes."

They became hushed again, with John not knowing what to say. The silence was frustrating. His eyes lit up, thinking of something that would break the quietness and answer some questions about the two of them. "Do you remember the last time we saw each other? In the hospital?"

Lisa dropped the menu. "Yeah?" Her face appeared shocked, meeting his gaze. He had her attention now.

"What happened after?"

"What do you mean?" she asked.

"That was the last time I ever heard from you," he continued. "I called several times. I stopped by your house. I wrote you several letters when I was at the school."

Her eyes darted back and forth before meeting his gaze again. "You wrote me letters?"

The waitress appeared and took their order.

"Yeah," John said. "Tons of letters asking how you were doing and where the school was. I couldn't leave the premises, but I was hoping you'd come visit or make a phone call. Something that told me you were OK."

"I…" She hesitated for a moment. "I didn't know about the letters. I never got them."

"Your parents," John concluded.

"It was all them," Lisa said. "I know you called and stopped by. I was grounded." Her cheeks turned pink. "They wouldn't let me answer the phone or come to the door."

"They didn't even open the door," he told her.

She shook her head. "I swear that I never knew you wrote me, and I didn't know where you were. They must have thrown away the letters."

He gave Lisa a double look, not quite sure what he heard. Now the real question. But how to ask? "Why did they press charges against me and send me away?" He said slowly and softly in order not to sound accusing. "I just… I don't see how that helped either of us, especially when you were pregnant."

"No, it didn't," Lisa confessed. "It was the worst thing they could do. They lied in court and made up the story of you taking advantage of me. They threatened to disown me." She paused and glanced at the table, then back up at John. "And then they kicked me out of the house because I allowed myself to get pregnant. I haven't seen them since."

"You're kidding!"

"No. That's why I work tons of hours almost every day. One time I had three jobs to support Marisa."

"That's terrible." John shook his head in disbelief and disgust. His face hardened by the mere thought of her parents. How she was kicked out of the house. How she was forced to work hard for Marisa. *That should have been me working hard for the two of them*, he thought. I would have done whatever was necessary to support my family.

The food came, lightening the mood. They dug into their meals.

He braced himself for the next question. He had to know. "Are you still mad at me?" She didn't reply at first, and he held his breath. His fork sat suspended in the air.

"I was when you took Marisa away," Lisa said, whereas his face winced, but then she chuckled, and he relaxed. "No, I'm not mad. Sorry about yelling. I was shocked that you found us, and I had told Marisa something different."

"Why did you lie to her?"

"What could I say?" She shrugged. "I slept with a guy when I was her age. What kind of example is that? Next thing I know, she'll sleep with every guy in town."

"I suppose you're right." He hesitated, searching for the right words. "But you do know that I would have helped you in raising Marisa, right?"

Lisa looked up at him, eyes wide.

"I should've been working three jobs to support you and Marisa," John said. "I would've done whatever it took. Stayed by your side. There wasn't a need for the court cases or for sending me away. That's why it took me so long to find you. I didn't know where you lived."

Lisa snorted, shaking her head before a quiet sob escaped her mouth. Her shoulders drooped and her eyes dropped to the table. "Believe me, I wasn't happy with my parents' decision," she admitted. "I was furious. Lying in court, sending you off, and kicking me out of the house. I would have done anything but what they did. After all that, I couldn't bring myself to ever see you again." She glanced up, making eye contact. "I'm ashamed of my own parents."

John remained silent, listening to her.

"Do you remember our dates?" she asked. "When you walked me home? At the mall before we went to your house?"

He nodded. "I kept glancing at my watch, keeping track of the time. You asked me why?"

His eyes lit up. He remembered. "Yes I do. Thought I had done something wrong."

She shook her head. "It was because of them. They were so strict. I had to lie to see you. Otherwise I couldn't have gone out. They wouldn't let me date. Even meeting you didn't help."

"What did you tell them?" he asked out of curiosity.

"That I was with my friends." She took a deep breath. "My parents were so hard on me and continued to disappoint me." She set her fork down. He wasn't eating either. "I heard from an old acquaintance that they had sold their house and moved away a few months after kicking me out, so I stayed here. They were another reason why I lied to Marisa about you. I was embarrassed by their behavior. Not giving you a chance. And it went downhill after that, but I honestly never thought I would see you again."

"All this time you lived here?" He raised an eyebrow.

"Yes." She nodded. "When my parents first kicked me out, I lived in a community shelter that helps young girls who are pregnant or have children but no help. Once I had a steady job and a little money, I moved to an apartment, and then to the house I have now. But I always remained in this area."

"We live so close to one another," John pointed out. "Surprised we never ran into each other before."

"I've never had a reason to enter your subdivision until now." She took a bite of her meal.

"True, but I mean at the stores and restaurants around here," John clarified. He took a sip of his drink, almost forgetting the food in front of them. "The first time I saw you was at the supercenter a few weeks ago."

She paused, looking up at him. "That's your parents' house, isn't it?"

He nodded, waiting for her to ask. It was getting easier to anticipate the question.

Sometimes knowing made it easier to discuss. Sooner or later, someone would ask. "I thought it looked familiar," she said. "Did they move?"

"I inherited their house and assets after they passed away..." he said softly.

"Oh, John." She covered her mouth with her hand. "I'm so sorry. What happened?" "Car accident."

Her eyebrows scrunched over. "When?" "A few months ago."

"I'm so sorry, John," Lisa murmured, her eyes darting all over his face. "I never knew." John threw his hand up, dismissing it. Better to dismiss it rather than dwell on it. Besides, now was the time to make his move. "If we could go back in time, how would things be?"

"If my parents hadn't sent you away, I would've accepted your help in raising Marisa." "What about us?" He leaned toward her.

"I would've stayed with you no matter what." Lisa blushed, and John smiled.

* * *

Someone stood behind her, holding her in place against her will. Marisa knew it was a person, a man by his strength, who wrapped their arms underneath her armpits and curled them upward over her shoulders. She started to scream, when one hand reached up and clamped over her mouth. The other hand folded around her neck.

"Scream, and I'll break your neck," a deep voice whispered in her ear.

She shut her mouth, whimpering. Panic seized her. The hands returned to her shoulders, steering her around until they faced the kitchen. The man used his body to push her forward, to get her walking. Her eyes darted around the house, looking for a way to escape. She grimaced, realizing that the man was big and muscular, when feeling his arms, chest, and legs brush against her backside. He guided her toward the kitchen, remaining behind her every step. She could feel his heart pounding viciously in his chest, and his hot, reeking breath on her neck. He smelled like sweat, urine, and beer. She held her breath, struggling not to gag from the stench.

Her choices were limited—walk or get run over. His hands kept veering her forward every time her pace slackened. The kitchen door stood in front of them. Marisa froze, knowing what kind of weapons the kitchen contained: knifes, pots, pans, all types of tools that could be used on her. Her mind raced over what someone could do with those tools to another human being. She heard stories on the news, read them in the newspaper and magazines. She heard plenty of stories, all right. Soon, her heart pounded in her chest, echoing in her eardrums. Sweat broke out on her forehead and neck.

Grunting, Marisa tried to struggle from the grip, but the man holding her was strong. She brought her hands up and over her head, clawing at his head, his arms, his neck—whatever she could get a hold of, trying to get him to let go of her. She leaned her head back to look at the man's face while scratching his arms, withering her legs and hands around. But he had on a ski mask and wore all black. She bent her leg back hard, smacking something solid and making the man grunt.

What's going on? she thought. *Who is this person? Why are they doing this?* The arms pulled together, fast and hard, shooting a bolt of pain. She felt her body crushed inward. Her arms slackened, falling by her sides, feeling limp, numb and stinging with fire.

"We can do this the easy way or the hard way," the deep voice continued. His thick, call used fingers traced up her neck, moving a strand of hair behind one ear. "If you cooperate, I won't hurt you. If you don't, I'll have to restrain you. We have some time before they get home. What's it going to be?"

Her eyes lit up when hearing the words. Not simply for their meaning; she knew he referred to her parents. She didn't want to think about that right now. What he might do to her before they came home. He was right—she would be alone for a few hours. But it was something else that caught her attention. Something irked in the back of her mind. She thought for a second that the voice sounded familiar.

Her head turned, looking over her shoulder at the ski mask and right at the eyes. The face averted her stare, looking the opposite way, and the arm unwound itself from around her. Marisa kept turning, trying to see their eyes as their bodies dipped together to the left slightly for a moment.

I know those eyes, she thought, straining to see when something hit the back of her head.

The surroundings slowly turned to black.

Marisa's eyes fluttered open, then shut, in focus, then blurry. A fierce headache pounded the back of her head. She moaned and stirred, only to taste a rag wedged between her teeth while her limbs felt asleep. Her eyes burst open. Her bearings came into focus, only to stare directly at her lap. Lifting her head, she faced the kitchen door. She tried to move her arms and legs around, thinking they had fallen asleep. But she couldn't. She glanced over her shoulder, spotting the rope around her wrists that were tied together behind her back. She moved her head forward, looking at her feet, where the rope wrapped around her ankles tight and secure.

She groaned and concentrated on flexing her hands and feet to gain back her movement.

The voice spoke from the left side, startling her. "You're not trying to escape, are you?"

Marisa turned her face to the voice, having forgotten all about them. There he stood, big and muscular, like she guessed, decked out entirely in black. The eyes and lips stared out of the ski mask, the gloved fingers laced together.

She shook her head no and narrowed her eyes, meeting his gaze.

He looked away. "Don't look at my eyes! I don't want to hurt you, kid. If you promise not to scream, I'll take off the gag. And if you promise not to escape, I won't hurt you. Can you promise me?"

She nodded, staring at the ground. The kitchen lights bounced off the walls. The rest of the house beyond the door sounded eerily quiet, empty. Dark. The clock ticked off the seconds. The house had only the kitchen light on and her bedroom light on. Her head tilted to the side, straining to hear the music. She listened hard and carefully, holding her breath before softly hearing it play in her bedroom.

"Don't look at me," the voice said. They slowly approached her, making a wide circle around the chair set in the middle of the kitchen.

Her eyes shifted to the ground, concentrating on how the house looked before she knocked out. How the house appeared when her parents left. His gloved fingers slithered into her peripheral vision, tugging on the rag at the back of her head. A few tugs and the rag fell onto her lap. Marisa closed her mouth, swallowed a few times, and stretched her jaw. A rotten taste remained—sour and raw. She returned to the one nagging thought that continued to surface.

How the house would appear when her parents came home.

His footsteps retreated to his place in the corner of the kitchen, standing wedged between the door and the counter. She sneaked a peek at him sideways while looking over the surroundings to see what else changed.

"I saw that," he barked. "There's no need to look at me. You already know who I am, don't you, kid?"

Marisa swallowed and then belatedly nodded. She knew all right. And she was not as surprised anymore. She peered at the kitchen door, seeing beyond it into the rest of the house. How many lights were on? The front-porch light, the front hallway light, her bedroom light, and the kitchen light. The usual lights were on. But the music was on in her room. The door should be open, revealing it was empty.

"Good." His eyes watched her. "Now I have some questions for you. And I need some answers."

When her parents came home, they would be led straight into the kitchen where she sat bound up. She then realized why he remained hidden. The door opened inward, meaning he would be concealed until they were inside the kitchen, until they reached her in a panic and started untying her. Her cheeks burned upon revealing his plan.

She was his bait!

His voice continued to ramble in the background. *I must stall him*, she thought, glancing at the clock. It won't be much longer now. I must create a lot of noise, or he'll hear when they arrive.

"I asked you a question, kid," the voice bellowed in her ear.

She shook herself and jerked her head upward, having forgotten that he had been speaking. "I'm sorry, but can I have some water, please?" she said instead. "I'm really thirsty."

"Answer the question," he ordered, sounding irritated and impatient. "Where did your parents go?"

She blinked a couple of times. "I don't know."

"Don't lie to me," the voice came closer, yelling into her ear.

Marisa flinched seeing the hands slither out toward her. "They went on a date," she yelled out, loud enough to freeze his movements. "But I don't know where."

"When will they get back?" the voice whispered, calm and collected. He hid again.

"I don't know."

I need to make some noise, somehow or someway. I need to set him off, she thought, veering her eyes out in front of her.

"You need to give me some answers," he bellowed, sounding agitated.

"You said you wouldn't hurt me," she answered, once spotting him move away from the corner and toward her. Marisa's body stiffened straight up after hearing the words echo in her ears. Those words sounded vaguely familiar. She heard those words before. Very recently. *Think, think already.*

His hands came out from his sides, and he circled around her. Her eyes opened wide and her head rose to the front door. That was where she needed him, directly in front of her. Then it clicked when he crossed over the chair. She saw that same image a few weeks ago in the exact spot. He said those words before, numerous times in the same spot, and in several spots around the house.

"I won't hurt you if you co-operate," he replied, continuing to circle around her, in wide sweeping arcs several feet away.

"She wouldn't want you to hurt me," she said. That line seemed to do the trick. He stopped in front of her. Her voice lowered and her head dipped back down. "I will never hurt you. I will always take care of you. I will never leave you. I should be the father. I should be the father. I should be her father! I love you…Lisa."

* * *

"Why did you change your name to Perez?" John asked. Lisa looked down before meeting his gaze again. "To hide."

"From me?"

"From everyone," she said softly. "Mainly my parents. I just wanted to start over." "You took your mom's maiden name," he pressed on.

"It's worked so far." She shrugged. "They have yet to track me down."

He nodded.

"By the way, how have you been doing?" she asked.

"Pretty good," he said. "Marisa and I are getting along really well." He took a sip of his drink.

"I mean with you." She extinguished a sigh. "I wasn't able to visit you. How was it? Were you able to cope?"

John looked down and didn't say anything. Memories he tried to bury returned on cue, haunting him. The long, lonely nights. He shook his head, trying to forget these memories. He didn't want Lisa or Marisa to know about his experience. It was best not to make it a big deal, to let these past events disappear and be thankful that things were getting better. He looked up at her. "The thought of getting you two back kept me going."

"Really?"

He nodded and took a deep breath, before working up his nerve. Now or never. He grabbed her hand. "I really missed you."

"I missed you too." She smiled, then cleared her throat, hesitating. Her smile disappeared and a frown remained. "I need to ask you something." Her eyes lowered briefly. "You've made it obvious why you came back. But...why...how...it's been thirteen years since we've seen each other. We're not the same two people we were for that brief period of time together." She paused again, her eyes darting over his face, searching. "You don't know the life I've had over the years and vice versa. What if you came back to find that... I was married? And even had another child?"

There was an awkward silence between them. John forced himself not to speak. Not to move. Breathe. Just breathe, already! A chill ran down his spine despite the warm atmosphere of the restaurant. Lisa, avoiding eye contact, studied the table and her hands, which were sweating. Breaking their clasp, she rubbed them on her lap. He focused on her until she looked up and made eye contact.

He broke the gaze, cleared his throat and swallowed. "I knew there was that possibility. I...I don't know. I kept pushing the idea away. If I dwelled on it too much, I wouldn't have the nerve to face you again. I couldn't even prepare myself mentally." He looked away momentarily and sipped his drink again to clear away the dryness. "I found out eventually through Marisa, but was too nervous upon seeing you to even register that fact." He let out a deep sigh.

Lisa glanced at his hands and at her own resting on the table. He followed her vision, noticing what she sought out and also looked over their ring fingers. Neither of them wore wedding rings or the trace of a lighter, wide arc shade on their fourth finger that developed from wearing a ring. He sensed her stare moving over his hand, up his arm, across his upper torso, and ended on his face, where he gave her a shy smile.

Seeing that it was all right, John did the same. This was the first time he really saw her up close and, in the light, so he took his time. The other times were late and for brief periods. Even then, he spent those times arguing with her rather than taking a moment to inhale her beauty. His eyes carefully examined everything he could see above the table. She was so gorgeous. She had matured and filled out, but she also remained exactly as he remembered. Finishing with her face, he smiled. "I wouldn't say we've changed too much. You're still breathtakingly beautiful."

She broke out in soft laughter, the same laugh he enjoyed thirteen years ago. They caught each other's glance and smiled, knowing everything was going to be better. They continued eating while filling each other in on what they missed together. The chatting turned into laughter at times, reminding them of how they use to be when they were younger. Pretty soon they were talking like nothing ever happened. There was still a spark between them. He knew it too. He was happy, gazing over at Lisa, listening to her story of what Marisa did when she was younger. It was all going to work out now.

After they finished the meal, they climbed into his car and headed over to her house. The ride back was relaxing and allowed more time for them to talk. The miles seemed to fly by quickly. Soon they arrived at her house. John jumped out of the driver's side and scurried over to hold the door open for Lisa, taking advantage of the little things he longed to do all these years. To spoil her and prove his love to her. For a moment it seemed like they were teenagers again, returning from a date. They walked to the front door hand in hand just like the old days. He squeezed her hand, freezing her movements from entering the house, not wanting the moment to end.

"I had a lovely time." He met her gaze. "So did I." She blushed.

John pulled her hand to him and stepped closer to Lisa, wrapping his arms around her body. Stroking her cheek with one hand, he cupped her face, leaned over, and kissed her on the lips. He felt her body press up against him, eagerly returning the kiss, wrapping her arms around him. When the kiss ended, they fell into each other's arms, holding on. He buried his face in her neck. One hand caressed her back; his other hand ran through her hair. He inhaled, taking in her scent, the smell of her perfume and shampoo, the feel of her in his arms, snug against him. He moved his hands over her arms, lightly stroking them. He lifted his head up to face her. They kissed again before untangling from one another.

Lisa smiled, fishing out her house key, bursting out with fits of soft laughter as he traced a finger along her arm and back before resting his hands on her waist. He held her and stood pressed against her backside. Then he remembered Marisa could be sleeping. He leaned his head forward, whispering the thought to Lisa, who fell silent. She managed to unlock the front door, and they noiselessly stumbled into the house, locked in each other's arms. He straightened up once seeing that the living room was quiet, and only a few lights were on.

The hall light was on, along with the kitchen light. He saw Marisa's bedroom door open with the light on. Music played softly in the background. Knowing his daughter, she probably fell asleep waiting for them to return. He smiled, remembering the numerous times he turned everything off in her room and tucked her into bed before hitting the sack himself. But then he realized they were at Lisa's house, and her stuff was still at his house. Tomorrow was a school day. But if she was asleep, John didn't want to disturb her.

I can drive by the house later and get her things, he thought. "It's later than I thought," Lisa whispered, glancing at her watch.

"Her things are at my place," he said softly. They headed to Marisa's room to check on her. "I can go get them real quick and come back."

She nodded, tiptoeing along. "Get your things too. You're not leaving me alone tonight." "Yes, ma'am."

That settled his other unspoken thought. Whether or not he would be staying over as well.

He didn't want to leave her now. Not after the great time they had. But he didn't know how to approach the subject. It was her house; therefore, it was her decision. The last thing he wanted was to offend her by asking. Even suggesting the idea could appear like he was rushing the relationship. Assuming things were all right between them and he could do as pleased. The tension lifted from his shoulders. Her comment confirmed it would be better. They could start over. They could sort out the other things—like custody—later. But tonight, he wanted to stay with her. He caught her gaze and smiled.

They reached Marisa's open bedroom door when a loud voice yelled from the kitchen. A male's voice, sounding deep and angry. Their heads jerked to the closed kitchen door. John clamped his hand over Lisa's mouth to keep her from making any noise.

"Shh," he whispered in her ear until she nodded. He glanced at her since she stood right beside him, and saw her body trembling. Grabbing her hand, he led her to the living room, near the door. They saw a dark shadow passing by, dimming the light that emerged from the bottom. The shadow passed again, but stopped right in the middle. Whoever it was stood on the other side. But were they facing the door or have their back to it? The shadow moved back and forth, crossing the kitchen. They had to be facing away.

"Shut up!" the deep voice shouted, erupting around the quiet house. "I said shut it!"

Marisa, he thought. His throat tightened and his hand gripped Lisa's. Looking over at her until their eyes met, she nodded, and he slowly pushed open the kitchen door.

CHAPTER 21

Marisa saw him in her mind clearly as that one day. He stood in the bathroom, fixing the toilet. Her mom stayed in the kitchen, cleaning up to keep busy and out of the way until he finished. He had been over before so Marisa never thought anything of it really.

But she sensed something different that one time.

As soon as her mom answered the door, she sensed it. He was too friendly. He delayed too long when her mom tried to show him what needed to be fixed, talking and asking too many questions. He lingered in the living room, looking around, making small talk, not seeming like he wanted to work but rather talk. He stood too close to her mom in the bathroom, when she pointed out what needed to be fixed. He made a comment casually about how he only came over for business, though he had known her mom for some time now. Perhaps he could come over for dinner one of these days. Her mom laughed it off like a joke and left him to do his work, but Marisa saw the hurt and anger flash in his eyes. Briefly, but he let it slip.

She watched it all from the shadows, moving to her bedroom doorway when they were in the living room, then remaining behind the open door. He went to work finally.

She saw him in the kitchen afterward, standing in the very corner. She watched with her arms crossed over her chest. Present because she was weary. She saw her mom wanted him to leave. He did his job; it was time to go. But he kept lingering with excuses to talk and stay, asking for water, bringing up all different subjects. Did her mom hear about this? What did her mom think about that? Marisa waited in the kitchen. Never speaking, only watching.

She stayed near the phone.

She rarely heard their conversations beforehand, hardly bothered to listen until that day. But she started paying attention once hearing the words spoken in the restroom. When he was alone. When he thought he was by himself.

Now she heard his words loud and clear, racing out of her mouth.

"Shut up!" he bellowed, inches from her face. He paced the floor in front of her. His back remained to the kitchen door, right where she wanted him. "You stop this right now."

Her voice rose. "I'll take care of you. I'll never hurt you. You can trust me. You can love me like I love you. I'll always be good to you, Lisa." She carefully kept her eyes on him when the door opened quietly.

"Stop it!" he yelled.

Their faces distorted. They slowly crept up closer and closer, soundlessly and carefully. Keep him distracted!

"What makes you think she'll love you," Marisa shouted. "You're nothing but a selfish bastard. She has never liked you and she'll never like you now. How could you even think that you stood a chance with her? That she would fall for you, you disgusting pig."

He came closer in big, broken strides. Her head lowered when his fist pulled back. Only to be stopped in mid-air. The man in black looked over his shoulder to find her dad standing right behind him, his hand wrapped around the wrist. "No!" the man yelled. "No!"

Her dad's free hand came over the man's shoulder and punched him in the face, hitting his eye. The man's head wrenched back, caught off guard by the blow. Her dad stepped forward, advancing on him, his step quick, heated, and angry. He threw punches left and right. The never-ending blows and his furious steps forced the man to retreat back to the kitchen counter, away from Marisa. Her eyes never left them. Both men yelled, shouted and grunted, each throwing punches with their fists and elbows, kicking and butting one another with their legs, feet, and knees. Some of the blows caught the man in black; some of them caught her dad. Some were in the face, some in the chest, and some below the belt.

They moved to a corner of the kitchen on Marisa's left side. She heard a voice yelling in her ear and looked up to find her mom, who began untying the restraints. Once she had an arm free, Marisa undid the rope on her other arm while her mom worked on her feet. When the binding was loosened, she wiggled her feet around and slid them out of the restraint. She stood up.

Her mom grabbed her arm and ran to the kitchen door, yanking Marisa along right as the men ventured over to the middle of the kitchen. She stood glued to the ground near the wall and counter, her heart racing, her breath short while watching them. They continued, struggling back and forth, hitting and thrashing around. When they moved over to the other side near the refrigerator, her mom ran over to the counter and snatched up the cordless phone. Averting her eyes for the moment, Marisa saw her mom dialing for help.

Turning her attention back to the struggle, the man in black picked up her dad by his shirt and threw him across the kitchen, where he landed hard against the wall. He slid down to the floor, causing Marisa to scream. But then he scrambled to his feet, charging toward the man. His head and arms collided into his chest, pushing him back until he fell over a kitchen chair and landed on the floor. The man in black struggled to get to his feet. Her dad stood over him, kicking him hard with his feet, hitting his legs, his arms, his chest and head, anything he could contact. He yelled and pounded away. The man's head bounced against the oven, the counter, and finally the legs of the kitchen table. The banging echoed throughout the house.

Someone must hear all this noise, Marisa thought. *Someone should be calling the police or coming over to check on us.*

Crawling over the floor on all fours, the man in black grabbed the kitchen chair that Marisa sat on moments earlier. She joined her mom's side. He threw the chair at her dad, who stood near the stove and oven. Her dad ducked, and the chair flew over him, hitting the wall before collapsing on the floor with a big bang. He grabbed the chair and pulled it over to him, yanking off one of the restraints. The man scurried to his feet since the blows stopped. He stood up, swaying a little, struggling to get his balance and catch his breath. Flexing his clenched fists, he faced her dad with his back to Marisa and her mother. Almost like he forgot about them.

Seeing her dad's intentions, Marisa grabbed the nearest chair from the table. Her mom also grabbed a chair. The man in black still faced her dad, who kept his distance, playing with the rope in his hands. She met her dad's gaze, and he continued to distract him. Casting her eyes over to her mom, they met each other's gaze and nodded. She lifted the chair over her head and threw it with all her might at the man in black at the same time as her mom. Her dad jumped out of the way at the last second. The two chairs smashed into the man's backside, knocking him to the floor. She held her breath and waited. The house turned silent.

Only this time the man didn't get up.

She released a deep sigh. Her dad stepped forward and pulled the man's hands behind his back. He tied the rope on. She retrieved the other bound from the ground and handed it over. As her dad secured the final restraint around the man's legs, her mom snatched off the disheveled black mask.

"You!" her mom exclaimed.

"Yes, it's me," Danny replied, moaning.

"Why?" her mom demanded.

Marisa glared at Danny, who also appeared angry despite the puffiness forming around his eyes, and blood dripping from his temple and lip. She glanced at her dad, noticing blood drip from a cut on his temple. Tearing her eyes away from him, she turned back to Danny, who lay on the floor on his stomach. He had such an incredible look of hatred; she almost didn't recognize him. He never took any care in grooming himself before, but now he looked worse than usual.

"You know this guy?" her dad asked.

"Unfortunately, yes," her mom replied.

"From where?"

"He went to high school with us," her mom answered. "His name's Danny."

Her dad's eyes widened; his face turned hard. "Danny! You kidding me?"

"You know him?" her mom asked.

"I'll tell you later."

Shrugging, her mom turned back to Danny. "Why did you do this?" The house became silent. They waited for an answer, but he didn't reply. Her mom kicked him in the chest, causing a moan to escape his lips. "Answer me," her mom yelled. "Why?"

They waited but Danny refused to talk. Instead, he glared at the floor, unmoving while catching his breath. He relented entirely.

"He likes you," Marisa interjected. Her parents exchanged glances with each other before turning their attention to her. "I heard him talking to himself in the restroom the last time he was here. When he thought he was alone. He likes you, and he wanted to be my father."

Her words echoed throughout the quiet house. Her dad walked around Danny and stood next to her mom, placing a comforting arm around her shoulders.

"Is this true?" her mom asked Danny.

She glanced down to discover him with his head on the floor and his eyes closed.

"He's not going to answer," her dad replied. "Come on, let's wait for the police to arrive and take him away."

Her mom's head lowered and her dad steered her away from Danny. She wrapped her arm around her mom's waist. The three of them exited the kitchen to the sound of sirens approaching their house.

It was late by the time the EMS left and the police left with Danny in custody. Her dad closed the front door and locked it, shutting away the authority figures, the noise of the sirens, and the dangers of the outside world. Marisa stood in the kitchen doorway. The sudden quietness hit her ears, comforting and soothing her nerves. Holding her elbows in her hands, she shivered despite the warmth in the house. Her back held the door open while she peered at the chaos. Her mom stood next to her, also inspecting the mess.

Chairs were scattered everywhere, some bent and some broken. Holes littered the walls, dents appeared in the appliances, and blood lay on the floor and on the table's legs. The table lay on its side, pushed into a corner. The knife stand and cooking utensil holder was turned over, scattering knives, spatulas, spoons, and forks. Small appliances were knocked to the ground. The canisters lay open, spilling brown sugar, flour, spaghetti, and sugar on the counter and floor.

Marisa exhaled a sigh, meeting her mom's gaze. Her dad joined them. He had a tiny white bandage covering the cut near his temple and a few bruises forming on his face. But other than that, he was fine.

"We need to redo the kitchen," her mom stated.

The night's events caught up with Marisa. Her limbs started shaking and her bottom lip quivered. She heard her mom ramble about how late it was. But she stopped paying attention. She felt relieved—but shocked, nevertheless. Relieved Danny was gone, but shocked he appeared out of nowhere. She couldn't believe what he did. She remembered her intentions to inform her mom what she overheard that day, but became distracted and completely forgot about him. Then again, she never knew he would go to such extremes. What would it have accomplished?

Marisa held onto the door trying not to collapse. She rubbed her wrists where the restraint was tied. Her ankles itched too. Her dad reached out his arms and pulled them to him. She sank her head on his chest and the tears instantly flew down her cheeks. She wrapped one arm around her dad's back, the other arm around her mom's back. Her dad held them tightly in his arms. She could feel her mom trembling next to her. Lifting her head up, she saw her mom sobbing on her dad's shoulder.

"Shh, it's OK," her dad whispered. "We're safe now."

Her mom also lifted her head, wiping her eyes. "Sweetie, are you all right?"

She nodded slowly.

"Are you sure? He didn't hurt you?"

She smiled when her mom checked one arm, rotating it back and forth. Her dad lifted her face, turning it to one side and then the other. He inspected her other arm, but no mark showed from the restraint. Shaking her head, Marisa also wiped away the fallen tears and took a deep breath. "I'm fine. Just a little shaken." She glanced at her dad. The bruises were bigger now, darkening around his eyes, nose, and mouth. Tomorrow was a school day. He couldn't show up looking like that. "What about your face?"

"I'll be fine," he said. "I'll go early and tell the principal we had an intruder."

Another silence filled the house. The three of them continued to hold each other, not wanting to let go.

"How did you know Danny?" her mom asked.

She looked over at her mom, who met her dad's gaze.

"I knew of him because he liked you," he replied. "My friends told me, but that was it. I remember seeing him once at the basketball game. He sat right above you and kept trying to get your attention."

"I don't remember him there."

"You seemed oblivious to him," he remarked. "He left the game after I smacked him with the ball."

Her mom's mouth dropped open. "That was him!" "Yeah."

"Oh," her mom said. "I didn't know him then."

She glanced back and forth between them, trying to keep up with their conversation but had no idea what they were talking about. This was before her time. She knew Danny attended the same high school as her parents, but left within the first year, though so did her dad. "I failed to mention how he acted the last time he was here," Marisa spoke up. "I'm sorry. I should have told you."

Her mom waved her hand, dismissing the comment. "I had already decided never to call him again."

"The last time?" Her dad's eyebrows burrowed over. "What was he doing here to begin with?"

"Fixing the bathroom," her mom replied. "He's a repairman."

"Has he been here a lot?"

"Every now and then," her mom answered. "I met up with him three years ago I think. I didn't know how to fix certain things when they broke. I called a repairman, and he showed up one day. He told me we went to high school together, but he had been expelled the first year. He always did his job, but last time he acted rather strange. More so than usual."

"What about tonight?" He looked at Marisa. "What happened before we arrived?"

"Right after you two left, I went to my room." She took a deep breath. "I heard a noise and came out here to inspect it when he grabbed me from behind. He knocked me on the head and I must have passed out. When I came to, I was tied to the chair."

"He just appeared out of nowhere?" her mom exclaimed. "How did he get in?" She shrugged.

"Did he say anything?" her dad questioned.

"He told me if I cooperated without screaming or trying to escape, he wouldn't hurt me," she continued. "Then he asked about you guys."

They exchanged glances. Her mom's eyes widened; her dad frowned. "What about us?" he demanded.

"He asked where you went and when will you get back," she replied. "I told him I didn't know." She paused, releasing a sigh. "Then I realized I was his bait. So I pissed him off and created some noise, keeping him in front of me and his back to the door until you guys came home."

"That was very brave," her mom said. "I'm so proud of you."

"But how did he even know you were by yourself?" her dad pressed on. "He couldn't have known that unless he …" He met her mom's gaze and his face turned hard. Cold and angry. "He's been following her around."

"For how long?" her mom asked him.

"Long enough," Marisa said. "He said parents when he asked about you two."

"I never told him about you." Her mom glanced at her dad. "It wasn't his business. I never told him anything about my life."

"If he's been following you around," he stated, "he could have figured it out. Marisa moved into my house a couple of weeks ago."

"You probably pissed him off showing up around here," Marisa added.

Catching her gaze, her dad raised an eyebrow. "He's been following the three of us for some time now."

She shuddered at the thought. The idea of anyone following and watching them was scary. Her dad was right; Danny had to have trailed them. How long exactly? A few weeks? Who knows what he saw? Enough to figure out when she was home alone. To know her parents were going on a date. It was too creepy to grasp.

Her mom shook her head. "All this time and we never knew." She let out a deep sigh.

"How could we know?" Marisa shrugged. "He was always strange, but I had sensed something else when he came over the last time. He was trying too hard. Really laying it on thick. Like he wouldn't take no for an answer."

"I sensed it too," her mom agreed. "But I don't know what gave him that idea. I never led him on. I didn't even like him. I knew he was hitting on me; I just kept brushing him off like I always did. I had to put up with his talking every time, but he was a good repairman, so I tolerated him. I wasn't obligated to him, because I paid him to do the job. I didn't owe him anything."

She glanced at her dad to find him looking back and forth between them. She laughed at his blank facial expression. Her parents also smiled, catching each other's glances.

"Apparently," her dad said, "he wanted more from you. He couldn't take the hint."

"Or he wouldn't," Marisa added.

Her mom nodded. "I guess so. But I'm glad he's gone now. Thank you for protecting us."

Marisa watched her mom raise her head, meeting her dad's eyes. One hand lingered on his back, and the other hand stroked his cheek. Her dad's face relaxed. She noticed how close her parents stood to one another, their bodies turned toward each other. Sensing that they wanted to be alone, she slowly backed out of their grips. They broke eye contact and glanced over at her. But not before holding each other. She walked backward toward her room.

Suddenly she remembered the date they went on, the reason she was left alone in the first place. She forgot all about it until seeing how they were wrapped in each other's arms. Though they did it after she broke out of their grips, it was done naturally. Like they were not even aware of it. They watched her retreat to her room, never breaking the hold on each other. Did this mean they were back together? They were certainly acting like a couple. She smiled upon seeing them still embraced, knowing they needed a moment alone.

"I'll just let you two finish your date." Marisa passed through her open bedroom door. She turned to her left and stood with her back braced against the wall, her ear pressed to the doorway. She concentrated on trying to hear their words. But she couldn't, for they were whispering. She leaned her head even closer and faintly heard their voices.

"I was wondering if you would give me another chance?" she heard her dad ask.

"I've been waiting all night for you to say that," she heard her mom reply, soft laughter escaping their lips. Marisa held her breath. "Yes."

She released her breath but no longer heard any talking. Peering around the wall, she looked through the open door into the living room. A smile appeared on her face upon seeing her parents locked in each other's arms, kissing passionately on the lips.

Yes! Her parents were kissing. She couldn't believe it. They would give their relationship another chance. Marisa began dancing all around her room while shouting, forgetting herself for the moment. She turned facing the doorway and froze, discovering her parents watching her. They exchanged glances with each other and shook their heads. She laughed despite herself, noticing they were still holding each other.

"Sorry." Her cheeks felt hot. "This means what I think it does, right?"

"You bet." Her dad smiled, then leaned over and kissed her mom again.

"It's about time." Marisa yawned loudly, causing them to laugh. "I'm going to bed. Good night, Mom. Good night, Dad."

She headed toward her parents to embrace them, when they froze this time. She stopped, seeing their mouths open and their eyes widen. "What?"

"You called him dad," her mom announced.

She tilted her head to the side, realizing they were right. Shrugging, she said, "He is my father." Her parents beamed. She hugged them and then retreated back to her room, but she stopped when she remembered something. They had already resumed kissing and reluctantly stopped.

"I thought you were going to bed," her mom said.

"I will, but first I want you to do me a favor," she stated.

"What?" her dad asked.

"Don't have another kid."

Meeting her dad's gaze, her mom nodded her head toward Marisa. "Get her."

Marisa ran into her room with her dad chasing after her. She quickly closed the door, laughing the entire time.

Kathryn Cervera grew up in Cibolo, Texas and moved to San Antonio. She graduated from St. Mary's University and the University of the Incarnate Word. She holds two master's degrees with a background in Communications and Writing. She is blessed with a boyfriend, her parents, an older brother, sister-in-law, and a niece and nephew. Her passion is writing young adult fiction novels about realistic life situations. She loves to laugh. She loves singing and dancing. She enjoys reading. Just don't ask who's her favorite author. That's a cruel question.

www.ingramcontent.com/pod-product-compliance
Lightning Source LLC
Chambersburg PA
CBHW070050080526
44586CB00013B/992